365 DAYS FOR ADHD MOMS

Practical Tips and Mindset Shifts for Everyday Life

CHRISTY LINGO

ISBN: 979-8-9945559-0-3

Book Cover by Mariem Khlifi (99designs)

First edition January 2026

To Q & A...

Everything I do, I do for you.

Table of Contents

Introduction

In hindsight, it probably wasn't the wisest idea to start writing a book during the busiest sports time of the year for our family and heading into the holiday season. But you know what it's like when that ADHD inspiration takes hold.

That inspiration came while I was reading the book *365 Days of Good Morning, Good Life* by Amy Landino and Sarah McCain. It dawned on me that short snippets of information each day, combined with action steps, could be the perfect way to learn about ADHD.

Each day features a different aspect of how ADHD impacts our lives, along with practical tips and mindset shifts you can apply to better understand your ADHD brain and make everyday life a bit easier.

The passages follow the flow of the year: cleaning and organizing in the spring, back-to-school at the end of summer, and the holiday season to wrap up the year. You may notice repeating themes, and that is intentional...because I know my ADHD brain needs info in bite-sized chunks and repeated often.

I also know each season brings different challenges or a need for fresh resources. And often, the challenges may be the same (like figuring out what to do), but the solutions I offer may be a bit different (the 1-3-5 rule, making a short daily to-do list, etc.).

And let's face it...we'll probably forget some things. So that repetition can help us remember.

If there is a particular passage you want to dive deeper into, you can consult the appendix to see what other days we discuss that same topic.

 I also included some of my favorite ADHD resources for additional support, as well as a link where you can download helpful checklists and support tools I created for my podcast audience and clients. Look for this symbol on passages to indicate there is a related download. You'll find the link in the Resources section.

And finally, the purpose of this book is education, tools, support, and hopefully a relatable chuckle along the way. I'm not a doctor, and this book isn't medical advice. But if you are looking for personal medical advice, mental health guidance, or a diagnosis, please reach out to a qualified health professional.

You can start with today or whatever day you want. You can skip days when you want (or when you forget) and come back when you're ready. Now that you've got it, this book isn't going anywhere (just make sure you know where it is).

Here's to less shame, more support, and a few good laughs along the way.

Ready? Let's do this.

Christy

January

What's Your Vision?

We all get the exact same 365 days.
The only difference is what we do with them. ~ Hillary DePiano

If we can't see something, there's a good chance our ADHD brain forgets it even exists. That's because ADHD brains thrive on visible cues to support memory.

It's also why the goals or projects we want to tackle in the new year can quickly slip into the "out of sight, out of mind" category if we don't keep them in view.

After a month of doing so much for everyone else, this is our chance to reconnect with what we want. This is why we're starting off the year by creating a vision board.

Seeing our goals regularly helps us remember not just what we want to work on, but why it matters. A vision board takes our goals out of our head and puts them somewhere we can actually see. It turns vague intentions into visual reminders of what we're working toward, helping us stay connected and motivated.

Make one by cutting out images and pasting them onto a foam board, creating a digital version for your phone or desktop wallpaper, or adding images to a journal (or one of the seventeen notebooks we've all accumulated).

And don't forget…a vision board only works if we see it. It's important to place it somewhere we naturally look so it can quietly remind us, again and again, what we're moving toward.

Put It Into Practice:

Make a vision board that reflects what you want in the upcoming year for your home, family, work, and, most importantly, yourself.

Goal Setting

January 2

Know Where You'll Go.

I've been on a calendar, but I've never been on time.
~ Marilyn Monroe

I used to scramble so often that I might as well have been an egg. I wouldn't realize something was happening until it needed to happen now. Or yesterday. This was likely due to my ADHD time blindness.

Flying by the seat of our pants can work, but when it becomes our main method of motivation, it starts to wear on our stress and anxiety levels.

A simple way to create more awareness around our time and commitments is to update our calendar before the year gets rolling. Take a little time now to add events you don't want to forget or miss, like:

- Birthdays
- School breaks
- Coupons and sales
- Deadlines
- Upcoming appointments
- Important events (especially those holiday ones we don't want to forget about next year)

By adding these ahead of time, we reduce last-minute mental load because we can actually see what's coming. And don't forget…ADHD brains thrive on reminders. So set a few while you're at it.

Put It Into Practice:

Add important events (with reminders) to your family calendar so they don't sneak up on you.

Planning, Time Management, Time Blindness, Time Investments

Start Small. Start Now.

The secret of getting ahead is getting started.
~Mark Twain

ADHD brains love doing something new... until we don't. Then the word "start" becomes the scariest word in the dictionary.

Task initiation relies on several executive functions (planning, prioritizing, time management, and organization) all working together. And when our executive function is spread thin, even thinking about starting a task can feel exhausting. Our brains run through every option and scenario before we've taken a single step... and by then, we're already worn out. No wonder starting feels so hard!

One of the best ways to overcome this is by breaking big, overwhelming goals into smaller, more manageable pieces. Instead of cleaning and organizing the entire kitchen, start with one drawer. Instead of planning an entire spring break trip, choose the dates and the location.

Starting small says to our brains, "See! We can do this!"

And each small win builds momentum and confidence, making the next step feel a little less intimidating.

We don't need to figure everything out to start. We just need to take a small step to prove to our brains we're capable of moving forward.

Put It Into Practice:

Pick one small step you can take to help you make progress on a task or project you've been avoiding.

Taking Action, Procrastination

January 4

Tell the World.

Accountability breeds response-ability.
~ Stephen Covey

It's no big secret that many ADHDers struggle with follow-through and completing tasks. My husband and I joked for years that I'm president of the 97% club because I'll often complete about 97% of a project, then decide to move on to another project. (I'm writing this book in order, so we'll see in December if I made it past 97%. Fingers crossed!)

Even before my official ADHD diagnosis, I discovered a secret for following through…accountability. And luckily, there are plenty of ways to use it to stay on track.

For instance, we can improve our chances of completing a task simply by telling the world we're going to do it.

When I decided to write this book, I told my girlfriends about it at brunch because I knew they would ask me about it… and that would keep me moving.

Send it in a text. Post it on social media. Make a bumper sticker for the back of the car. How we tell people isn't important, but making sure we do is.

Put It Into Practice:

Tell someone (or several someones) about a goal you have for the upcoming year.

Accountability, Goal Setting, Taking Action

Prep for Your Rest.

Without enough sleep, we all become tall two year olds.
~ JoJo Jensen

Many of us struggle with sleep. Probably because ADHD impairs the regulation of brain activity, making it harder to wind down and stay asleep. Add in busy mom brains that never quite turn off, and it's a wonder we get any rest at all.

If we're looking to improve the quality of our sleep, it can help to look at our sugar, caffeine, and alcohol intake. High sugar intake (especially near bedtime) can lead to energy spikes and crashes, making it harder to stay asleep and feel well-rested.

Caffeine may boost focus during the day, but consuming it too close to bedtime impacts our ability to wind down while increasing nighttime waking.

And while alcohol may make us sleepy at first, it disrupts the amount and quality of our REM sleep, which is essential for learning, emotional regulation, and executive function.

The good news is that all three of these sleep thieves are within our control. By limiting them in the hours leading up to bedtime, we can significantly improve both the quality and duration of our rest.

Put It Into Practice:

Cut off your sugar, caffeine, and alcohol intake 2–3 hours before you head to bed if you struggle to fall or stay asleep.

Sleep, Productivity, Executive Function

January 6

Check Yourself Before You...

When we look closely, we recognize the same balls being dropped, over and over...We know the patterns. We see the costs. It's time to try something else. Try a checklist. ~ Atul Gawande

There are so many executive functions involved with completing a task. We have to:

- Remember what we want to do
- Remember all the steps
- Remember to start
- Remember where we left off if we get distracted or switch tasks midstream

Let's just say, completing a task, even a small one, can feel overwhelming for someone with executive function challenges.

But that doesn't mean it's impossible. It just means we might need some support for our executive function.

Might I suggest the humble checklist?

A written structure like a checklist takes the pressure off our working memory to remember all the steps. It reduces decision-making by showing us what comes next and reduces overwhelm by breaking tasks into smaller, more manageable steps. And as a bonus, every time we tick off a line on our checklist, we get a little hit of that sweet, sweet dopamine to keep us going.

Put It Into Practice:

Create a simple checklist for a regular task, activity, or routine. Think morning routine, bedtime routine, or cleaning a room.

Checklists, Productivity, Executive Function

The Sandwich Process.

Setting a goal is not the main thing. It is deciding how you will go about achieving it and staying with that plan. ~ Tom Landry

As a second grader, my son had an assignment to write down all the steps in the peanut butter sandwich making process. Nearly every child in the class wrote "start by putting the peanut butter on the bread," to which the teacher replied, "No, the first step is getting out the plate to make the sandwich on."

This is a simple but important reminder as we look at the goals we want to achieve in the coming year. We can't dive into spreading peanut butter on the bread if the peanut butter and bread are still in the pantry.

If breaking goals into manageable tasks feels overwhelming, think of it like making a peanut butter sandwich. The early steps, like getting out the plate or opening the jar, might feel small or obvious, but they're the foundation that makes the rest of the process possible.

Progress doesn't start with big action, it starts with preparing the next small step.

Put It Into Practice:

Think through the entire process for a project or goal and write down each step, no matter how small, to help with task initiation and reducing feelings of overwhelm.

Goal Setting, Taking Action

January 8

Explanation, Not Excuse.

Awareness is the greatest agent for change.
~ Eckhart Tolle

ADHD is more than forgetfulness, chronic tardiness, and hyperactivity. And everyone's ADHD looks a little different.

When we build awareness around how our unique version of ADHD looks, we can better see where support and coping strategies might help.

Exploring resources like books, blogs, podcasts, and support groups helps us understand our ADHD. This newfound awareness allows us to understand why we behave the way we do, why certain situations feel harder than others, and why some skills or systems matter more for us than for someone else. It shifts our experience from confusion or self-criticism to clarity.

Improved ADHD awareness also helps us to explain, not excuse, why we behave or react in certain ways to family, friends, and co-workers. When we understand our own patterns, it becomes easier to communicate our needs, seek support, and make intentional changes. Without that understanding, it may be hard to know what needs adjusting or to believe we're capable of thriving at all.

Put It Into Practice:

Educate yourself on your unique version of ADHD, even if you've been dealing with it for years. Then share your findings with a trusted family member or friend for added support.

Awareness, Relationships, Mindset

Sweat Out Your Stress.

You can't stop the waves, but you can learn to surf.
~ Jon Kabat-Zinn

Exercise is one of the (if not *the*) best non-medicative ways to manage ADHD. On top of that, it helps manage comorbid conditions like anxiety and depression, which many of us ADHDers also struggle with.

And here's the fun science-y part: regular movement boosts serotonin, the neurotransmitter that helps lift our mood, and gamma-aminobutyric acid (GABA), which helps calm the brain and counteract stress and anxiety.

Exercise also quiets activity in the amygdala, the brain's fear center, helping reduce our emotional reactivity to everyday stressors.

In other words, regular exercise won't just boost dopamine to help with our focus, planning, and executive function. It will strengthen multiple aspects of our brain chemistry, supporting mental health, reducing stress, and improving overall well-being.

Even small, consistent bursts of movement can make a noticeable difference in how we think, feel, and respond to the world. As little as 10–20 minutes of increasing our heart rate can help boost our mood and neurotransmitters.

Put It Into Practice:

Add movement into your daily routine. Remember, it doesn't have to be long or intense to see the benefits.

Exercise, Anxiety, Emotional Regulation, Mental Health

January 10

Bye-Bye, Bad Vibes.

When you let go of what doesn't serve you, you make space
for what's meant to be. ~ Ava DuVernay

When it comes to getting organized this year, our mindset may need some decluttering, too. Rejection Sensitive Dysphoria (RSD) is common among ADHDers and can make negativity or shame feel more intense than our neurotypical counterparts.

While RSD isn't an official ADHD symptom or medical condition, it's closely linked to the executive function of emotional regulation. When experiences like embarrassment, failure, criticism, or comparing ourselves on social media spike our emotions, it can be difficult to regulate our response in the moment.

Emotional reactions to these situations are completely normal. The difference is that many of us with ADHD feel this pain, embarrassment, or criticism more deeply and for longer periods of time.

That is why it is so important that we work to curate what we allow into our mental space, choosing input that supports positivity, aligns with our values, and moves us toward the goals we're trying to achieve.

Put It Into Practice:

Take time today to unfollow 5 social media accounts that don't inspire you, support you, or align with your goals.

RSD, Emotional Regulation, Mindset, Time Investments

Who Put Mood in Charge?

I don't want to be at the mercy of my emotions. I want to use them, to enjoy them, and to dominate them. ~ Oscar Wilde

Emotional regulation and dopamine play a big role in irritability, a short fuse, and emotional overdrive. Which is why stress, anxiety, depression, and burnout often hit ADHDers harder, especially during high-demand seasons (hello, holidays)…and even the recovery period afterward.

Researchers are still working to fully understand emotional dysregulation in ADHD brains. It may be connected to impaired executive function, which lowers our ability to inhibit responses. Or overstimulation, which can reduce our capacity to regulate stressful or emotionally charged situations. For some, Rejection Sensitive Dysphoria (RSD) adds another layer, intensifying emotional pain in response to real or perceived rejection.

While we can't change how our brain is wired, we can gather tools to help when emotional dysregulation strikes. By looking back at past emotional flare-ups and identifying the triggers that influenced our mood, we can plan ahead and respond with more intention the next time.

Put It Into Practice:

Identify what tends to trigger strong emotional responses. Use that awareness to decide where you may need boundaries, support, or a pre-planned coping strategy.

Emotional Regulation, Overstimulation, RSD

January 12

You Deserve a Break Today.

Wisdom is knowing when to have rest, when to have activity, and how much of each to have. ~ Sri Sri Ravi Shankar

Is it better to take a break or breakdown?

When we build rest into our days as ADHD moms, we give our brains the pause they desperately need.

These "brain breaks" improve our executive function by reducing mental fatigue and restoring our capacity to focus, plan, and regulate.

Rest also boosts creativity. Instead of pulling from an empty tank, we refill our energy reserves, making it easier to think clearly and problem-solve.

And when we rest, we activate our parasympathetic nervous system (PNS), the body's "rest and digest" mode, which lowers stress hormones that impact our physical, mental, and emotional health... and potentially our longevity.

It may feel counterintuitive to think rest, relaxation, or taking a break can help us achieve more. But as fulfilled, healthy, and well-rested moms, we have more energy to do the things we love with the people we love.

Put It Into Practice:

Take a break today and do something just for you. It doesn't have to be time-consuming or expensive...just intentional. Then do it again tomorrow.

Burnout, Productivity, Emotional Regulation

Learn Your Way Forward.

Do something today that your future self will thank you for.
~ Sean Patrick Flanery

It's the season for goal setting…and many of us don't realize there are two types of goals.

Learning goals focus on building skills or increasing knowledge. They bring instant rewards like a dopamine hit from learning something new or mastering a small step.

Performance goals, on the other hand, focus on a specific outcome. They often take longer to achieve and don't provide much immediate payoff along the way.

It's probably no surprise that many ADHDers lean toward learning goals due to their instant gratification. This also helps explain why long-term goal setting can feel so difficult when rewards are delayed. But that doesn't mean we should avoid performance goals. We just need to build learning into the process.

One effective strategy is to build learning goals into your performance goals. For example, instead of focusing solely on the performance goal of losing ten pounds, you might set a learning goal of attending two different gym classes each week and learning from different instructors. The learning goal keeps you engaged and motivated, while naturally supporting progress toward the larger performance goal.

Put It Into Practice:

Find ways to pair learning goals with your performance goals to help keep you motivated and making progress.

Goal Setting, Consistency, Taking Action, Productivity

January 14

Reach Out. Refill. Repeat.

No distance of place or lapse of time can lessen the friendship of those who are thoroughly persuaded of each other's worth. ~ Robert Southey

None of us mean to ghost the people we love. We just get so caught up in going, going, going that checking in with the people who matter slips through the cracks. Missed birthdays, unanswered texts, or forgotten holiday emails can feel embarrassing, or even shame-inducing, but those moments say far more about how busy and overloaded we are than how much we care.

And here's the important part: the people who love us still want to hear from us. Even late. Even awkwardly. Even without a perfect explanation. And deep down, we want to connect with them, too.

Connection matters…especially as busy ADHD moms flying by the seat of our pants. Staying connected reminds us that we're supported, seen, and not doing life alone. It grounds us in something bigger than the never-ending to-do list.

Put It Into Practice:

Reach out to a friend or family member that you haven't connected with in a while. Make the call. Send the text. Write the email. It doesn't have to be perfect, it just has to be real. You'll be glad you did.

Relationships, Mom Life, Self-Care

Invest to Stay Accountable.

Invest in yourself to get the best interest.
~ Debasish Mridha

I hate paying for something and not getting a return on my investment. From produce in the fridge to kids' classes at the rec center, if I paid for it, I'm going to make sure it gets used. The expectation creates motivation.

I really noticed this during my third round of Weight Watchers after my second child was born. Paying for the app and logging my points created built-in accountability and structure. For me, that made all the difference. It helped me stay engaged and see progress in a way nothing else had. And I've been investing in myself to create accountability and help me reach my goals ever since.

When we invest time, money, or energy, we naturally expect a return. That upfront investment creates accountability, lowers friction, and gives our ADHD brains a reason to follow through. And while the cost may feel uncomfortable at first, the payoff can be significant.

So, when a resolution feels stuck, consider whether an investment might help create momentum. It could be hiring a personal trainer or joining a gym to stay consistent, paying for childcare or a cleaning service to free up time, or using paid tools that add structure and reminders. It's not an indulgence…it's support!

Put It Into Practice:

Brainstorm where you can invest time, money, or energy to add accountability or reduce barriers as you work toward a goal.

Accountability, Time Investments, Goal Setting

January 16

Oooh, That Smell.

Housework can't kill you, but why take the chance?
~ Phyllis Diller

Are there leftovers lurking in the back of the fridge? It's usually around this time in January when I realize I have no food storage containers left. Not because we're using them, but because every single one is holding a half-eaten remnant of holiday meals past.

It's also around this time when I have to be honest with myself that no one is going to eat the last cinnamon roll from Christmas morning. And those seven remaining New Year's Eve hors d'oeuvres? They've officially missed their moment.

Clearing out the fridge isn't just about eliminating mystery smells (though that's a nice bonus). For ADHD brains, visual clutter creates mental clutter. When the fridge is overstuffed and disorganized, meal planning feels harder, decisions feel heavier, and we're more likely to default to takeout…again.

Making space helps us see what we actually have, reduces decision fatigue, and makes feeding our families feel just a little more manageable.

Put It Into Practice:

Do a quick fridge reset today. Toss anything your family isn't going to eat, plus anything rotting or expired. And don't forget to check the condiments for expiration dates.

Cleaning and Organizing, Eating and Meal Planning, Time Investments

Quitter's Day.

When it comes to team success, accountability isn't a burden, it's a gift. ~ Patrick Lencioni

The term "Quitter's Day" was popularized by a fitness company in 2019 after they noticed a distinct drop-off in the number of people using their app by mid-January.

Many of us lose steam after setting goals, New Year's resolutions or otherwise. But a proven way to push past your motivation and consistency hurdles is accountability.

For ADHDers, external accountability is extra powerful because of the Hawthorne Effect, which shows that people change their behavior when they know someone is paying attention or expecting follow-through. That outside awareness creates just enough urgency to help us take action.

External support not only boosts motivation, it increases our chances of sticking with our goals long enough to see real progress. Accountability can look like regular check-ins with a friend or family member, joining a group with similar goals, or hiring a coach or trainer to help keep us on track.

Put It Into Practice:

Choose one goal then add the extra layer of external accountability …someone, somewhere, or something that helps you show up consistently.

Accountability, Consistency, Goal Setting

January 18

Why Am I So Tired?

Life is one long process of getting tired.
~ Samuel Butler

Some days it feels like my brain is running on fumes…even before breakfast. This is likely because ADHD is, in an oversimplified nutshell, a struggle with inconsistent dopamine regulation.

Normal dopamine levels support focus, concentration, motivation, and a balanced mood. But low dopamine can make even simple tasks feel exhausting. Brain fog, mood swings, fatigue, and difficulty concentrating are all common when our dopamine dips.

Add in the pressures of modern motherhood and more distractions keeping us awake than in all of human history, and it's no wonder many of us are one long blink away from falling asleep.

Once we understand why we're tired, we can start to address it. Are we running on too little sleep? Too little dopamine? Or perhaps too few boundaries? Each cause has different strategies, but awareness is always the first step.

Put It Into Practice:

Identify why you feel exhausted. Once you pinpoint the source, you can take steps to restore energy, whether it's by setting boundaries, scheduling rest, or adding movement to boost focus and mood.

Energy Management, Sleep, Self-Care

Outsource Your Overwhelm.

There is no way to be a perfect mother, and a million ways to be a good one. ~ Jill Churchill

After over a decade as a mom, I have yet to discover any bonus points, prizes, or trophies for doing it all myself. But I also realize there are all sorts of reasons why moms don't ask for help.

Maybe someone won't do it the way we want. Maybe it feels faster to just do it ourselves than to explain it. Maybe we worry asking makes us look weak or incapable. Or maybe we're just too tired today and tomorrow feels like a better day to try again.

But riddle me this…is it better to make some progress than none at all?

For ADHD brains, delegation isn't just a convenience…it's a strategy. When motivation is low, energy is depleted, or distractions abound, handing off part or all of a task helps us keep moving forward without hitting burnout. Delegation prevents us from becoming our own roadblock, freeing mental space for the things that truly require our attention.

Put It Into Practice:

Make a list of tasks or projects where you could use extra support. Who can help lighten the load? Could you outsource part of it to a friend, family member, or professional? Remember, even small delegations create momentum and protect your energy.

Taking Action, Energy Management, Productivity, Mom Life

January 20

The Year of No.

*Half of the troubles of this life can be traced to saying yes too quickly
and not saying no soon enough. ~ Josh Billings*

In 2013, my oldest was 18 months old, I was pregnant again, and my organizing business was taking off. I felt completely overwhelmed by life. Which is why my New Year's resolution was to say "no" more often.

Yes, I did worry that I'd be viewed as negative, disappoint people, or miss out on opportunities. But my exhaustion outweighed my worry. I knew something had to change.

Confidently saying "no" starts with slowing down to evaluate the opportunities that come our way, which can be a challenge for our impulsive ADHD brains. But try asking questions like:

- Do I want to do this?
- Do I have time for this?
- Will this take time away from something that's a priority for me?
- Will there be an opportunity for me to do this in the future?

While saying "no" might feel uncomfortable at first, over time we will notice the positive impact of filling our day with tasks, people, and opportunities that energize rather than drain us.

Put It Into Practice:

Practice saying "no" to opportunities that don't align with your priorities. Over time, you'll create more space for the people and activities that truly fill your cup.

Mindset, Productivity, People-Pleasing

Dopamine vs. Deadlines.

If it weren't for the last minute, nothing would get done.
~ Rita Mae Brown

Is procrastination part of ADHD? Well…yes and no. It happens when a bunch of executive functions decide to short-circuit, making progress feel almost impossible.

Initiating a task requires us to decide where to start, break the task down into manageable pieces, prioritize the steps, and sustain interest. For ADHD brains, that's a lot of exhausting executive function work before we even begin.

But as deadlines draw closer, we start to develop a sense of urgency, which triggers a burst of adrenaline. The energy from adrenaline makes it easier for us to lock in and complete those tasks or projects we've been avoiding.

While this procrastination-adrenaline cycle can work to help us complete tasks, it also leads to an increase in stress and burnout along with a lower quality of work. But when we give our brains a dopamine boost upfront to kick our executive function into gear, we don't have to rely on panic and urgency to get moving.

Put It Into Practice:

Boost your dopamine to boost your motivation. Try sunlight, dancing to your favorite music, a cold shower, or eating spicy food instead of relying on last-minute deadlines and stress.

Procrastination, Executive Function, Productivity, Dopamine

January 22

Do It As a Hot Dog.

If there's something hard you've gotta do and you can't do it in the tub, do it as a hot dog. ~ Kristen West

The ADHD brain loves new, different, fun, and exciting things. That's why routine tasks often feel...well, mundane. And when something feels mundane, there's a good chance our brains won't produce enough dopamine to overcome motivational hurdles.

Injecting a bit of novelty and fun into our tasks can make it easier to start those necessary, boring tasks that keep our homes and families functioning.

One of my all-time favorite TikToks is from Kristen at The Centered Life Co. She suggests dressing up as a hot dog to do the dishes, vacuum, and clean the tub if motivation is low. The novelty and silliness of doing boring chores dressed as a hot dog releases dopamine, the neurotransmitter we need to initiate tasks, focus, and follow through.

No hot dog? No problem! Fun or novelty comes in many forms. Try changing up the environment, adding in music, or turning the task list into a game.

Put It Into Practice:

Boost motivation and interest in tedious tasks by adding a layer of fun, silliness, or novelty. Small changes can make boring tasks easier to start and maybe even enjoyable.

Taking Action, Productivity

Consistently Persistent.

Consistency is contrary to nature, contrary to life. The only completely consistent people are the dead. ~ Aldous Huxley

Habits make everyday ADHD life easier because they reduce the executive function needed to remember, decide, and act. But doing the same thing consistently, day after day, can feel incredibly unsatisfying to our ADHD brains.

We can build habits while satisfying our need for spontaneity. And it starts with shifting from consistency to persistence.

Consistency is about maintaining a regular pattern. Persistence is about continuing in some form, even when it's hard, when we don't feel like it, or when life throws obstacles in our way. Thanks to neuroplasticity, each time we follow through despite resistance, we strengthen our ability to follow through in the future.

So, as we look to establish new habits this year, aim for persistence and continual effort rather than rigid consistency. It's the small, repeated acts of persistence that lead to lasting change.

Put It Into Practice:

Evaluate a recent goal for ways you can make incremental progress. Focus on showing up in some way rather than the exact way.

Goal Setting, Taking Action

January 24

Messy Desk, Messy Mind.

*If a cluttered desk is a sign of a cluttered mind, of what,
then is an empty desk a sign? ~ Albert Einstein*

Keeping desk clutter at bay is a constant battle for many ADHD moms. When our workspace is filled with visual clutter, the extra stimulation makes it harder to start tasks, filter distractions, and stay focused. And since many desk tasks (paying bills, meal planning, or updating the family calendar) require concentration, visual overload can make them feel even harder.

It's like all those intrusive, distracting thoughts take a physical form of unopened mail, old to-do lists, and random sticky notes. And we need every ounce of focus to stay on track and ignore distractions.

Simple steps to tidy a workspace include:

- Clearing any trash or items that don't belong
- Grouping like items (lists, notes, or items to file together) to process later
- Scheduling time to process the piles and reset the space for the next work session

Creating a workspace with fewer visual demands helps us focus and give our brain a boost to zero in on just the task at hand.

Put It Into Practice:

Schedule time to declutter your workspace to help improve focus and prevent distractions.

Cleaning and Organizing, Time Investments, Productivity

Stop Paying for Nothing.

Most of what we say and do is not essential...Ask yourself at every moment, 'Is this necessary?' ~ Marcus Aurelius

Many of us have forgotten subscriptions. Maybe it's a free trial we forgot to cancel, an app we downloaded that we no longer use, or one of the dozens of streaming platforms we pay for to watch TV or listen to music but rarely touch.

A 2025 CNET survey[1] found that on average, subscribers spend about $17 a month, or about $200 per year, on subscriptions they don't use or forget they have. For ADHD brains, remembering these small but recurring expenses can be tricky. I'm willing to bet we all have a few subscriptions quietly draining our bank account each month.

Taking control of forgotten subscriptions isn't just about saving money, it's about creating a small but meaningful win in our lives. The key is to schedule a specific time to review and cancel them. Treating tasks like appointments increases the likelihood they get done. Blocking specific time for it makes "someday" actionable, giving the ADHD brain a clear signal to follow through.

This isn't about a huge money makeover but a small financial win that will add up and help simplify our life.

Put It Into Practice:

Schedule a subscription audit. Cancel anything you don't use, forgot about, or cringe seeing on your bank statement.

Money Management, Time Investments

January 26

Your Focus Impacts Your Fork.

Your body is the direct result of what you eat as well as what you don't eat. ~ Gloria Swanson

"Eat healthier" often tops our lists of annual goals. But for ADHD brains, planning, prepping and eating food requires a lot of executive functions. We need to organize, make decisions, and manage our time just to create a meal plan, grocery list, or meals.

It's easy to miss a meal when we're hyperfocusing on work, hobbies, or life in general. Then, when hunger finally hits, we want food immediately, whatever is quickest and within reach, rather than what's most nourishing. Add impulsivity into the mix, and stopping once we start eating something enjoyable is difficult because that dopamine hit feels too good to pause.

When we understand how executive function impacts eating, we can use coping strategies that actually work for our brains. By planning ahead, we can ensure we get the protein, nutrients, and energy we need to stay focused, motivated, and balanced throughout the day.

Put It Into Practice:

Set alarms to remind you to take a break and eat. Make a list of healthy "grab-and-go" snacks to keep on hand. And purchase pre-portioned items to help keep portion sizes in check.

Eating and Meal Planning, Executive Function, Self-Care

Which Brain is the Boss?

*When awareness is brought to an emotion, power
is brought to your life. ~ Tara Meyer Robson*

We often talk about the brain in two parts. The thinking brain, located in our prefrontal cortex, where reasoning and executive function reside, and the emotional brain, located in our amygdala and limbic system, where automatic responses live.

For the neurotypical population, these two systems work together in intense or emotional situations to reduce stress and find resolutions.

For ADHD brains, however, the connection between thinking and emotional centers isn't always as strong. The emotional brain can easily override the thinking brain, leading to floods of emotion, mood swings, and difficulty letting go.

With time and practice, we can work to enhance our emotional regulation skills. Mindfulness practices like deep breathing, meditation, or yoga can help. And simply naming the emotion we're feeling can also improve recognition, processing, and help us reframe negative responses for the future.

Put It Into Practice:

Choose a regulation tool for your toolbox to start improving your emotional regulation skills the next time life flares up.

Emotional Regulation, Mental Health

January 28

Your Battery is at 15%.

Self-care is never selfish, but it may feel that way when you live a frenzied life. ~ Arthur Ciaramicoli

I can't tell you how many times mom friends or clients have told me they simply don't have enough time to take care of themselves while managing everything else.

Mamas…we deserve better than this.

Part of the issue may be that we've lost the plot when it comes to what "self-care" means. It doesn't have to be expensive or time-consuming. Ideally, it's something we do regularly, maybe even daily.

In fact, here are ten free self-care ideas we can do in around ten minutes on a daily basis:

- Meditate
- Show gratitude
- Write affirmations
- Move our bodies
- Take deep breaths
- Laugh hard
- Contact a loved one
- Read something
- Make something
- Celebrate what we've accomplished today

For ADHD brains, small, consistent moments of self-care are powerful. They help recharge our energy, reduce overwhelm, and improve focus, making it easier to show up for everything else in our busy lives.

Put It Into Practice:

Pick one or two easy self-care practices you'd like to start incorporating into your daily life. Remember…if it's something you're doing just for you, it counts as self-care.

Self-Care, Mindset, Mom Life

Do You Need Inside Shoes?

I firmly believe that with the right footwear one can rule the world.
~ Bette Midler

File this under the "TikTok made me try it and I'm a convert" category...

If you're struggling to initiate a task or find your focus, try putting on shoes. Psychologists speculate that wearing shoes at home may trigger signals to our brain that it's time to be active and productive. For ADHD brains, these small cues can help jumpstart executive function and focus.

Wearing shoes can act like a sensory cue...a physical signal that tells your brain it's time to shift into "go mode." It's similar to how stimming works as a physical behavior that helps us self-regulate. While stimming often includes physical actions like rocking, vocal behaviors like humming, or object manipulation like clicking a pen, it also includes sensory actions to help us self-regulate or manage emotions. For many ADHDers, these behaviors give the brain the feedback it needs to settle, focus, and engage.

Next time we're stuck on initiating a task or trying to maintain focus on something we've already started, put on shoes and see if it signals to the brain, "Let's go!" If there's a no-shoes rule at home, consider keeping a special "productivity pair" or shoe-like slippers to wear strictly for work or task time.

Put It Into Practice:

Put on shoes to stimulate motivation and focus the next time you're struggling to start or follow through on a task.

Fidgets and Stimming, Taking Action, Productivity

January 30

Less Stuff. More Focus.

Organizing is what you do before you do something, so that when you do it, it is not all mixed up. ~ Winnie the Pooh

Decluttering can feel overwhelming for the ADHD brain, especially when we don't know where to start or the task feels massive. But even small steps to pare down what's around us can create big benefits for ADHD moms.

A less cluttered environment reduces stress and overwhelming feelings caused by unfinished tasks. It helps us concentrate at our desks, sleep more peacefully in our bedrooms, and put items away more quickly when they're actually visible. Less clutter also saves time searching for lost items…and money when we don't replace things we already have.

Even tiny decluttering projects can make a noticeable difference, not just in our physical space but in our mental clarity, focus, and motivation. For ADHD brains, seeing progress, even small wins, can boost dopamine and make it easier to tackle the next task.

Put It Into Practice:

Choose one small area to declutter today. Maybe a drawer, your purse, or that catch-all basket on your kitchen counter. Take it one step at a time and notice how it makes your space, and your brain, feel.

Cleaning and Organizing, Distractions

No Success Too Small.

Happiness is all about celebrating small wins.
~ Abdul Jawad Khattak

Executive functions like focus, planning, and task initiation rely on dopamine, the reward chemical that signals to our brain, "Hey, let's do that again!"

But because ADHD brains have lower dopamine levels and faster dopamine reuptake, we're constantly hunting for stimulation or reward to get that sweet dopamine hit.

Combine our dopamine deficiencies with self-esteem hits from missed deadlines, forgetfulness, and low motivation, it's easy to end up a Negative Nelly instead of Positive Polly.

Luckily, ADHDers respond incredibly well to positive reinforcement, even when it comes from ourselves. In fact, we may be our own best cheerleaders, since we spend a lot of time with us.

And the best part? Our celebrations can come from everyday actions. Shower today? Woohoo! Eat lunch? Way to go! It may feel silly, but acknowledging small wins gives our brain the dopamine it craves while reinforcing positive behavior.

Put It Into Practice:

Celebrate a success you had today. Big or small, celebrate it all (to get the dopamine hit)!

Dopamine, Mindset

February

First Attempt In Learning.

Success is stumbling from failure to failure with no loss of enthusiasm.
~ Winston Churchill

Today is National Get Up Day, established in 2017 by the U.S. Figure Skating Association to remind us to pick ourselves up when we fall and give it another try.

For many ADHDers, fear of failure can feel particularly intense. It might stem from people-pleasing tendencies, worry about how failure affects others, Rejection Sensitive Dysphoria (RSD) that amplifies the sting of criticism, or perfectionism that makes starting feel impossible unless we can do it perfectly.

But what if we trained our brains to think of failure as a stepping stone instead of a roadblock...a First Attempt In Learning? (Get it?)

Neuroscience shows that through practice and repetition, we can create new neural pathways, making what once felt impossible become possible...eventually. See, we can teach an old dog new tricks.

Put It Into Practice:

Practice reframing lessons as wins. Identify a situation where you thought you failed in the past and find something positive or instructive that came from it. Celebrate that insight as a win.

Mindset, RSD, Taking Action

February 2

Good. Better. Best.

*Do not fixate on one path, because then you are likely to give up
when that path is blocked. ~ Po Bronson*

Some days are easier to ADHD than others. But when we don't adjust our expectations on low-energy, low-dopamine days, it's easy to feel discouraged...and even less motivated to get started.

One strategy that helps is creating a range of options for what success can look like. Personally, I like to think in terms of good, better, and best:

- Good is the minimum we need to do to keep the wheels turning.
- Better is the baseline plus a little extra to help prevent feeling behind.
- Best happens when we do it all, assuming all the stars align and our dopamine is firing on all cylinders.

It's perfectly OK if not every day is a best day. What matters is aligning our expectations with our schedule, availability, and energy. Scaling tasks to our current capacity helps prevent shame, reduce overwhelm, and keep progress moving forward.

Put It Into Practice:

Review your to-do list and identify tasks you've been avoiding. Look for places to scale any tasks back from "best" to "good" or "better" so you can actually get started and check them off.

Energy Management, Taking Action, Procrastination, Mindset

You Spin Me Right Round.

Overthinking is a symptom of underacting.
~ Adam Grant

Making decisions can feel exhausting…particularly when there are too many options from what to eat for breakfast to what to watch on TV.

Choice paralysis, also known as analysis paralysis, happens when we get stuck overanalyzing, feel overwhelmed by an abundance of options, or fear making the wrong choice. Since every decision requires executive function, the more options we have, the more mental energy it takes to move forward.

So how do we stop the spin when our brains are stuck in a swirling cyclone of possibilities? We reduce the number of choices so we can take action.

For example, when deciding where to go on vacation, limit the options based on factors like budget, accommodation availability, or destinations everyone agrees on. Or limit options by setting a deadline because limited time to research forces us to choose from the information we already have instead of endlessly collecting more.

Remember…fewer choices mean fewer decisions and less overwhelm.

Put It Into Practice:

Decide in advance how many options you'll consider or how long you'll spend researching so you can move forward instead of creating even more choices.

Decision-Making, Productivity, Taking Action

February 4

Less Hot Mess Express.

*Burnout isn't just a problem to be solved; more importantly,
it's a relationship to be addressed. ~ Eva Selhub, MD*

The ADHD burnout cycle goes something like this…We say "yes" too often, overcommit, and pour all our energy into meeting expectations, especially when we don't want to disappoint others.

At the same time, we underestimate how long things will take and how much we're already juggling, leading to dopamine depletion.

As our energy drops, motivation, focus, and follow-through get harder. Progress slows, pressure builds, stress rises, mistakes happen, and suddenly it's all aboard the Hot Mess Express (toot, toot!).

Eventually, we hit physical, emotional, and mental exhaustion. We withdraw, push through on fumes, and use every last ounce of energy just to survive.

Sound familiar? To break the cycle, start with awareness…notice the patterns that lead us to overcommit, underestimate our capacity, and run ourselves ragged. When we can spot those patterns, it's easier to say "yes" less, step back from commitments, and protect time for rest and recovery. With practice, burnout becomes something we can interrupt instead of endure.

Put It Into Practice:

Notice what shows up right before burnout hits. Awareness is the first step toward making changes that reduce stress and prevent burnout in the future.

Burnout, Anxiety, Self-Care

Passwords Managed.

Passwords are like underwear: you don't let people see it, you should change it very often, and you shouldn't share it with strangers. ~ Chris Pirillo

ADHDers often struggle with remembering details, which is why many of us reuse the same password over and over. It feels easier. But speaking from experience, it isn't worth the risk.

I learned this the hard way when someone hacked my Walmart account and ordered AirPods in a state over a thousand miles away. Cleaning up that mess was stressful, time-consuming, and completely avoidable.

On top of our own logins, many of us manage accounts for our kids and sometimes even a spouse or family member. That's a lot for an ADHD brain to track. A simple password system supports our memory, protects our information, and gives us peace of mind in an increasingly digital world.

The system doesn't have to be complicated. It might be a printed list of accounts and passwords stored securely. Or a password manager (like Google Password Manager, LastPass, or NordPass) that creates strong passwords, saves them, and autofills when needed.

Put It Into Practice:

Choose a system (paper or using a password manager) and start updating your passwords so your brain doesn't have to remember them all.

Time Investments, Cleaning and Organizing, Memory Support

February 6

Executive Function vs Dinner.

*You can't cook quick, healthy meals if you don't have a plan
and ingredients on hand. ~ Carolyn Williams*

We all have to eat, but many of us with ADHD struggle to feed ourselves and our families. And like many ADHD challenges, it comes down to executive function.

Decision fatigue creeps in when we have to decide what to make and what to buy. Initiating the tasks of grocery shopping or cooking can feel impossible, especially at the end of the day when dopamine reserves are low. Add in organization (knowing what we have), time management (planning when to eat), and impulse control (hello, grocery store aisles), and meal planning can feel downright overwhelming.

No wonder drive-thrus and takeout seem so much easier. But if our budget or bellies don't agree, the solution isn't trying harder. It's making things simpler. Repeating meals or themes each week reduces decisions, streamlines shopping, and lowers the mental load. And remember, we don't need Martha Stewart–approved dinners every night to feed our families well.

Put It Into Practice:

Choose five simple dishes for a weekly meal plan and list the ingredients. Repeat the same meals next week or rotate them to build a few go-to weekly menus to reuse when your brain is tired.

Eating and Meal Planning, Executive Function, Mom Life

DIFF It.

Small deeds done are better than great deeds planned.
~ Peter Marshall

DIFF It stands for "Do It For Five minutes." I created this acronym when I began working out again after my cancer treatment. It was hard to motivate myself to rebuild the routine. But I knew it was so important because all my doctors and physical therapists kept telling me it was.

So I made a deal with myself to work out for 5 minutes. Some days I kept going. Some days I stopped. Either way, I did something rather than nothing.

Since then, I've applied DIFF It to a multitude of tasks I'm feeling less than motivated to do like folding laundry, sanding drywall repairs in my kids' bedroom, and writing scripts for YouTube videos.

DIFF It works because it removes pressure, lowers the barrier to starting, and gives our ADHD brains a quick win. Even if that's all we do, 5 minutes feels doable, non-threatening, and often enough to get some momentum going.

Put It Into Practice:

Do something you've been putting off for just five minutes today. If you want to keep going after the timer goes off, great. If not, remember 5 minutes of progress is more than no minutes.

Taking Action, Productivity

February 8

Start Your Day Your Way.

How you spend your morning can often tell you what kind of day you are going to have. ~ Lemony Snicket

A morning routine acts like a warm-up for our brain and body. It creates predictability and structure for our ADHD brains, helping us transition from sleep to action without immediately draining our executive function. And no…it doesn't need to start before the sun rises to be effective.

A simple morning routine helps reduce the number of decisions we make early in the day, preserving precious dopamine and mental energy for later. It gives us a moment to orient ourselves to what's coming up, where our energy may be needed, and how to pace ourselves before the day takes over.

Morning routines also offer built-in support for emotional regulation. When we start the day feeling grounded and cared for, we're less likely to feel reactive or overwhelmed as demands pile up. And when we include something just for us, like movement, quiet, creativity, or connection, it becomes easier to stay consistent because our needs aren't always last on the list.

Put It Into Practice:

Start building your morning routine by choosing 2–3 simple things you'd like to do each morning to support your ADHD brain and set yourself up for a smoother day.

Morning Routine, Self-Care, Energy Management

End Your Day Your Way.

The way to a more productive, more inspired, more joyful life
is getting enough sleep. ~ Arianna Huffington

Sleep is essential for ADHD brains because it supports executive function, emotional regulation, and memory. Without enough rest, focus, decision-making, and impulse control can feel even harder.

But many ADHDers struggle to wind down at the end of the day. That doesn't mean we have to accept sleepless nights.

Perhaps what we need is a "sleepy time launch sequence." A simple, regular routine like "dim the lights, shut down screens, wash our face, brush our teeth, and work on a Sudoku puzzle" that signals to our brain it's time to wind down and move toward sleep.

Since quick transitions are often difficult for ADHD brains, setting up a routine that slowly introduces the idea of winding down helps us get to sleep at a reasonable hour within a reasonable amount of time. Will it work immediately? Probably not. But over time, it will help train our brain and body.

Put It Into Practice:

Choose 3-4 simple actions to include in a bedtime routine that helps your brain and body wind down. For bonus points, set a nightly alarm to remind you to start your routine.

Sleep, Self-Care

February 10

Flying (Time) Blind.

Time moves slowly but passes quickly.
~ Alice Walker

When we look at the clock and think, "Where did the last 3 hours go?!?" we're experiencing what is known as time blindness, or the inability to sense that time has passed or accurately estimate how long a task will take.

Neurobiologists believe perceiving and estimating time is linked to activity levels in the prefrontal cortex of the brain. Struggling to pull ourselves out of a hyperfocus hole or underestimating how long a task will take makes sense when we remember ADHD brains often have weaker structure and function in this area. This makes planning, prioritizing, and staying on schedule extra challenging.

The best way to avoid getting sucked into hyperfocus is to plan how to stop a task or project before starting. Set an alarm, limit the scope of work to certain steps, or ask someone to check that we've stopped. Doing this gives our ADHD brain external cues to manage time, so we can stay on track and avoid blindly losing hours.

Put It Into Practice:

Plan how you'll break your hyperfocus before starting a task or project that might suck you in. Consider alarms, timers, or accountability partners to help you manage your time.

Time Blindness, Time Management, Productivity

Take a (Brain) Dump.

Your mind is for having ideas, not holding them.
~ David Allen

Having an ADHD brain is kind of like having 47 browser tabs open at once. Thoughts swirl around constantly, pulling our attention in every direction. We may get distracted by a new idea or worry we'll forget something important, and before we know it, we're spinning our wheels instead of getting anything done.

What we need is a place to dump all these thoughts. A brain dump supports ADHD memory by giving our brain a place to park the information we want to remember later. It reduces mental clutter by storing thought distractions outside our brain for better focus or creativity.

Since many of us with ADHD are visual thinkers, brain dumps give us a physical list of our intrusive thoughts so we can organize, prioritize, and take action later (if needed).

There are no rules for a brain dump…jot your thoughts on paper, type them in a Word doc or Notes app, or record a voice memo to revisit later, whatever works best in that moment.

Put It Into Practice:

Create a brain dump when you're struggling to wind down or focus your busy brain. Revisit the list later to organize, prioritize, and take action as needed.

Memory Support, Distractions, Productivity

February 12

Mom Brain or ADHD.

It's not easy being a mom. If it were easy,
fathers would do it. ~ Betty White

Motherhood can feel exhausting. And overwhelming. And stressful. And all of this can contribute to feelings of anxiety and depression.

Anxiety may make us restless or hyperactive, struggle to focus, make impulsive decisions, or have trouble sitting still. Depression can bring lack of focus, forgetfulness, and difficulty with motivation and decision-making.

Do motherhood challenges along with anxiety and depression symptoms sound remarkably similar to ADHD? Why, yes. Yes, they do. The major difference between everyday, run-of-the-mill mom brain and ADHD is the intensity and duration of symptoms.

With mom brain, our forgetfulness, distractedness, and mood swings typically resolve within a few years of giving birth for the final time. With ADHD, it's very likely we've experienced these symptoms throughout our life.

Regardless of the root cause, it's important to seek support if any of our symptoms impact our everyday life. Seeking support shows strength.

Put It Into Practice:

Call or message your primary care doctor or a mental health provider to discuss an ADHD evaluation if you feel your symptoms go beyond typical mom brain or you have additional symptoms that need to be addressed.

Mom Life, Mental Health

What's Yours Like?

Every brain comes with its own challenges but it's when you acknowledge those challenges and learn to optimize your strengths then you will really begin to understand what you are capable of. ~ Lisa Castenada

A few years back, I needed new tires for my car. My mechanic recommended an online place because it was cheaper. But when the tires were delivered to the shop, they were the wrong size for my tiny car. They would have worked for someone else's car, just not mine.

In much the same way, not every ADHD coping strategy fits every ADHD mom. Our unique version of ADHD is a combination of strengths, challenges, upbringing, and life experiences. That's why it's so important to understand our personal variant before diving into coping skills.

Reading books, listening to podcasts, watching videos, or discussing life with a mental health professional can help pinpoint the areas where we need support. Once we understand our ADHD, we can start building the strategies that help us thrive in a world that wasn't designed for us.

Put It Into Practice:

List the strengths and challenges you experience to better understand your unique version of ADHD. Then start to research coping strategies that align with your needs.

ADHD Symptoms

February 14

Love and ADHD.

A great marriage is not when the "perfect couple" comes together. It's when an imperfect couple learns to enjoy their differences. ~ Dave Meurer

I know I'm easier to love some days than others. I can be hyperactive, forgetful, and my lack of impulse control makes me loud, filter-less, and prone to a hair-trigger temper that rears its ugly head at the strangest times. And don't get me started on my lack of motivation to do the dishes.

But I'm also the one who'll drop everything when someone needs to process feelings or act the fool to get the party started on the dance floor.

Developing awareness around our ADHD symptoms and how they impact others goes a long way in strengthening our relationships, whether it's romance or friendship. Discussing our struggles helps others understand our behavior and opens lines of communication to prevent future conflict.

These conversations aren't about shaming us or masking what makes us unique. Instead, they explain how our ADHD impacts our life and clarifies the support we need from the people who love us.

Put It Into Practice:

Talk with someone you love about the ADHD symptoms that challenge you most to help them understand and support you better.

Relationships, Mindset, ADHD Symptoms

The Positive Power of No.

Don't be afraid of losing people, but be afraid of losing yourself trying to make everyone happy. ~ Naguib Mahfouz

From chocolate to wine to making other people happy, too much of a good thing can become not-so-good if we aren't careful. And us ADHD moms are particularly prone to people-pleasing traps.

It may be due to Rejection Sensitive Dysphoria (RSD) and our desire to avoid negative interactions. Or it could be poor impulse control, time blindness, and decision-making difficulties that lead to overcommitment. Maybe making others happy gives us a much-needed hit of dopamine.

But unchecked people-pleasing has consequences. Burnout and resentment can creep in, straining our relationships and leaving us feeling unfulfilled. We may neglect our physical and emotional well-being because we're too busy ensuring everyone else is happy.

When exhaustion and resentment show up, our best tool is the word "no". It takes practice. And fighting through a bit of guilt. Acknowledge those feelings, but remember that feeling guilty doesn't mean saying "no" is wrong. Saying "no" is an act of self-respect, protecting time, energy, and well-being so we can show up fully for the people and things that matter most.

Put It Into Practice:

Build confidence in protecting your time and energy by practicing saying "no" to low-stakes requests.

Relationships, Mindset, RSD, Self-Care

February 16

Scheduling vs Planning.

The key is not to prioritize what's on your schedule,
but to schedule your priorities. ~ Stephen Covey

For most ADHD moms, family life would be absolute chaos without a schedule. Our ADHD brains thrive on structure and clear boundaries because, without them, we can easily get pulled into distractions, hyperfocus on the wrong thing, or forget important tasks entirely.

Although the terms schedule and plan are often used interchangeably, they serve different purposes when it comes to productivity and time management.

Scheduling creates awareness around commitments and availability so we can better plan what to do and when to do it. Planning shows us the exact steps we need to take to go from now to completion.

Without both a solid plan and a schedule, many tasks and projects, even the ones we're really excited about, may idle in the realm of eventually or someday for eternity. For our ADHD brains, having both is like giving our executive function a roadmap and turn-by-turn directions to stay on track.

Put It Into Practice:

Create a step-by-step plan for an important task or project on your to-do list. Then schedule each step at a specific time so you'll have dedicated moments to actually work toward completion.

Planning, Time Management, Productivity

A Hanger Hack.

I really like doing the laundry, because I succeed at it. But I loathe putting it away. It is already clean. ~ Jenny Holzer

I hate laundry almost as much as I hate dishes. Almost. I think it's because there are just so many steps involved that it's hard for my ADHD brain to get motivated...unless I realize my 12-year-old has worn the same pants three days in a row.

For me, laundry isn't one task. It's a whole chain of tasks, and ADHD brains tend to stall when there are too many steps between starting and done. One small trick that gets me over the hurdle of putting laundry away is keeping all the empty hangers at one end of the closet bar, instead of scattered between clothes.

It turns out that the extra step of hunting for empty hangers (when I'm already tired, already bored, and already low on motivation) was just one step too many. My brain would hit that friction point and decide, "Never mind, I'll do this later."

With all the empty hangers together, I can grab what I need immediately. That tiny reduction in effort lowers the activation energy enough to make it more likely I'll finish the task. It may feel laughably simple, that is exactly the point. When we remove even one energy-draining step, follow-through becomes much more possible.

Put It Into Practice:

Pick a closet. Any closet. And gather all the empty hangers at one end of the bar. If you're feeling particularly energetic, repeat in another closet.

Cleaning and Organizing, Mom Life

February 18

I Can't Move.

*A mother continues to labor long after
the baby is born. ~ Lisa-Jo Baker*

When we've got a work deadline, projects of our own, summer camp sign-ups to handle... and then suddenly realize the jersey our kid needs for tomorrow's game is still dirty from last week, you'd think all that urgency would light a fire under our motivation.

But instead, our ADHD brain (already juggling challenges with motivation, task initiation, working memory, and decision fatigue) says, "That's it. I'm out." This experience is often referred to as ADHD paralysis.

ADHD paralysis happens when our brain becomes so overloaded processing too much information that it essentially shuts down, making even simple tasks feel impossible to start or complete.

When we slip into paralysis mode, a simple action plan can help interrupt it before it fully takes hold. Helpful strategies include moving your body, verbally processing what you're feeling and what needs to happen next, and working to let go of perfectionist tendencies.

Put It Into Practice:

Develop a plan for interrupting paralysis so you're ready when it strikes.

Paralysis, Burnout, Self-Care

Eating with Intention.

When walking, walk. When eating, eat.
~ Zen Proverb

Struggles with distraction, memory, decision-making, time management, and focus don't just impact our productivity, they also impact our daily eating habits. When we skip meals, we lose the fuel our ADHD brains need to manage symptoms and create that all-important dopamine that powers our executive function.

Practicing mindful eating and using external cues can help keep our eating habits on track, ensuring we get the nutrients our brains and bodies need.

Start with simple strategies like setting reminders for meals during tasks that may lead to hyperfocus. Keep a short list of easy "grab and go" foods on hand to reduce decision fatigue and make eating easier. When possible, aim for options that include protein and complex carbohydrates to support neurotransmitter production and stabilize blood sugar.

And try not to multitask while eating. While focusing solely on eating may feel inefficient, it helps our brain register fullness and reduces the mental fatigue that comes from task switching.

Put It Into Practice:

Practice intentional eating by setting mealtime reminders, keeping brain-boosting foods on hand, and focusing on eating during your meals.

Eating and Meal Planning, Self-Care

February 20

Share the Work.

The first rule of management is delegation. Don't try and do everything yourself because you can't. ~ Anthea Turner

I am a massive fan of checklists…probably because I've forgotten steps, items, or where I left off in a project more times than I can count. For ADHD brains, holding multi-step tasks in working memory is exhausting, and checklists take that pressure off.

Another reason I love checklists? They make delegation so much easier. A checklist shows someone the exact steps needed to complete a task from start to finish and allows them to take over from wherever we left off without needing extra explanation.

If we work in an office or run our own business, we've probably come across the term SOP, which stands for Standard Operating Procedure. An SOP is simply a standardized checklist that allows anyone to follow the same steps and achieve consistent results.

But SOPs aren't just for the workplace. We can standardize everyday tasks, like cleaning the bathroom or paying the bills, so other people can step in and help without adding more mental load.

Put It Into Practice:

Create an SOP for one task or routine in your home. It doesn't need to be fancy. Simply write down the steps in the order you want them done, and, voilà! You're done.

Checklists, Mom Life, Productivity

February 21

Self-Care Isn't Optional.

Self-care is your fuel...Whatever the road ahead or the path you've taken, self-care is what keeps your motor running and your wheels turning. ~ Melissa Steginus

Burnout is defined by the World Health Organization as "a syndrome conceptualized as resulting from chronic workplace stress that has not been successfully managed." But burnout isn't limited to the workplace...especially for moms.

Between the expectations placed on us as humans, parents, partners, and workers, it's no wonder we feel stressed so often. For ADHD moms, that stress is often amplified by the ongoing mental load of managing executive function challenges day after day.

And while there are plenty of questionable statistics floating around about higher rates of burnout in the ADHD community, personal experience tells me this much: burnout happens. A lot. Like...*a lot* a lot.

One reliable way to reduce burnout in our busy ADHD mom lives is by intentionally building in regular self-care. While massages and girls' trips are lovely, self-care doesn't have to be elaborate. Sleep, nourishment, movement, and meaningful connection are simple, sustainable ways to care for ourselves every day.

Put It Into Practice:

Brainstorm a short list of self-care options you can realistically incorporate into your routine to help reduce burnout.

Burnout, Self-Care

February 22

Making Deadlines Work.

I love deadlines. I like the whooshing sound they
make as they fly by. ~ Douglas Adams

A client once came to me for support as she applied to grad school. She wanted to apply the year before but waited too long to gather all the required pieces, and as a result, she missed the deadline.

For many ADHDers, breaking a large project with multiple steps into smaller tasks can feel surprisingly difficult because our brains initially register the project as one step.

Then, as the deadline approaches, reality sets in. We realize it isn't just one step (apply for grad school) but a series of smaller steps like requesting recommendations, drafting a thesis statement, and creating a CV. And each of those steps takes time. Potentially time we don't have.

When we break large projects into smaller steps early, and assign each step a deadline, it becomes easier to initiate action. Smaller steps feel more manageable, less overwhelming, and more doable.

As a bonus, each completed step provides a small dopamine boost, which helps keep our ADHD brains motivated and moving forward toward the larger goal.

Put It Into Practice:

Take one large project you've been putting off and break it into smaller tasks. Schedule time to work on one step this week. Acknowledge each win as you go.

Procrastination, Planning, Time Management, Taking Action

Inbox Detox.

The email of the species is deadlier than the mail.
~ Stephen Fry

Not too long ago, my personal Gmail inbox had well over 10,000 emails. I cringed every time I opened it. Along with feeling overwhelmed, I avoided checking it altogether because it was so distracting.

That avoidance meant I missed a reminder to renew the business license for my professional organizing company (I keep it active…just in case). It wasn't the end of the world to reactivate it, but it was a preventable problem that cost me time and energy I could have used elsewhere.

Decluttering our inbox makes it easier to spot important messages, reduces distractions, and prevents ADHD task paralysis that makes us avoid email altogether.

Cleaning out an email inbox doesn't have to be one big, overwhelming task. We can delete old emails one day, bulk-delete messages from a specific sender another day, or spend a few minutes unsubscribing from newsletters so the inbox doesn't refill as quickly.

Breaking an overwhelming task into smaller, manageable steps lowers the barrier to action and makes progress feel possible.

Put It Into Practice:

Choose one specific email-decluttering task and spend a little time getting your inbox in order.

Cleaning and Organizing, Time Investments, Productivity

February 24

Forget Me Not.

The only thing faster than the speed of thought is the speed of forgetfulness. ~ Vera Nazarian

I joke about my need to put everything on an external hard drive. I rely heavily on reminders and alarms to stay on track. I make notes and lists constantly, and there's rarely a pad of sticky notes out of reach.

My need for memory support comes down to working memory, the brain's temporary workspace that holds information long enough for us to decide what to do with it.

I like to describe working memory as a waiting room. Information walks in and takes a seat, waiting for the nurse to direct it to the room to see the doctor. But sometimes, instead of waiting, that information turns right around and walks out the doors…never to be heard from again.

That's why creating external supports is so important for ADHD working memory. These reminders are like leaving a note in the waiting room that says, "If this comes back up, here's where we left off." They bridge the gap between intention and follow-through when our brains can't reliably hold onto information on their own.

Put It Into Practice:

Identify one way to support your working memory externally. This could look like carrying a small notebook, recording voice memos, or keeping a running list in the notes app on your phone.

Memory Support, Executive Function

Think and Chew Gum.

For me, the dumbest rule is that you can't chew gum in school. For some reason, chewing gum for me gets my brain going. ~ Brie Larson

I chew through four to five packs of Extra Polar Ice gum each week. And it turns out it might actually help me focus.

A 2022 study published in the Journal of Cognitive Psychology[2] found that repetitive motor activity, specifically gum chewing, can improve sustained attention in adults with ADHD.

Yep. All those years we were told not to chew gum in class…imagine how much more we might have been able to focus.

Researchers are beginning to better understand that so-called "mindless" fidgets, like chewing gum, are actually forms of stimming or repetitive movements and behaviors that help regulate attention, emotions, and sensory input.

For many ADHDers, fidgeting isn't about being disruptive. It's often an outward sign of the brain trying to stay engaged, calm itself, or maintain focus. When the body has something simple and repetitive to do, the brain may have an easier time settling into the task at hand.

Rather than fighting these instincts, allowing small, supportive fidgets can be a surprisingly effective way to work *with* our ADHD brains instead of against them.

Put It Into Practice:

Keep your favorite gum on hand and chew a piece when you need to focus. Notice if the added sensory input helps with your attention.

Fidgets and Stimming, Focus, Productivity

February 26

The Need to Be Alone.

Please kindly go away, I'm introverting. ~ Beth Buelow

Not all ADHDers are extroverted, energetic, and talkative. In fact, ADHD introverts often go undiagnosed because the energy we associate with ADHD isn't always visible. Instead, the hyperactivity happens inside the ADHD introvert's brain.

Unlike their extroverted counterparts, who recharge via social interactions and external stimuli, introverted ADHDers need quiet and solitude to recharge.

Social interactions, overstimulation, and constant multitasking can be extra draining for ADHD introverts. Conversations with coworkers, small talk at school events, or coordinating logistics with other parents can quickly burn through their mental bandwidth...even if those interactions are positive.

Because of this, ADHD introverts benefit from being intentional about protecting and replenishing their energy. Making space for alone time isn't selfish...it's necessary.

For example, my introverted husband works an extroverted customer service job where constant interaction and small talk drains his energy. He recharges by spending time alone and listening to music, which helps him reset and show up more fully for his next shift.

Put It Into Practice:

Schedule intentional alone time after people-heavy days to refill your energy and prevent burnout if you're an ADHD introvert.

Introverts, Self-Care, Energy Management

Decisions Take a Village.

You cannot make progress without making decisions.
~ Jim Rohn

Decision-making requires a significant amount of executive function. We have to evaluate and prioritize options, hold relevant information in mind, make time to consider our choices, and stay flexible if something changes. Honestly, I'm exhausted just writing about it. It's no wonder decision-making can completely drain an ADHD brain.

If we've ever opened an email, read it, thought about responding, struggled with what to say, decided we need more information, and told ourselves we'd come back later...only to find that email still sitting in our inbox two weeks later, we've experienced ADHD decision paralysis.

Our brain spirals trying to craft the "perfect" response, manage the emotions tied to the message, and anticipate outcomes all at once. And when that feels like too much, task avoidance kicks in.

But we don't have to stay stuck. Boosting dopamine through movement, novelty, or working during your best focus window can make decisions feel more manageable.

Put It Into Practice:

Boost your dopamine first (through movement, music, or novelty), or tackle decisions during your highest-energy time of day.

Decision-Making, Productivity, Executive Function

February 28

Low Dopamine is Good?

Anything worth doing is worth doing slowly.
~ Mae West

Imagine starting the day driven by intention and calm rather than stress and immediate gratification. Sound like a fantasy? It doesn't have to be.

A low-dopamine morning routine starts the day with calm, low-stimulation choices to preserve dopamine and support executive function.

Instead of jumping straight into high-stimulation activities like scrolling social media, consuming sugar or caffeine, or doing an intense workout, we opt for gentler ways to ease into the day that encourage calm and sustained attention.

It's not about deprivation…it's about regulation. By avoiding early dopamine spikes, we reduce the likelihood of crashing later in the day and feeling unmotivated, scattered, or overwhelmed. When our brains get a big dopamine hit first thing in the morning, they often spend the rest of the day chasing that same level of stimulation, making it harder to focus on what actually matters.

Put It Into Practice:

Think of ways you can ease into your day rather than starting with a dopamine burst. Swap screens for sunlight. Delay sugar and caffeine in favor of water. And try to avoid stress-inducing activities when possible (we are mothers after all).

Morning Routine, Self-Care

March

March 1

Adventure Awaits.

Actually, the best gift you could have given her
is a lifetime of adventures. ~ Lewis Carroll

Spring break is right around the corner, and travel planning requires a lot of executive function. There's decision-making about where to go, how to get there, and what to do. There's organizing transportation and accommodations, and following through with bookings and payments, which is typically the least exciting part of travel.

Many ADHD moms gravitate towards the fun parts of travel planning, like where we'll eat or what activities we'll do before nailing down the important details like dates, transportation, and accommodations.

When we understand how our ADHD impacts trip planning, we can put simple strategies in place to make sure everything is handled and actually enjoy the trip… as much as a mom can enjoy a vacation (aka parenting in a different location).

By creating a travel planning checklist that includes all those boring but important details, we ensure they're addressed for upcoming and future trips…and *then* we can move on to the fun stuff.

Put It Into Practice:

Create a travel-planning checklist that covers where you're going, when you're going, how you'll get there, what to bring, and what needs to happen at home before you leave.

Travel, Checklists, Planning, Mom Life

March 2

Who? What? When?

You may delay, but time will not.
~ Benjamin Franklin

Many years ago (and before my ADHD diagnosis), I attended a yearly planning workshop as part of a business coaching program, and it seriously stressed me out.

I couldn't wrap my brain around what I wanted to happen in three, six, or twelve months. It wasn't because I wasn't trying or I didn't want to do the work. It was more likely because my ADHD brain struggled to plan and problem-solve for anything not in the immediate future.

A "time horizon" is how far into the future a task or project feels real enough to act on. And time horizons for ADHDers tend to be much shorter than for neurotypical brains.

This shortened time horizon helps explain why we struggle with timeliness and procrastination…but it doesn't mean we're stuck that way.

When we list the steps we need to take and assign target dates, we effectively shorten our time horizon and bring what feels like the distant future into the present.

Put It Into Practice:

Create a simple timeline for a project you'd like to start sooner rather than later. Write out what needs to happen and when, so you can clearly see the next step and its due date.

Procrastination, Time Blindness, Time Management

Your Sweat Weapon.

Take care of your body. It's the only place you have to live. ~ Jim Rohn

The single most important tool in our ADHD management toolbox is regular movement.

Beyond acting as an outlet for our pent-up energy, which is especially important for us hyperactive-type ADHDers, exercise releases neurotransmitters like dopamine. And when we get that all-important shot of dopamine, we often see improvement in our planning, organizing, focus, and time management.

Regular movement can also help normalize brain-derived neurotropic factor (BDNF), a key molecule in the brain affecting learning and memory. Since movement releases endorphins, it can also help those of us with ADHD who struggle with depression or anxiety. And regular movement helps many of us both fall and stay asleep.

It doesn't have to be super hard, sweaty, or even what is traditionally considered "exercise." We get the brain-boosting benefits with just 10–15 minutes of elevated heart rate doing something we enjoy like playing with the kids or pets, active chores, or dance parties in the living room.

Put It Into Practice:

Find a way to move your body regularly to support both your brain and your overall well-being.

Exercise, Self-Care, Dopamine, Executive Function

March 4

Now vs. Not Now.

People with ADHD cannot deal with time, and that includes looking back to look ahead, to get ready for what's coming at you...The now is more compelling than the information you're holding in mind. ~ Dr. Russell Barkley

According to Dr. Russell Barkley, clinical psychologist and ADHD expert, ADHDers perceive time in two ways...It's either "Now," meaning currently on our radar. Or it's "Not Now," meaning it's in the future and doesn't require our attention...yet.

Because of this, those of us with ADHD often wait to act, even on something we feel excited or passionate about, until it becomes absolutely necessary. Or until it's already too late.

While the urgency, fear, and anxiety caused by procrastination can help our ADHD brains lock in and focus, the stress that comes with it takes a toll on both our brain and body.

There is a way to hack our brain's urgency trigger by creating a due date and adding accountability. A deadline or knowing we have to report progress helps our brain interpret a "Not Now" task as something that needs attention now.

Put It Into Practice:

Assign a due date to the task or next step of a project when you're struggling to make progress. Bonus points for asking a family member or friend to hold you accountable for finishing that step by the due date.

Time Blindness, Procrastination, Time Management

I See You.

Accountability is the glue that ties commitment to results.
~ Will Craig

Maybe it's our people-pleasing tendencies, but working alongside others can be incredibly motivating for ADHD brains.

Body doubling simply means working at the same time as someone else, either in person or online. It's based on the *Hawthorne effect*, which suggests that people tend to behave differently when they know they're being observed.

In other words, when we are supposed to be working and people can see us, we're more likely to follow through and do the work.

That "seeing" doesn't have to be in person. We can join online body-doubling sessions through platforms like Flow Club or Focusmate, tune into livestreams on YouTube or TikTok, or schedule a Zoom call with a friend. Just remember to keep the socializing to a minimum until the work is done.

And body doubling isn't only for "work" work. This strategy can help with any task we're struggling to start, from spring cleaning to writing a grocery list.

Put It Into Practice:

Schedule or join a body-doubling session to help you focus, start, and follow through.

Body Doubling, Accountability, Productivity, Taking Action

March 6

Revision Permission.

Expectations are dangerous when they are both
too high and unformed. ~ Lionel Shriver

ADHDers are incredible big-picture thinkers. We know we're capable of amazing feats, but we often forget that our strengths don't always lie in planning the steps, following through, or managing time well enough to bring those ideas to life.

Basically…our creative brains write checks that our ADHD brains can't always cash.

This doesn't mean we should think small or give up on big, exciting goals. But if a project feels overwhelming, sparks anxiety, or doesn't get started because it can't be done perfectly, it's okay to revise the plan.

Instead of finishing the whole project, aim to complete one portion by the original deadline. And then set a new deadline for the next step. Look for ways to delegate so progress continues even when we're not actively working on it. And accept "good for now" as an option for calling a project done, knowing we can always revisit and refine later.

Put It Into Practice:

Give yourself permission to revise. Break big projects into smaller steps, delegate when possible, and scale back the "perfect" version so you can make progress…at least for now.

Perfectionism, Procrastination, Goal Setting, Taking Action

Delete Dryer Delay.

Nothing got cleaned just because it got to the laundry room.
~ Craig D. Lounsbrough

If I had a nickel for every time I've started a load of laundry in the evening only to forget about it until the next morning, I could give this book away for free.

It stinks…both literally and metaphorically.

Because when we forget to switch our laundry, we pay the ADHD tax. We pay with more detergent. We pay with more water. And we pay with more time because we have to start over.

A few years back I discovered one of the many settings on my washer I typically ignored…the delay button. And that's when it dawned on me.

What if I loaded the washer at night but delayed starting the cycle until right before I woke up? That's when I'd actually remember to switch it over anyway. And then I added a reminder on my phone to change the laundry in the morning.

Since discovering this hack, I've saved myself many unnecessary rewashes…and reduced my ADHD tax burden.

Put It Into Practice:

Check if your washing machine has a delay cycle and try it the next time you start a load at night. And don't forget to set a reminder to switch it over in the morning.

Cleaning and Organizing, Mom Life, Memory Support

March 8

EF This Clutter.

*Don't own so much clutter that you will be relieved
to see your house catch fire. ~ Wendell Berry*

Clutter and motherhood often go hand in hand. And for us ADHD moms, managing clutter can feel particularly hard because organizing requires multiple executive functions working together.

There's decision-making around what stays and what goes, and where things should live. We rely heavily on visual cues because of forgetfulness, which can unintentionally contribute to visual clutter. And estimating how long an organizing project will take often feels overwhelming due to challenges with time management.

Motivating ourselves to start an organizing project can also be difficult when there isn't a strong enough reason to initiate the task…but hold on tight when our mother-in-law suddenly needs to stay in the guest room where we've been hiding all the bags and piles.

We can hack our executive function with simple strategies: using a body double for motivation and accountability, researching realistic project timelines, and choosing storage that keeps things visual and contained.

Put It Into Practice:

Pick one executive-function support for your next organizing session (a body double, a timer, or a realistic time estimate) and use it to make steady progress.

Cleaning and Organizing, Executive Function

What Lies Beneath.

The mind is like an iceberg, it floats with one-seventh of its bulk above water. ~ Sigmund Freud

When I was growing up in the 1980s, ADHD (or ADD as they called it back then) was basically ten-year-old boys who couldn't sit still. Obviously, I'm paraphrasing a little.

And even with advancements over the past few decades, it's still the outward-facing ADHD symptoms like fidgeting, distractibility, hyperactivity, and impulsivity that tend to get noticed by parents and teachers, leading to diagnosis and the development of coping strategies.

But there's a whole layer of ADHD symptoms that lie beneath the surface. And these often have a bigger impact on our overall well-being.

We may experience emotional dysregulation with mood shifts that get labeled as depression or anxiety, even when they stem from underlying ADHD. We may not connect struggles with relationships, information processing, or even taking a shower to our ADHD. Sleep and eating challenges are also tied to these less visible symptoms.

When we bring awareness to how these hidden ADHD symptoms show up in our lives, we can replace self-criticism with understanding and begin building coping skills that address what's really going on.

Put It Into Practice:

Research a few internal (less-visible) ADHD symptoms and use what you learn as a starting point for supportive coping strategies.

Awareness, ADHD Symptoms

March 10

I'll Have What She's Having.

One cannot think well, love well, sleep well,
if one has not dined well. ~ Virginia Woolf

I love food. I love cooking food. I love baking food. I even love shopping for food (when I have the time). But what I don't love is deciding what to eat or what to make.

I think it's because I feel overwhelmed by the sheer number of recipe options on Pinterest and all the new items to try at the grocery store. To make this easier on my ADHD brain, I limit my choices by using a set breakfast and lunch menu.

Instead of coming up with new breakfast and lunch ideas each week, I asked my family for their favorites and created a simple menu. They pick what they want for the upcoming week before we go grocery shopping.

This simple system streamlines what to serve and what to buy, and it reduces the daily mental load of figuring out what to eat.

Put It Into Practice:

Create a menu of favorite foods by asking your family what they enjoy (or listing go-to meals you already know work). Let them choose from it before your next grocery trip.

Eating and Meal Planning, Mom Life, Decision-Making

When You Can't Decide.

The more choices we are forced to make, the more the quality of our decisions deteriorates. ~ Greg McKeown

When the decision-making part of our brain is toast by 5 p.m., we're likely experiencing "decision fatigue."

Decision-making relies on multiple executive functions, including planning, working memory, and impulse control. When you combine that with the sheer number of choices we face throughout the day, it's no wonder our brains feel exhausted.

But if we can find a way to intentionally reduce the number of decisions we have to make, we can help prevent decision fatigue.

Establishing routines limits decision-making because we already know what to do…no deciding required. Using a checklist for a routine further reduces decisions by clearly showing what comes next.

We can also conserve decision-making energy by streamlining our options. Eating the same breakfast each morning or wearing a daily "uniform" frees up mental energy for the decisions that actually matter.

Put It Into Practice:

Pick one daily decision to eliminate this week. Bonus points for making a checklist so your routine runs on autopilot.

Decision-Making, Productivity

March 12

Jump First. Focus Later.

All creative activity begins with movement.
~ Joseph C. Zinker

There's a TikTok trampoline workout trend going around and it turns out that bouncing isn't just fun. It's also a powerful way to support the ADHD brain before asking it to focus.

Along with providing an outlet for excess energy, jumping stimulates the vestibular system (in the inner ear), which helps regulate balance and sensory input. The pressure from bouncing also activates proprioceptive input, supporting sensory regulation, grounding, and focus.

Bouncing also increases our heart rate, leading to boosts in neurochemicals like the mood-enhancing serotonin, focus-fueling norepinephrine, and executive-function–supporting dopamine. And because jumping is fun, it also releases endorphins, helping lower stress and improve overall mood.

Bottom line: when we jump first, we set our brains up to focus better later.

Put It Into Practice:

Boost your brain by bouncing. No trampoline or rebounder? Try exercises like jumping jacks, jump squats, or jumping rope for a similar effect. Or just blast some House of Pain and "Jump Around."

Exercise, Fidgets and Stimming, Focus, Self-Care

Mise en Place.

*Give me six hours to chop down a tree and I will spend
the first four sharpening the axe. ~ Abraham Lincoln*

The French culinary term "mise en place" translates to "put in place," meaning we gather and prepare the ingredients we'll need for a dish before we start cooking.

When everything is already in place, the barrier to entry is lower, making it much easier to jump in when we're ready.

This same principle supports task initiation for ADHDers because taking action is much easier when we don't have to hunt for supplies or make extra decisions before we start.

Think: laying out workout clothes the night before so we don't have to decide what to wear in the morning. Or keeping a cleaning checklist and supply caddy ready so we don't have to remember the steps or gather everything before getting started.

By reducing the energy and executive function required to prep for a task, we can redirect that effort into actually doing the darn thing.

Put It Into Practice:

Choose a task you struggle to start and decide how you can put everything in place ahead of time to make beginning easier.

Taking Action, Productivity

March 14

Address Your Stress.

Stress is not caused by what happens to us, but by our thoughts about what happens to us. ~ Kelly McGonigal

Burnout is what happens when stress runs too long without enough recovery. And while we may not be able to eliminate all stress from our lives as busy moms, we can lessen its impact on our bodies, minds, and relationships by identifying what's actually driving it.

In 1999, researchers at the University of California at Berkeley[3] identified six major stressors that can lead to burnout:

- Feeling chronically overloaded with work
- Lack of autonomy or control
- Lack of recognition or reward
- Lack of supportive relationships
- Carrying an unfair portion of the workload
- Spending significant time on tasks that don't align with your values

When we bring awareness to which of these stressors show up most often in our lives, we're better equipped to develop coping strategies and reduce the likelihood of future burnout.

Put It Into Practice:

Identify what's truly behind your stress so you can choose one boundary that protects you moving forward.

Burnout, Mental Health

Eat the Elephant.

There is only one way to eat an elephant, a bite at a time.
~ Desmond Tutu

When our spring cleanup plans feel like too much, we often don't start at all. Which is why I want to talk about elephants…eating elephants, to be precise.

And no…sadly, they aren't some mystical power source that suddenly gives us motivation or energy.

The idea of devouring an entire elephant is overwhelming. But when we focus on the small bites required to make progress, the task becomes far more manageable.

Instead of "I need to clean out the garage," we think "I'll start with this tool shelf." Instead of "I need to deep clean the kitchen," we think "I'll start by decluttering and wiping out this drawer."

Small tasks have a lower barrier to entry, making them easier to start. And each small win provides a dopamine boost that helps build momentum to keep going.

Put It Into Practice:

Eat your elephant by breaking down an area you want to clean or organize this spring into smaller, easily digestible tasks. Then start with just one bite.

Taking Action, Cleaning and Organizing

March 16

Your Spring Cleaning Roadmap.

*No wise pilot, no matter how great his talent and experience,
fails to use his checklist. ~ Charlie Munger*

Knowing the route ahead of time makes it much easier to get from point A to point B. And since many of us with ADHD struggle to get tasks from point A to point B, a roadmap can make all the difference.

Checklists are an easy way to chart our route through tasks, even ones we've done a million times. Or the ones we don't feel like doing. Checklists:

- Help us remember what needs to be done and keep track of the steps.
- Make it easier to pick up where we left off if we get distracted or run out of time.
- Make it easier to delegate because the steps are already spelled out.

When it comes to creating a cleaning checklist, we have options. We can start from scratch, download one, or use it as a template. We can group tasks by room, by type, or by day. There's no right or wrong way to do it... the best checklist is the one you'll actually use.

Put It Into Practice:

Create or print a cleaning checklist that works for your ADHD brain. Save it so you can reuse and update it next year.

Cleaning and Organizing, Checklists, Mom Life

Why You're Lucky.

I prefer to distinguish ADD as attention abundance disorder. Everything is just so interesting, remarkably at the same time. ~ Frank Coppola

Looking back, one reason I delayed an official ADHD diagnosis was fear of the label. But in the years since my diagnosis, I've learned not only what the symptoms are and how they affect my life but also how my ADHD brain can be a strength.

ADHDers are often incredibly creative and valued for our big-picture thinking and outside-the-box problem-solving. We tend to bring enthusiasm and empathy into our relationships. We're adaptable because doing the same thing over and over doesn't come naturally to us. When we learn how to work with hyperfocus instead of against it, we can be incredibly productive. Not to mention, if someone is looking for a night of spontaneous fun, we're usually the first call.

People with ADHD have achieved extraordinary things including Olympic gold medalists like Simone Biles and Michael Phelps, who have openly shared their ADHD diagnoses. And while we can't know for sure, some researchers have speculated that innovators like Albert Einstein, Thomas Edison, and Alexander Graham Bell may have had ADHD traits as well.

ADHD isn't just something to manage, it's something that can make us uniquely capable, creative, and resilient.

Put It Into Practice:

List some of the ADHD-related strengths or benefits you notice in your own life, even if they sometimes show up alongside challenges.

Mindset

March 18

Hack Your Hacks.

*Adapt what is useful, reject what is useless, and
add what is specifically your own. ~ Bruce Lee*

I use a lot of "hacks" to stay on track in my ADHD mom life. And almost none of them worked perfectly the first time. Most required a few rounds of trial and error before they actually fit my brain and my family.

Unfortunately, many of us ADHDers tend to operate from an "if at first we don't succeed, throw in the towel and hyperfocus on researching a completely new solution" mindset, rather than reworking a system we've already invested time and energy into.

It often takes time and tweaking to figure out what truly works for us. When we come across a hack we think might help, treat it as a baseline or jumping-off point, not a rigid rule.

If it works exactly as described by the creator, great! And if it doesn't, that doesn't mean the hack is useless or that we've failed. It may just need a little zhuzh to better match our routines, energy levels, or current season of life.

Put It Into Practice:

Dust off an ADHD hack you tried in the past that didn't work the way you hoped. If it felt too complicated or hard to maintain, simplify it or modify it so it better fits your flow.

Productivity, Mom Life

Busy House. Busy Brain.

Clutter smothers. Simplicity breathes.
~ Terry Guillemets

Decluttering matters for the ADHD brain. And I'm not just saying that as a former professional organizer.

Reducing clutter clears our physical space, making it easier to find what we need when we need it. It also clears mental space by reducing sensory overload and limiting visual distractions constantly competing for our attention.

Yep! The physical clutter in our homes can fuel intrusive thoughts while we're trying to concentrate. And we really don't need any more of those, thank you very much.

If you don't have hours, days, or weeks to declutter, that's okay. Small projects, done consistently, still make a meaningful impact.

As the saying goes, "Start where you are. Do what you can." Every item removed means fewer things to manage, fewer decisions to make, and less to sort through going forward.

Put It Into Practice:

Grab a box. Any box. Ask each family member to add five items they no longer need. Set a weekly reminder to add five more items. When the box is full, add "drop off donations" (or "schedule a pickup") to your to-do list.

Cleaning and Organizing, Distractions

March 20

Time to Move On.

Transitions are difficult for ADHD brains...Every time you switch tasks, your brain engages in four different tasks...Stop, Switch, Start, Focus. ~ Sue Rapp

When people picture ADHD, they often imagine jumping willy-nilly from one task to another. And while distractibility and hyperactivity can lead to frequent task-switching, many ADHDers also struggle to stop a task and transition to something new, especially when we're hyperfocused.

Difficulty moving on from a task is often rooted in...that's right... executive function challenges. Planning and time management challenges can mean we don't leave enough time to finish, making it hard to stop once we've finally found our flow. Working memory challenges can make us worry we'll lose an idea, information, or progress if we don't keep going.

Support strategies build awareness around our hyperfocus and transition tendencies. We can try:

- Setting timers to signal when it's time to wrap up.
- Planning buffer time between tasks to allow space to reset.
- Creating a brief wrap-up routine to help capture where we want to pick back up next time.

Put It Into Practice:

Add transition support like alarms, buffer time, or a wrap-up routine to make switching easier and help you stay on track.

Time Management, Time Blindness, Planning

First Day of Spring.

If we had not winter, the spring would not be so pleasant.
~ Anne Bradstreet

It's officially spring…bringing warmer weather, flowers, and seasonal allergies. The change of seasons is a great reminder to knock out home and personal maintenance tasks we might otherwise forget. These small time investments can reduce the ADHD tax like higher utility bills from clogged filters or costly repairs from neglected car maintenance.

For your home and property, remember to:

- Check and replace smoke detector batteries
- Change the furnace and refrigerator water filter
- Change the oil in the car
- Clean out the dryer vent

For you and your family:

- Replace toothbrushes
- Wash makeup brushes
- Delete unwanted digital photos
- Back up the computer's hard drive
- Drop off the donations in the back of the car

Put It Into Practice:

Schedule time this week for a few seasonal maintenance tasks for both your home and your family.

Time Investments, Cleaning and Organizing

91

March 22

Why Is This Taking So Long?

Most people overestimate what they can accomplish in a year and underestimate what they can achieve in a decade. ~ Tony Robbins

When scheduling organizing projects this spring, ADHD time blindness may convince us that we need less time than we actually need. Or that we can accomplish more in a given window than is realistic. Here are rough estimates for how long common organizing projects often take:

- Home Office – 6–18 hours
- Garages/Basements – 8–20 hours
- Closets – 2–8 hours
- Toy rooms – 4–8 hours
- Kitchens – 4–8 hours

Actual time will vary based on factors like how much there is to sort through, whether there's help, and how many distractions pop up. And I know these numbers might feel surprisingly long, but deciding what to keep, what to let go of, and where everything belongs is mentally exhausting and particularly taxing for the ADHD brain.

Put It Into Practice:

Schedule your next organizing project using the estimates above and build in more time than you think you'll need.

Cleaning and Organizing, Time Blindness, Time Management

This Mess Won't Clean Itself.

Spring is the time of plans and projects.
~ Leo Tolstoy

Unfortunately, time doesn't magically appear for the things piling up on our to-do list. So if spring cleaning is a priority, we have to intentionally make time for it by giving it space on our calendar.

Scheduling cleaning tasks like appointments turns them from vague wishes into real projects with clear start times, stop times, and expectations. Appointments support task initiation because we're more likely to follow through when something feels like a commitment rather than an optional "someday" task.

Knowing there's a defined endpoint can also make less-than-exciting cleaning tasks feel more manageable. Our ADHD brains are far more willing to start when we know we don't have to do it forever.

Effective cleaning task scheduling starts with deciding ahead of time what you'll work on, then blocking that time on your calendar. Setting a timer helps prevent hyperfocus and keeps us from neglecting other responsibilities. And if help is available, ask for it. We don't have to clean it all ourselves.

Put It Into Practice:

Block specific time for specific spring cleaning tasks on your calendar to increase the chances they actually get done.

Cleaning and Organizing, Time Management, Taking Action, Mom Life

March 24

Stuck Before You Start.

*Aiming for perfection causes frustration at best
and paralysis at worst. ~ Sheryl Sandberg*

As a recovering perfectionist, there are many passion projects I've quit before I started. Sometimes I felt intimidated by what I didn't know. Sometimes I was overwhelmed by the number of steps. Other times, I feared failure. Whatever the reason, I simply couldn't get my brain on board.

ADHD task paralysis happens when we feel mentally stuck. We're hesitant or unable to begin or keep working, even when we want to.

Although they're often used interchangeably, procrastination and task paralysis aren't the same. Procrastination involves a conscious decision to delay starting. Task paralysis, on the other hand, is an involuntary freeze response. It feels like our brain is stuck in an endless loop of inaction.

And now that we have a name for why we're stuck, we can create a plan to get unstuck. Strategies like breaking tasks into smaller steps, reducing the commitment required to start, and identifying positive outcomes can lower the barrier to entry and help us take that first step.

Put It Into Practice:

Make the first step in starting a task smaller and smaller until it feels doable.

Paralysis, Perfectionism, Procrastination, Taking Action

Spending Time Dollars.

We all know our money isn't infinite, yet we end up treating our time, energy, and attention as if they are. ~ Shane Parrish

When we meet with a financial advisor to better manage our money, one of the first things they suggest is figuring out where our money is currently going. We can't change our spending habits if we don't know where it's going.

The same is true when it comes to managing our time. Both time and money are finite resources...we only have so much of each. So if we want to better manage our time, we first need to understand where it's actually going.

By tracking our day from wake-up to bedtime, we can spot patterns like how much time we spend driving kids around, cleaning the house, working, resting, or scrolling on social media.

Once we're aware of our current time habits, we can decide where small adjustments might help. This doesn't mean deleting TikTok or making the kids ride the bus every day. It simply gives us information so we can make intentional shifts that support what matters most to us.

Put It Into Practice:

Spend a few days tracking how you use your time from morning to night. Then look for small, realistic shifts that could help you make room for tasks or activities you're struggling to fit in.

Time Management, Planning, Mom Life

What's a DOOM Pile?

Clutter is nothing more than postponed decisions.
~ Barbara Hemphill

When we scoop everything from the counter, bed, couch, or car into a box, bin, bag, or pile and move it out of the way with every intention of dealing with it later, we create what is known as a DOOM pile.

DOOM stands for <u>D</u>idn't <u>O</u>rganize, <u>O</u>nly <u>M</u>oved. DOOM piles are a common ADHD coping strategy for quickly reducing visual clutter when our executive function is exhausted. Making decisions about what stays, what goes, and where things belong takes energy we often don't have. Add in time blindness and suddenly we're cleaning at the last minute with no time for proper follow-through.

Over time, those DOOM piles tend to accumulate in other spaces. And when we finally look at them again, they feel overwhelming. There's no category, no order, and there's way too much to process all at once.

Luckily, DOOM piles don't have to be tackled in one giant organizing session. We can sort and put away one pile a day. Or one a week. We can even pair the task with something enjoyable, like watching a show or listening to a podcast, to make it easier to start.

Put It Into Practice:

Find a DOOM pile. Any will do. Sort the contents and put everything away. If you still have energy, you can always tackle another.

Cleaning and Organizing

Leave Space for Chaos.

If you are always racing to the next moment,
what happens to the one you're in? ~ Zig Ziglar

Most moms' schedules are jam-packed from sunrise to sunset...commitment after commitment, slamming into each other with no wiggle room if we hit traffic or suddenly need to run our kid's violin to school.

Maybe it's our difficulty estimating time, convincing us we can fit far more into a window than is realistically possible. Maybe our time perception fails us when we're hyperfocused and lose track of what's next. Or maybe our people-pleasing tendencies make it hard to say no because we want to be helpful and seen as a team player.

Regardless of the cause, it's nearly impossible to get a handle on time management without intentionally building in buffer time.

Buffer time is like an emergency fund for our schedule. If we don't end up needing it, great! We've found extra time. And if we do need it, there's far less ripple effect on the rest of our day.

Put It Into Practice:

Add margin or buffer time between appointments or commitments on your schedule to leave time for the unexpected.

Time Management, Planning, Mom Life

March 28

Oops.

A person with ADHD has the power of a Ferrari engine but with bicycle-strength brakes. ~ Dr. Ned Hallowell

In 1998, I went to the mall and came home with a $1,200 teacup Maltese puppy. I had to set up a payment plan to buy her. And did I mention that my apartment had a very strict "no dogs" policy?

When impulse control is challenging, we tend to act first and think later, reacting before we've had time to consider the consequences.

Impulsivity can show up in many areas of our lives. It can affect our eating habits when it's hard to stop once we start eating something we enjoy. It can impact our financial health through frequent impulsive purchases that add up quickly. It may even influence our physical health or relationships when we struggle to pause, wait our turn, or think through long-term outcomes.

The goal isn't perfection or eliminating impulsivity entirely. But by practicing the pause, building awareness around what triggers our impulsive responses, and creating supportive boundaries, we can begin to slow things down and respond more intentionally.

Put It Into Practice:

Think through situations where impulsivity tends to show up for you and plan an alternative response ahead of time. The more you practice pausing before acting, the easier it becomes.

ADHD Symptoms, Executive Function

Let's Get It Started!

Ideas are easy. Execution is everything.
~ John Doerr

Initiating tasks is often difficult for ADHDers due to differences in the prefrontal cortex and dopamine regulation.

When you add in fear of failure, anxiety, decision fatigue, perfectionism, and distractions (squirrel!), it's no wonder we so often procrastinate.

This is why checklists are such a powerful tool for ADHD brains. They support task initiation and routines by reducing the executive function energy we spend deciding where to start or what to do next.

Checklists also make big tasks feel more approachable because we can see the small steps required to move forward. They provide a visual way to track progress…what's done, and what's left. And let's not forget the dopamine boost we get when we check something off the list.

When creating a checklist, the goal is simply to get the steps out of your head and into a visible format. It doesn't have to be perfect because chances are it will evolve as we use it. Write it down, type it up, print it out, and place it somewhere we'll actually see and use it.

Put It Into Practice:

Create a simple checklist for a regular task or routine in your home and place it where it's easy to see and use.

Checklists, Procrastination, Taking Action

March 30

Externalize Your Memory.

The only thing faster than the speed of thought is
the speed of forgetfulness. ~ Vera Nazarian

I'm pretty open about my forgetfulness. For a long time, I beat myself up for forgetting things like why I came to the grocery store… only to remember on the drive home.

But once I better understood my ADHD and how working memory functions, I realized I wasn't broken, I just needed to do things differently. My brain needed to externalize steps of a task and reminders for regular activities. And once I accepted that, it was such a relief to start "remembering" again.

ADHD impacts working memory, which is responsible for temporarily holding and processing information before it's stored in long-term memory for later recall. It's believed our ADHD brains take in information, but distractions interrupt the process, and the details get lost along the way.

That's why, at any given point in the day, you'll likely find me writing things down, setting alarms, or checking a list. These tools help ensure important tasks, ideas, and details don't slip through the cracks.

Put It Into Practice:

Support your memory by externalizing it. Use a notebook or Notes app, set reminders or alarms, and write down systems and routines you rely on regularly.

Memory Support

Rinse & Repeat.

It's easier to keep up than to catch up.
~ Gretchen Rubin

Maintenance is often the most overlooked step in the home organizing process. After all, if we've invested the time, energy, effort, and money into organizing a space, it makes sense to want to keep it functional, right?

Maintenance (keeping a space organized) typically takes only a fraction of the time of the original project. We've already decluttered excess items and established homes for what we're keeping. That groundwork matters.

It's far easier to spend a little time each week or month maintaining an organized space than it is to let things slide until it feels like we're starting from scratch again.

Another bonus? The steps for maintenance are the same ones we use when starting any organizing project:

- Block time on the calendar
- Break the task into manageable steps
- Let someone know what we're working on so they can help keep us accountable

And just like with any skill, repetition matters. The more we practice maintaining our spaces, the easier it becomes to reset them, again and again.

Put It Into Practice:

Schedule regular time to reset a space you've already organized, even if it only takes a few minutes.

Cleaning and Organizing

April

April 1

You're No Fool.

If you judge a fish by its ability to climb a tree, it will go its whole life believing it's stupid. ~ Albert Einstein (Maybe)

In 1949, neuropsychologist Donald Hebb introduced what's now known as Hebbian Theory to explain how brain pathways are formed and reinforced. He famously said, "Neurons that fire together, wire together."

Many ADHDers grow up absorbing negative messages, from others and from ourselves. We're labeled lazy or loud. We feel unreliable because of time management struggles, or "stupid" because of careless mistakes. And as Dr. Hebb's work shows, repeated negativity can wire itself into our brains, contributing to low self-esteem and mental health challenges.

But this same principle of neuroplasticity also brings good news. Our brains are capable of change at any stage of life. Just as those negative pathways were formed over time, we can intentionally build and strengthen positive ones too.

Consistent exposure to positive thoughts and experiences helps reinforce new neural connections. Practices like noticing moments of gratitude or intentionally celebrating even small wins can begin to undo years of negative feedback...both from others and from ourselves.

Put It Into Practice:

Find one positive moment or small win to acknowledge today. Then do it again tomorrow.

Mindset, Mental Health

April 2

Pick Your No's.

*When you say yes to others, make sure you're not
saying no to yourself. ~ Paulo Coelho*

Response inhibition is an executive function that helps us pause and think before we respond. Because it's an executive function, many ADHDers struggle to slow down long enough to weigh the pros and cons of a commitment before jumping in.

When response inhibition challenges combine with people-pleasing tendencies, it's no surprise that many ADHD moms find themselves stressed and overcommitted.

Learning to say "no" when we're already stretched thin helps reduce burnout and protects our time, energy, and effort. And saying "no" doesn't mean we're being selfish or unhelpful, it means we're being intentional. Every "no" creates space to say "yes" to the things that matter most and bring us joy.

Like any skill, setting boundaries gets easier with practice. The more often we pause before responding, the more natural it becomes to choose commitments that truly fit our capacity.

Put It Into Practice:

Practice slowing down your response when a new request or obligation comes up. Give yourself permission to pause, then decide whether it truly fits your current energy, availability, and priorities.

Executive Function, People-Pleasing

One Mess at a Time.

My idea of housework is to sweep the room with a glance.
~ Erma Bombeck

It can be easy for us ADHD moms to talk ourselves out of starting our ambitious spring cleaning plans when they feel big or overwhelming.

That's why the first step in any spring cleaning project should be breaking it down into the smallest, most easily digestible tasks possible.

Tiny tasks have a much lower barrier to entry, making them easier to start. We may not always have the time or energy to deep-clean every window, blind, or baseboard in the house…but we can clean one window, one blind, or one room.

And every small task we complete comes with a dopamine boost from checking it off our list. That little reward may be just enough to build momentum and tackle another small cleaning task.

Spring cleaning doesn't have to happen all at once. Progress adds up, even when it happens one mess at a time.

Put It Into Practice:

Break your spring cleaning list into small, easy-to-start tasks and choose just one to work on today.

Cleaning and Organizing

April 4

Control Closet Clutter.

If you want to improve your life, clean out a closet.
~ Cheryl Richardson

Decluttering a closet supports ADHD mom life in more ways than just making it easier to find clothes or put away clean laundry. It reduces decision fatigue by limiting how many choices we face when getting dressed and helps minimize visual clutter in our bedroom, which can otherwise contribute to distraction and low motivation.

A calmer, less cluttered closet can even support better sleep. When piles of clothes are the last thing we see at night and the first thing we see in the morning, they can quietly increase stress levels.

To pare down closet clutter, try these simple steps:

- Block out specific time to work on this project.
- Group like items together (t-shirts, jeans, cardigans) to see how many you have.
- Decide how many of each item you realistically wear or need.
- Return only those items to their homes (designated spots).

If decluttering the entire closet feels overwhelming, focus on just one category at a time or enlist an accountability helper to share the work.

Put It Into Practice:

Schedule time to declutter a closet. If doing it all at once feels like too much, start by grouping like items, then work through one category at a time.

Cleaning and Organizing

Control Calendar Clutter.

The bad news is time flies. The good news is you're the pilot.
~ Michael Altshuler

Is it possible to raise well-rounded, activity-filled children without feeling overwhelmed or stuck in constant FOMO?

As far-fetched as that may sound, it is possible when we actively manage our schedules instead of letting our schedules manage us.

Many ADHD moms struggle with people-pleasing and saying "yes" too often, which can quickly lead to overloaded calendars and chronic overwhelm. Creating clear boundaries around what we commit to helps prevent paralysis caused by sensory and schedule overload.

When we take back control of our calendars, we make room for what truly matters. We align our time with the priorities we've set for our families and ourselves. And whatever discomfort or fear comes with letting go of events that don't support those priorities tends to fade once we experience the extra time, energy, and calm that comes from protecting our schedule.

Put It Into Practice:

Pause before adding a new event or commitment to your calendar. Consider what you may need to say "no" to in order to say "yes" to something new.

Time Management, People-Pleasing, Energy Management

April 6

The First Step Freeze.

A journey of a thousand miles begins
with a single step. ~ Lao Tzu

ADHDers often struggle to start. Maybe a task is unfamiliar or feels difficult. Maybe we're distracted by everything else on our to-do list. Or maybe it's just not what we feel like doing right now...or ever.

Whatever the executive-function-related reason, we either do nothing or switch to something else...neither of which helps us begin the task we actually need to do.

If this pattern feels familiar, there's good news! Overcoming task initiation challenges starts with identifying why we're stuck so we can choose strategies that help us move forward:

- Try breaking a task into smaller, easier steps so starting doesn't feel so overwhelming (ChatGPT is a big help with this).
- Gather everything needed ahead of time to reduce the energy required to begin.
- Plan to work for at least 5–10 minutes.
- Make the environment more enjoyable by changing locations or playing music.

Remember, it's not about finishing the task in one go. It's about getting started. Momentum often follows action, not the other way around.

Put It Into Practice:

Make starting easier by identifying your biggest "first step" obstacle and adjusting the task to be smaller, shorter, simpler, or more fun.

Taking Action, Procrastination

DUST Busters.

*The dread of doing a task uses up more time and energy
than doing the task itself. ~ Rita Emmett*

Procrastination is more than just putting off tasks. There's usually a reason behind the delay.

Graham Allcott, author and founder of Think Productive, identifies four common reasons we procrastinate in his book *A Practical Guide to Productivity*. He calls it the DUST model, which suggests we avoid tasks because they feel Difficult, Unclear, Scary, or Tedious.

If a task feels difficult, we may be missing skills or information. Follow-through is easier when we pause to learn what we need to know.

If a task feels unclear, it needs better definition. Breaking it into small, specific steps can make starting feel far more manageable.

If a task feels scary, fear of failure or criticism may be holding us back. Adding accountability can create the external motivation needed to move forward.

And if a task feels tedious, it's simply boring. Playing music, changing locations, or gamifying it can make the work more engaging.

Once we know why we're procrastinating, we're no longer stuck. Now we can choose a strategy that actually addresses the problem.

Put It Into Practice:

Identify which DUST factor is at play when you notice yourself procrastinating. Then use a matching strategy to help you get started.

Procrastination, Taking Action

April 8

iPhone vs. Android.

There are many paths to the top of the mountain,
but the view is always the same. ~ Chinese Proverb

When we read a blog post or hear a podcast and think, "this could be really helpful for me!", only to realize there are too many steps or it's hard to maintain, it may not mean we're doing something wrong. It may simply be that the system wasn't designed with our ADHD brain in mind.

I like to think of neurotypical and neurodivergent brains as similar to iPhones and Androids.

Both are designed to accomplish the same outcomes. We can make calls, send texts, and download apps for social media, games, or productivity. But iPhone apps don't work on Android devices because they aren't built for that operating system.

The same is true for our brains. ADHD brains need coping strategies and systems designed for the way we operate. So if that meal-planning tip or productivity system we heard on a podcast doesn't work for us, it doesn't mean we failed…it may just mean we need an ADHD-friendly version that's built for our brain.

Put It Into Practice:

Identify a strategy that hasn't worked for you and look for an ADHD-friendly version designed to support how your brain works.

Awareness

Progress Over Perfection.

Perfectionism doesn't make you feel perfect.
It makes you feel inadequate. ~ Maria Shriver

Decision-making with an ADHD brain can feel exhausting or even impossible. Often, this comes from a fear of making the wrong choice or worrying that if we choose poorly, the outcome won't be perfect.

This is where redefining what "finished" can look like helps us move forward.

Take meal planning…The idea of planning meals and making a grocery list can feel completely overwhelming when we've convinced ourselves that every meal needs to be homemade and totally different from what we served last week.

But that's just the *best* version. A *better* version might include a mix of from-scratch meals and frozen family favorites. And a *good* version might rely entirely on premade or super-simple options.

All three versions accomplish the same goal of feeding our family. But when decision fatigue is high, the good version often requires the least energy and actually gets done.

Progress doesn't come from making the perfect choice. It comes from making a choice we can follow through on.

Put It Into Practice:

Brainstorm a few versions of what "done" could look like when you're stuck trying to make the perfect decision. Choose the one that fits your current energy and capacity.

Perfectionism, Decision-Making

April 10

When Time's Not Ticking.

*Time management is a misnomer; the challenge
is to manage ourselves. ~ Stephen Covey*

It's easy to fall into a hyperfocus hole and suddenly realize we've spent far too long organizing a sock drawer. Or we try to squeeze in a full garage cleanout before our kid's basketball game at noon.

Managing time requires multiple executive functions like decision-making, planning, organizing, and prioritizing. When we add in time blindness (challenges with time perception and estimation), it's no wonder so many of us struggle to manage our time effectively.

As with many ADHD challenges, awareness is the first step toward creating supportive strategies. When we make time more visible and concrete, it becomes easier to work with. Simple ways to improve time awareness include:

- Using analog clocks or visual timers to help us see time passing
- Timing tasks so we can better estimate how long they'll take in the future
- Reviewing schedules to identify where extra time is needed for travel or transitions
- Setting alarms as external reminders that a transition is coming or it's time to wrap up

Put It Into Practice:

Pick one strategy to improve your time awareness and try it today.

Time Management, Executive Function

Just Get on Base.

Don't let the fear of striking out hold you back.
~ Babe Ruth

It's spring, and it's baseball season. Truth be told, I'm not the sportiest sports fan, but I did enjoy my share of Chicago Cubs games back when I lived in Chicago.

I was there during the famous home run race of the early 2000s between Sammy Sosa and Mark McGwire. During that stretch, Sosa hit an incredible 243 home runs. But what's talked about far less is that he also got on base another 257 times.

In other words, he helped his team not only by hitting home runs, but by simply getting on base.

As moms, we often view tasks in all-or-nothing terms…a home run or a strikeout. But we forget that progress is still being made when we get a hit and get on base.

We don't have to hit a home run every time. We just have to get on base so we're in position to score (aka eventually get the task done).

Put It Into Practice:

Choose a task you've been avoiding and identify one small action that would help you "get on base," even if you don't finish it right away.

Taking Action, Productivity

April 12

Find Your Fob.

I remember things that happened sixty years ago, but if you ask me where I left my car keys five minutes ago, that's sometimes a problem. ~ Lou Thesz

I once lost the key fob for our Honda Pilot for nearly two years. And just when we were about to fork out almost $200 to order a replacement, it magically reappeared in my work bag.

By "magically," I mean I found it in a pocket I could have sworn I checked more than once during those two years.

After that, I changed my system. Now both car key fobs live in the front pocket of my purse, and I don't remove them unless I absolutely have to. If I need something from the car or trunk, I take my entire purse with me and keep it right next to the vehicle.

This works because I always have my purse when I leave the house. And even though it's not very large, I'm far less likely to lose an entire purse than a tiny key fob. Bigger items are easier for my ADHD brain to track than small, easily misplaced ones.

Put It Into Practice:

Create a permanent home for your key fob in a purse or bag pocket, especially if you frequently misplace it. And practice returning it there every time.

Memory Support, Mom Life

Dividing Dinner Duties.

Meal planning shouldn't be a one-woman show. Sharing the load teaches kids life skills and gives moms back their evenings. ~ Jenna Marshall

I really do enjoy cooking…just not at the end of a long day when my executive function is tapped out, I can't decide what to make, and my motivation to go to the store is near zero. Unfortunately, that's most nights for our family.

We can simplify supper by sharing the load. Implementing family-friendly, age-appropriate steps can significantly reduce the strain that meal planning and prep places on our executive function.

Start by having each family member add their favorite meals to a shared list, then let them help choose what's on the menu for the week. You can also create simple theme nights like "Meatless Monday" or "Taco Tuesday" and rotate who gets to decide.

And don't forget about prep. Toddlers can help wipe counters or add pre-measured ingredients. Older kids can gather supplies, measure, and practice supervised knife skills. Teens can learn to follow recipes from start to finish, skills they'll definitely appreciate once they're cooking for themselves.

Sharing dinner duties doesn't just reduce the workload, it builds independence and keeps meals from resting entirely on our already-full plate.

Put It Into Practice:

Invite your family to help with meal planning and prep to lighten your mental load and build their kitchen skills.

Eating and Meal Planning, Mom Life

April 14

Breath Before Brew.

Just one small positive thought in the morning can change your whole day.
~ Dalai Lama

The way we start our day often shapes how we work, respond, and feel for all the hours that follow.

That's why beginning the day with a moment of mindfulness can help quiet the mental noise running through our busy ADHD brains. Reducing this mental clutter supports focus, emotional regulation, and a greater sense of calm as we move through whatever the day brings.

Mindfulness goes far beyond meditation. There are many simple, accessible ways to practice it in the morning. We might try a brief body scan by starting at the feet and slowly moving upward, noticing how each part of our body feels. Or we could sit quietly and focus on the rhythm of our breath as we inhale and exhale.

If movement feels better, try gentle stretching, yoga, or a mindful walk, pausing to notice sights, sounds, or sensations all around. And if journaling resonates, writing a few lines of gratitude or visualizing how we'd like the day to unfold can help set a positive tone.

Mindfulness doesn't have to be long or elaborate to be effective. It just has to be intentional.

Put It Into Practice:

Choose a quick, simple morning mindfulness practice and try it tomorrow. Then try it again the next day.

Morning Routine, Mindset, Self-Care

The ADHD Tax.

If you think nobody cares if you're alive,
try missing a couple of car payments. ~ Earl Wilson

The ADHD Tax is what we pay in time, energy, effort, or money as a result of our ADHD symptoms.

It might look like paying late fees because we forgot to pay a bill. Or tossing yet another planner in October that we only used for two weeks in January. We may own multiple staplers because we keep misplacing them and buying replacements. Or we rely on takeout because the food in the fridge goes bad before we remember to eat it.

Sometimes the ADHD Tax is bigger, like paying an extra $60 to expedite a passport because we remembered to renew our kids' passports but forgot to send in our own… and need it immediately. I speak from experience on this one.

While the ADHD tax is common, it doesn't mean we're doomed to keep paying it forever. We don't have to accept late fees, lost items, or constant last-minute scrambles as inevitable. We can reduce the ADHD tax by:

- Creating reminders for bills and deadlines so they're paid on time
- Developing organizing systems to give important items a consistent home
- Planning meals in a way that works for our brains so food gets eaten instead of wasted

Put It Into Practice:

Identify one place where you're paying the ADHD tax with your time, energy, or money. Then choose one simple support like a reminder, system, or routine to help reduce it.

Memory Support, Time Investments

April 16

Set It. Save It.

If you're saving, you're succeeding.
~ Steve Burkholder

ADHD money management challenges often stem from executive function struggles like impulsivity that leads to overspending or inattentiveness that results in missed bill payments. But when we automate parts of our financial life, we offload the executive function required to track, remember, and manage all the details, helping us avoid costly mistakes.

One way to do this is with automatic savings. According to a 2025 Bankrate Emergency Savings Survey[4], 24% of those surveyed have no emergency savings to provide a safety net for unexpected expenses.

Setting up a regular, automatic transfer to savings is a simple way to build an emergency fund over time. And if you're thinking, "I don't have extra money to save," consider the small, everyday expenses that add up like grabbing coffee while running errands or tossing a few unplanned items into the grocery cart. Even $5–10 a week, saved automatically, can begin to create a meaningful financial cushion.

Automation removes the need to decide, remember, or rely on motivation…and that's exactly why it works so well for ADHD brains.

Put It Into Practice:

Set up a recurring, automatic transfer to a savings account to begin building your family's emergency fund.

Money Management, Time Investments, Mom Life

Ding! You're Done.

How did it get so late so soon?
~ Dr. Seuss

The kitchen timer has symbolized the passage of time for decades...the familiar ticking counting down the seconds and the loud bell signaling it's time to take dinner out of the oven.

While many neurotypicals sense the seconds ticking by and know when it's time to move on internally, ADHD time blindness makes it difficult for us to sense the passage of time. Add in hyperfocus, and we may miss or ignore internal cues to transition altogether.

But when we externalize time, we create support systems that help us function more effectively in a neurotypical world.

One simple way to build time awareness is by setting a timer.

Timers let us know when the time we've allotted for a task has passed and it's time to wrap up or switch gears. They can also make dreaded tasks feel more manageable by turning them into a short, defined challenge...play "beat the clock" and move on.

Over time, regularly using timers helps us develop a more accurate sense of how long tasks actually take, making it easier to plan and schedule realistically in the future.

Put It Into Practice:

Set a timer before starting a task, either to limit how long you work on it or to track how long it actually takes, to help improve your awareness of time passing.

Time Blindness, Time Management, Productivity

April 18

Power Saving Mode.

*Telling an introvert to go to a party is like telling
a saint to go to Hell. ~ Criss Jami*

Energy management needs to stay top of mind for all ADHDers, but it's extra important for ADHD introverts who regularly expend extroverted energy through work, social, and family obligations.

When our energy is low, executive function and dopamine regulation become even harder. Tasks like following routines, making decisions, or regulating emotions can suddenly feel overwhelming. Add in an event that requires more extroverted energy than we naturally enjoy, and it's no surprise we feel depleted before we even begin.

One key strategy for managing energy as an introverted ADHDer is being intentional about what we do before an energy-demanding activity. Reducing executive-function–heavy tasks and limiting stimulating activities beforehand helps conserve energy for what's next.

For example, if you need to give a presentation at work, spend some quiet time alone beforehand. Choose low-dopamine, low-demand activities so you have more energy available when it matters.

Managing energy this way isn't about avoiding responsibilities. It's about supporting the nervous system so we can show up more fully when it matters.

Put It Into Practice:

Look at your upcoming schedule. If you're an ADHD introvert with an extroverted event coming up, plan low-energy, low-dopamine time beforehand to conserve energy.

Introverts, Energy Management, Self-Care

Move More, Sleep Better.

A ruffled mind makes a restless pillow.
~ Charlotte Brontë

Poor sleep quality can worsen ADHD symptoms like forgetfulness, distractibility, and difficulty following through on tasks. And when we head to bed ruminating on everything we didn't finish that day, our sleep suffers even more, fueling a cycle that repeats itself.

There is a way for us to improve our sleep quality and help break this cycle...movement.

In addition to helping burn off excess energy, regular movement supports better sleep by increasing the amount of deep, slow-wave sleep, the most restorative phase of the sleep cycle.

A 2020 controlled trial[5] found that High Intensity Interval Training (HIIT) workouts improved sleep quality, including how long participants slept and how often they woke after falling asleep. But the sleep benefits aren't limited to intense workouts. Even as little as 10–15 minutes of elevating our heart rate can make a difference.

Put It Into Practice:

Move your body today, whatever that looks like for you, to support better sleep tonight.

Sleep, Exercise, Self-Care

April 20

Remind Me to Remember.

Lost time is never found again.
~ Benjamin Franklin

I once spent an entire Saturday evening deep-diving into celebrity legal issues on YouTube and somehow became an "expert" on conservatorships. A prime example of ADHD time blindness.

And there's nothing wrong with getting lost in something we enjoy or find interesting. The problem comes when getting lost in it pulls us away from other responsibilities or commitments.

Many of us, ADHD or not, struggle with temporal discounting, or the tendency to choose immediate rewards over delayed rewards with a bigger payoff. When we add ADHD challenges with impulse control, self-awareness, and a natural inclination to live in the moment, it's easy to see how we can lose track of time entirely.

That's why relying on our internal sense of time often isn't enough. Instead, we can create external time reminders to help anchor us. Alarms and reminders on our phones or digital assistants are simple, effective tools for this.

While we still have to choose to switch tasks when an alarm goes off, these reminders help interrupt hyperfocus and make us aware of time passing...something our brains may not naturally register.

Put It Into Practice:

Set alarms or schedule reminders to help you notice the passage of time and cue transitions throughout your day.

Time Management, Productivity

April 21

TRIM Your To-Do List.

*Our dilemma goes deeper than shortage of time; it is basically
a problem of priorities. ~ Charles E. Hummel*

Prioritization, or deciding what to work on first, is an executive function many ADHDers struggle with. One common prioritization tool is the Eisenhower Matrix, which sorts tasks by what's urgent/not urgent and important/not important.

While helpful in theory, this system can be difficult for ADHD brains. Answering vague questions like "What's important?" takes a lot of decision energy. Time blindness can make everything feel urgent, especially when emotional motivation is required to take action.

That's why I created the TRIM Method, a more concrete way to identify priorities. Instead of ranking importance, ask whether a task is:

- Time Sensitive – Has a due date
- Required – Must be completed to move forward
- Impactful – Creates meaningful positive change
- Money Related – Makes or costs you money

If the answer is yes to any of these, it's a priority...and deserves time on your calendar.

Put It Into Practice:

Use the TRIM Method to identify which tasks on your to-do list truly need your attention first.

Productivity, Taking Action

April 22

Go Touch Grass.

In every walk with nature, one receives far more than he seeks.
~ John Muir

Today is Earth Day…which feels like the perfect time to talk about how spending time outdoors can support our ADHD brains.

In 1989, Stephen and Rachel Kaplan introduced Attention Restoration Theory (ART) which suggested that time in nature helps restore our ability to focus by giving our attention a break from the constant indoor distractions competing for it.

Beyond improving focus, being outdoors also activates the parasympathetic nervous system (PNS), the part of our nervous system responsible for rest and regulation, helping lower heart rate and reduce cortisol, the body's primary stress hormone.

To feel present and grounded while outside, try the 5-4-3-2-1 technique by noticing:

- 5 things you can see
- 4 things you can touch
- 3 things you can hear
- 2 things you can smell
- 1 thing you can taste (just don't swallow it)

Even a few intentional minutes outdoors can help calm our body and reset our focus.

Put It Into Practice:

When you're struggling to focus, step outside. Take a walk, visit a park, or sit in your yard and try the 5-4-3-2-1 technique.

Self-Care, Executive Function

Simplify Your Subscriptions.

*The ability to simplify means to eliminate the unnecessary
so that the necessary may speak. ~ Hans Hofmann*

Research from The Radicati Group in August 2025 reported that there are over 9.8 billion emails sent in the United States each day. And I am pretty sure that half of them end up in my inbox.

Digital clutter can be just as distracting as physical clutter. We open our email looking for a message from our child's teacher, notice a sales email from a company we vaguely remember liking, and before we know it, we've fallen down a rabbit hole of clicks, deals, and diversions.

Every extra email is another opportunity for distraction. Luckily, we can reduce the noise. Legitimate email lists are required to include an "unsubscribe" link, making it possible to declutter our inbox one list at a time.

And if that still feels like too much, there are tools that can help. Services like Leave Me Alone, Clean Email, or Unroll.Me can handle unsubscribing in bulk, saving our time and executive function for more important mom things.

A quieter inbox means fewer distractions, less decision fatigue, and a calmer digital space.

Put It Into Practice:

Reduce inbox clutter by unsubscribing from email newsletters you rarely open or no longer find useful.

Cleaning and Organizing, Productivity, Distractions

April 24

Park Your Thoughts.

Distractions destroy action. If it's not moving towards your purpose, leave it alone. ~ Jermaine Riley

Managing external distractions like noise or clutter is often easier for ADHDers than managing internal distractions like intrusive or racing thoughts. These concentration challenges are linked to differences in how our brains switch between networks.

The Default Mode Network (DMN) is responsible for internally focused activities, such as creativity, memory processing, and mind-wandering when we're at rest. The Task Positive Network (TPN) takes over when we need to focus, plan, and problem-solve.

In neurotypical brains, there's a relatively smooth handoff between these two networks. In ADHD brains, however, the DMN often stays active even when the TPN is engaged, leading to increased distraction, rumination, and wandering thoughts while we're trying to concentrate.

When this happens, it can help to create a place to park those thoughts. Writing them down or capturing them elsewhere allows us to move forward with the task at hand, knowing the thoughts are saved and can be revisited later if needed.

Put It Into Practice:

Create a "parking lot" for intrusive thoughts, such as a notebook, notes app, or sticky note, so you can refocus on the task now and return to those thoughts later.

Distractions, Productivity

Find Your Fidget.

We have good evidence that fidgeting itself seems to be associated with better attention. ~ Dr. Julie Schweitzer

If you regularly find yourself squirming in your seat, pacing, chewing the inside of your cheek, or tapping a pen, you may be fidgeting as a form of stimming…self-stimulating actions that help regulate the brain and body.

For those of us with ADHD, fidgeting often shows up when we're trying to focus, organize our thoughts, or calm down after an emotionally reactive moment.

Fidgeting can help manage hyperactivity and anxiety by giving the body an outlet for pent-up energy. It can support focus by increasing alertness and helping regulate attention. And it can redirect that building discomfort so we feel calmer and more grounded.

To tap into the benefits of fidgeting, choose something that doesn't disrupt others and can be done without pulling attention away from the main task.

Put It Into Practice:

Find a mindless fidget the next time you're feeling anxious or struggling to focus. Try tapping your foot, chewing gum, doodling or coloring, pacing, using a textured object, or bouncing gently on an exercise ball.

Fidgets and Stimming, Executive Function

April 26

Embracing Messy Action.

Perfectionism is the enemy of progress.
~ Winston Churchill

Messy action means moving forward on a task or goal even when we don't have the perfect plan or everything figured out.

Far too often, even the most researched, detailed plan will eventually need to be edited, updated, or changed. Maybe in two weeks...maybe in two months. But at some point, it will evolve.

This book is a perfect example. With each month I write, I think of something I want to add, adjust, or improve in previous or future sections.

If I waited until everything was perfect before I started writing, it might take two decades to publish. And chances are very good I'd still end up changing my "perfect" plan anyway.

So if we know the plan is going to change, why not embrace action instead of waiting for certainty? Messy action creates momentum...and momentum is often what our ADHD brains need most.

Put It Into Practice:

Take one step of messy action on a task, project, or goal you've been avoiding. Then celebrate the progress. Each small step creates a dopamine reward that helps you stay motivated.

Perfectionism, Taking Action, Productivity

April 27

Break It Down.

The secret of getting started is breaking your complex overwhelming tasks into small manageable tasks, and then starting on the first one. ~ Mark Twain (Maybe)

It can be hard to tackle a task when it feels big. And when something feels big, our brain may interpret it as a threat to our energy, sending a quick message of "We don't have the capacity for that." (Thanks, limbic system.)

That's why breaking a project into smaller pieces makes it easier to begin. When the task looks smaller, it feels more doable and our brains are less likely to shut down before we start.

There are lots of ways to create smaller steps. We can work backward from the end result and identify what has to happen first. We can verbally process the steps using a voice memo (or talk it out while someone else takes notes). We can mind map to organize ideas in a non-linear way, or do a full brain dump and then reorder the steps from start to finish.

And to work smarter, not harder, we can always look up a task checklist online or ask ChatGPT to break it down.

Put It Into Practice:

Break your tasks and projects down into smaller, manageable steps and choose just one to begin.

Procrastination, Taking Action, Productivity

April 28

Running on Empty.

Burnout occurs when your body and mind can no longer keep up with the tasks you demand of them. Don't try to force yourself to do the impossible. ~ Del Suggs

Awareness is power when it comes to combating burnout as an ADHD mom. When we learn what burnout looks like in our own body and mind and build in strategies to pull back before things get dire, we're already interrupting the burnout cycle.

One way burnout can show up is in our performance. Instead of feeling emotionally overwhelmed first, we may notice that our ability to do things starts slipping. Signs can include completing fewer tasks than usual, taking much longer to finish things, procrastinating more often, or abandoning projects that we would normally follow through on. We may stop showing up altogether…not because we don't care, but because we've run out of capacity.

If you've been struggling to keep up, stay motivated, or function in ways that feel unlike your normal self for an extended period of time, it may be a sign you're running on empty.

The answer isn't to push harder. It's to pause. Rest. Reduce mental load. Simplify where you can. Then return to the task when you feel more resourced.

Put It Into Practice:

Do a burnout self-check. If starting or following through is harder than normal, you may be heading toward burnout. If so, take a break before you break down.

Burnout, Taking Action, Self-Care

Recognizing RSD.

You must be at one with your emotions,
because the body always follows the mind. ~ Bruce Lee

Since emotional regulation is an executive function, it can be difficult for ADHDers to regulate and respond when something spikes our emotions. That emotional pain can feel so intense that it impacts motivation and keeps us from trying new things for fear of failure.

We may feel anxiety before rejection or negative outcomes even happen. We may strive for perfection to avoid disapproval. And we may interpret anything that isn't overly positive as rejection. This is known as Rejection Sensitive Dysphoria (RSD).

And yes, anyone can experience these emotions depending on stress, hormones, sleep, or life circumstances. The difference is that for many ADHDers, this happens regularly, sometimes daily, and it repeats over and over. We hold on to those feelings and ruminate. We can't always be like Elsa and just "let it go."

We can reduce the intensity and duration of RSD when it strikes. Create some distance from the trigger when feelings start to bubble up. Redirect your brain away from rumination. And remind yourself of past successes to quiet fear of failure.

Put It Into Practice:

Learn to recognize when RSD is showing up. When it does, use coping strategies to pause, ground yourself, and slow your response.

RSD, Emotional Regulation

April 30

I'm Grateful For...

Gratitude makes sense of our past, brings peace for today, and creates a vision for tomorrow. ~ Melody Beattie

Our limbic system plays a major role in emotion and behavior. And practicing gratitude can stimulate it to release feel-good neurochemicals like dopamine. Over time, repeated gratitude practices can strengthen positive neural pathways, supporting motivation, mood, and the executive functions we rely on for memory, planning, and decision-making.

Gratitude doesn't just influence dopamine. It can also support serotonin, a neurotransmitter that helps regulate mood. That means a consistent gratitude practice may help reduce symptoms associated with depression, anxiety, anger, and low self-esteem.

Learning to redirect and reframe negative thought patterns through gratitude can also be helpful for Rejection Sensitive Dysphoria (RSD), the ADHD tendency to experience perceived rejection, failure, or criticism more intensely than neurotypical brains.

Regularly noticing what we appreciate helps train our brains to focus more on abundance and what we have, rather than what we lack.

Put It Into Practice:

Grab a notebook or the Notes app on your phone and list five things you're grateful for today. Then set a reminder to do it again tomorrow...and the next day.

Gratitude, RSD, Mindset, Self-Care

May

What's a Body Double?

For folks with ADHD whose minds tend to wander and get off task, the body double somehow works as an external motivator to stay on task. ~ Billy Roberts

Is it easier to work at the office, exercise with a group, or fold laundry while the family is nearby? Then welcome to the wonderful world of body doubling.

Body doubling means doing a task in the presence of another person, either in person or online, especially for things we find boring, frustrating, or hard to start. There's something about having someone else around that jump-starts our motivation and helps us stay on track.

A typical body-doubling session includes two or more people choosing a time to work, briefly sharing what they plan to do, and then checking in afterward to report progress.

A body double doesn't need to do the same task as you. The benefit comes from setting aside focused time to work in the presence of someone else.

And body doubling doesn't always require direct interaction. We can get a similar effect by working in a coffee shop, joining an online session, or even following a "Clean With Me" video on YouTube.

Put It Into Practice:

Brainstorm a few easy ways you can body double and use this strategy the next time you're struggling to start.

Body Doubling, Accountability, Taking Action, Productivity

May 2

Adulting.

Adulting is too hard. Let's play something else.
~ Tanya Masse

Today is National Life Insurance Day, and many of us are either on team "Wait, what is life insurance even for?" or team "ugh, I keep forgetting to research life insurance."

Common "adulting" tasks like enrolling in insurance, financial planning, maintaining health, and managing property require extensive executive function. And let's be honest, they're not very exciting. This may explain why these vital tasks often fall through the cracks.

Reviewing our 401(k) or scheduling a colonoscopy simply isn't as dopamine-rewarding as playing a game on our phone or binge-watching Netflix.

That's why creating a dedicated block of time for life admin each week can help keep important tasks from being endlessly postponed. When we treat adulting tasks like scheduled appointments, we're far more likely to follow through.

Take it from the mom who put off scheduling her first mammogram for four years only to discover she had breast cancer. Preventive care and planning aren't just "nice to do"…they protect us and our families.

Put It Into Practice:

Schedule regular life admin blocks to stay on top of important tasks related to your health, finances, and future.

Mom Life, Taking Action

The Spoon Theory.

Energy is currency. Spend it wisely.
~ Sarah F. Taylor

Despite what we like to tell ourselves, energy is a finite resource. And some days we may have less than others.

As an ADHD mom, managing energy may be more important than managing time, especially when it comes to burnout prevention.

Which brings us to The Spoon Theory, created by Christine Miserandino to explain the limited energy and mental resources many people with chronic illness or other conditions must manage each day.

In The Spoon Theory, each person starts the day with a certain number of "spoons." Every activity, from showering and cleaning to making dinner and parenting, costs a few spoons. More often than not, we run out of spoons long before we run out of tasks that require them.

When we become aware of how many spoons we have and what different activities tend to cost, we can make better choices about what to commit to, what to simplify, and what to skip while protecting our energy and reducing the risk of burnout.

Put It Into Practice:

Estimate your daily "spoons." Small tasks might take 1–2, while bigger responsibilities may take 3–4. Pay attention to when your energy dips to better understand your typical spoon budget.

Energy Management, Burnout, Self-Care

May 4

Forget Fewer Steps.

We forget all too soon the things
we thought we could never forget. ~ Joan Didion

There's a lot of executive function involved in initiating and completing tasks. And the longer we're working, the more our dopamine supply can dwindle, making it easier to forget steps, lose focus, or rush just to be done. That's why external supports for memory and executive function are so vital for ADHD moms.

It's easy to focus so much on finishing and moving on that we skip important steps, make mistakes, or waste time redoing what we already did.

One of the simplest ways to prevent missed steps is to create checklists for just about everything. Yes, even the things we've done a million times and swear we'll never forget.

And for ADHD moms raising ADHD kids, checklists can be a game-changer, particularly during morning routines when it often feels like the blind leading the blind.

A checklist turns a routine into a visible path, so you don't have to rely on memory to know what comes next.

Put It Into Practice:

Create a checklist for a routine or recurring task to reduce missed steps and make follow-through easier.

Checklists, Memory Support, Productivity

Merry Maycember.

*24/7 – Once you sign on to be a mom, that's the only
shift they offer. ~ Donna Ball*

Maycember, a term coined by the Holderness Family on YouTube in 2016, describes the chaotic month of May before school lets out. Basically, it's December…without the cookies, twinkle lights, and socially acceptable week of doing nothing to recover.

When we combine a month where time is in high demand with ADHD struggles like overcommitting and people-pleasing, we can end up starting summer already overwhelmed and burned out. But as with so many ADHD coping strategies, awareness gives us the power to plan ahead.

Start by listing the events and activities coming up, then sorting them into must-do's and would-like-to-do's. If that feels difficult, ask:

- Is this the last or only time my child will do this?
- Do I actually enjoy this, or do I feel obligated to go?

If commitments overlap, call in support from grandparents, extended family, or friends so everyone has someone cheering them on. And don't forget to schedule recovery time, either during May or immediately after the school year ends.

Put It Into Practice:

Review your May calendar and make a plan for reducing overcommitment to protect your energy while still supporting your kids.

Mom Life, People-Pleasing, Time Management, Burnout

May 6

Pacing with Purpose.

Motion keeps the mind sharp.
~ Brian Tillery II

Ever feel an uncontrollable need to walk around? Many ADHDers recognize that we need an outlet for pent-up energy when we're trying to focus, feeling restless, or getting overstimulated. And it turns out pacing is an excellent choice in these moments.

Pacing can be a form of stimming or self-stimulating movement used by many neurodivergent people to regulate emotions, reduce sensory overload, and manage restlessness.

It supports hyperactivity and anxiety by giving our body a physical outlet for stress. And it helps improve focus by increasing alertness and helping engage the prefrontal cortex, where executive function lives.

Pacing can be particularly helpful when we need to focus during a phone call, process information, or calm down when emotions start to rise. The steady rhythm of movement can help organize our thoughts, release excess energy, and bring our nervous system back to its baseline.

Movement supports focus. And pacing gives our body something to do while our brain gets to work.

Put It Into Practice:

Try pacing when you need to focus or regulate your emotions (as long as it isn't disruptive or distracting to others).

Fidgets and Stimming, Focus, Executive Function

Travel Timeline.

Don't talk about going to Borneo. Book a ticket, get a visa,
pack a bag, and it just happens. ~ Alex Garland

I've had my fair share of travel disappointments, like Airbnbs disappearing or flights selling out because I waited too long to book. That's why creating a travel planning timeline is so helpful for ADHD moms.

ADHD time blindness can make future events feel like "not now," which means they don't get attention until they suddenly become urgent. But with travel, waiting until it feels like "now" can mean missing out on your favorite options.

A travel timeline solves this by assigning smaller due dates to the tasks that make a trip happen. That way, a future vacation becomes important now because one piece of it has an upcoming deadline.

Our travel timeline might include dates for choosing where to go and when, booking transportation and accommodations, reserving activities, and applying for any travel documents we may need.

Put It Into Practice:

Create a travel planning timeline for your summer vacation so you don't miss out on your best options.

Travel, Planning, Time Management, Time Blindness

May 8

It Needs a Home.

A place for everything and everything in its place.
~ Benjamin Franklin

I used to tell my organizing clients "organizing isn't about bins and pretty labels, but about finding what you want when you need it." Sure, the bins and labels are nice, but if the basket doesn't actually contain what the label says, it's really just décor.

When we give items a permanent home and then practice returning said item to said home, we save ourselves the time, effort, energy, and mental bandwidth it takes to search for them later.

Think about the items we frequently look for...keys, remotes, shoes, backpacks, jackets, lunchboxes (and those are just the things I've had to find this week). These are the best items to start with when assigning "homes."

It's important to make the "home" work for our brain, even if it doesn't make sense to the general population. If it makes sense to keep our car keys on the nightstand because we always grab our phone off the charger before we leave, put a hook or tray there.

Making it easy to follow through makes it easier for us to stick to it.

Put It Into Practice:

Choose one frequently lost item and give it a permanent home. Then practice returning it to that home until it becomes automatic.

Cleaning and Organizing

Mom Brain Drain.

A suburban mother's role is to deliver children; obstetrically once and by car forever after. ~ Peter De Vries

If we never change the oil and top off the fluids in our car, it will eventually break down. And if we deny our ADHD mom brain what it needs to function well, it can burn out and shut down too.

There are simple ways we can protect and support our busy mom brain:

- Ease task overwhelm by asking for help from family or friends
- Reduce isolation by connecting with other moms
- Prioritize sleep to recharge your brain
- Use external reminders to reduce executive function load
- Eat brain-supporting foods like fish, beans, eggs, whole grains, and dark, leafy greens when possible

And don't forget grace. We're doing a great job… even on the days we're pretty sure something we said will come up in our child's therapy later.

Put It Into Practice:

Choose one way to support your mom brain today. Then do it again tomorrow.

Mom Life, Mental Health, Self-Care

May 10

Afraid to Start.

Leap and the net will appear.
~ John Burroughs

Ever have a great idea...only to overthink it and never start? Chances are, we've built protective walls to shield ourselves from criticism, perceived failure, or not achieving the success we know we're capable of.

Whether it's due to low self-esteem, perfectionism, Rejection Sensitive Dysphoria (RSD), or a combination of these, many ADHDers struggle to act on our ideas and ambitions because we're afraid of failing.

And that's a huge loss...because ADHDers are incredible at thinking outside the box and creatively solving problems. But fear can keep those gifts stuck in our heads instead of shared with the world.

Luckily, there are small, simple steps we can take to help us start:

- Visualize the benefits of taking action
- Focus on the first step, not the final outcome
- Celebrate past successes (proof we can do hard things)

Put It Into Practice:

Choose one task or project you've been afraid to start and identify one small way you can begin today.

Taking Action, Mindset

May 11

ChatGPT My ADHD.

The advance of technology is based on making it fit in so that you don't really even notice it, so it's part of everyday life. ~ Bill Gates

ChatGPT can be a powerful support tool for managing ADHD mom life when we use it to narrow choices, clarify next steps, and reduce the mental load of planning.

We can ask ChatGPT to help with:

- Household planning by making a meal plan
- Task management by breaking big projects into smaller tasks
- Creating family routines like checklists
- Decision support like suggestions for family activities

To use ChatGPT effectively, we need a good prompt. And a good prompt follows a simple framework:

- The situation - what we're working on
- The goal - what we need help accomplishing
- The format - how we want the answer delivered

For example, instead of asking "Can you help me make dinner?", try "I have chicken, broccoli, and rice at home (the situation). Can you give me a 20-minute recipe (the format) that uses those ingredients (the goal)?" The more specific the prompt, the more helpful the response.

Put It Into Practice:

Start a log of prompts you can use to plug-and-play in ChatGPT for areas where you frequently need support.

Productivity, Mom Life

149

May 12

Motivation > Procrastination.

It's a job that's never started that takes the longest to finish.
~ J. R. R. Tolkien

Procrastination happens when we consciously choose to avoid a task or project. And when our busy ADHD mom brains are exhausted and low on dopamine, we often don't have enough in the tank to fire up executive function and motivate ourselves to act.

To kick-start motivation and overcome procrastination, we need to hack our dopamine delivery system.

Dopamine is a key neurotransmitter involved in executive functions like deciding what to work on, planning the steps, prioritizing what comes first, and sustaining attention long enough to finish.

Trying to motivate ourselves without enough dopamine is like trying to drive a car without gas…we can't expect to go anywhere if we can't even get started.

But once we understand what's happening, we can plan for ways to "refuel" when we're stuck. Listen to a favorite song. Take a short walk. Step outside for sunlight. Dance around for a minute. Just keep the dopamine boost brief so it supports the task instead of replacing it.

Put It Into Practice:

Choose a quick dopamine booster you enjoy when you're struggling to start. Then ride that momentum into the task.

Dopamine, Taking Action, Procrastination

Stop Learning. Start Doing.

An idea not coupled with action will never get any bigger than the brain cell it occupied. ~ Arnold Glasow

Those of us with ADHD often gravitate toward learning goals because they deliver a near-instant dopamine reward when we discover something new or develop a skill.

But there are also performance goals, or goals focused on outcomes, which usually take longer to see results. And since patience, motivation, follow-through, and consistency all require executive function, it makes complete sense why many ADHDers lean into learning over action. It feels like progress.

In reality, it's the illusion of progress. We know more… but we're still in the same place.

Once we recognize this pattern, we can shift from learning into doing. We can set limits on how much research we do before starting. We can choose one strategy and test it. And we can embrace messy action before we've explored every possible option.

Put It Into Practice:

Set a research budget, like 15 minutes or three sources, before you start researching. When you hit the limit, stop learning and take one small action step (even if it's messy).

Procrastivity, Goal Setting, Procrastination, Taking Action

May 14

Ready. Set. Go!

Time is what we want most but what we use worst.
~ William Penn

Our ADHD time management struggles often encompass more than running late or trying to cram too much into a day.

They also stem from time blindness, our difficulty sensing and estimating time accurately, and time perception challenges, our difficulty feeling the passage of time. That's why external time support is so important for ADHD brains.

One simple way we can build better time awareness is to time ourselves during common tasks. Start a timer or note the clock when we begin, then record how long the task actually takes. Over time, this "task time list" gives us real data we can use to better plan our day.

Instead of guessing how long something should take, we'll know how long it usually takes us specifically. And that makes time blocking and scheduling much more realistic.

This also helps reduce the shame we may feel if we consistently run out of time. It just means we're human…with an ADHD brain and time-estimation issues.

Put It Into Practice:

Create and use a task time list to better estimate how much time you need to block for your regular tasks.

Time Blindness, Time Management, Productivity

Swimsuits. Socks. Sanity.

When preparing to travel, lay out all your clothes and all your money. Then take half the clothes and twice the money. ~ Susan Heller

ADHDers are notorious over-packers, often because decision fatigue makes it hard to choose what to bring, and past forgetfulness convinces us we need to cover *every* possible scenario.

That decision fatigue (and one too many forgotten essentials) is what led me to create a basic travel packing checklist that I print before every trip, even short weekend getaways. Honestly, it's the "It's only a couple days... I won't forget anything important" trips when I've forgotten shirts for my kids... and even my wallet.

Start the checklist with broad categories like clothes and shoes, documents, toiletries and medications, electronics, and things to double-check before walking out the door (like your wallet). Once the categories are listed, we can add specifics that fit our family and trip.

And here's the best part: because we use a printed checklist, my kids can pack themselves. Sure, I still give their suitcases a quick once-over to make sure it isn't all sweatpants. But most of the work is theirs, which means fewer tasks for my overworked ADHD mom brain before we take off.

Put It Into Practice:

Create a printable travel packing checklist. Start with basic categories, customize it for your trip, and save it with a name you'll remember so you can reuse it next time.

Travel, Checklists, Mom Life

May 16

Less Friction. More Action.

Start where you are. Use what you have. Do what you can.
~ Arthur Ashe

I used to work out every morning in our family room. That was until my husband set up a gym in our detached garage and moved the weights out there. For the first couple of weeks, I didn't mind walking out to the garage. But eventually, it started to feel like too much effort, and I stopped working out altogether.

Because task initiation requires executive function, the more obstacles we face, the harder it is to start. That's what friction is...the tiny barriers that make a task feel harder than it should.

When we can reduce friction, we can make good habits easier to start like laying out clothes the night before or clearing off a desk so we can sit down and get to work faster.

And when we add friction, we can make not-so-helpful habits less convenient like storing chips on the top shelf where we need a step stool to reach them.

I'm happy to report that I've resumed my workouts by moving my weights to my bedroom and doing apartment-friendly workouts that don't wake my kids. Less friction, more action.

Put It Into Practice:

Choose one habit or routine you want to maintain and identify one way to reduce friction so starting takes less effort.

Taking Action, Productivity

Consistency Creates Calm.

You can't always control what goes on outside, but you can always control what goes on inside. ~ Wayne Dyer

ADHDers have a real love/hate relationship with structure. We know it helps… and yet, routines can feel boring. Blech.

But for the many ADHD adults who also struggle with anxiety, routines can be essential. They reduce the number of decisions we have to make each day, which frees up mental energy for other executive functions like emotional regulation, focus, and task initiation.

Routines also create predictability. They give us a clearer sense of what comes next and set expectations that make the day feel more manageable. Since anxiety often grows when we feel uncertain or out of control, predictability can reduce worry by helping us know what's coming and reminding us we've handled it before.

And routines act as external guides for time management, helping reduce tardiness and improve transitions because we're familiar with the flow from one task to the next.

Put It Into Practice:

Add one simple routine to your day to reduce decision fatigue and create more calm and predictability.

Anxiety

May 18

Lean, Mean, Dopamine Machine.

The evidence is indisputable: Exercise has a more profound and sustained positive effect on mood, anxiety, cognition, energy, and sleep than any pill I can prescribe. ~ Anna Lembke

As ADHDers, we are on a constant quest for dopamine to help power our executive function. One free and effective way to boost dopamine and other important neurotransmitters is through regular physical activity.

When we move our bodies, our nervous system kicks into gear and releases dopamine and norepinephrine, brain chemicals that support focus, motivation, and mood. Over time, regular movement can strengthen dopamine pathways and may even help dopamine stay active in the brain longer, which can support attention and emotional regulation for hours afterward.

A 2020 review of studies[6] on physical activity and dopamine found consistent increases in dopamine levels for physically active participants, lower instances of depression and anxiety, and improved neuroplasticity with as little as 10 minutes of movement per session.

It's not about becoming a fitness influencer. It's about fueling your brain.

Put It Into Practice:

Move your body regularly. If traditional exercise isn't your thing, try dancing, ping pong, taking the stairs, yard work, or any movement you enjoy.

Exercise, Dopamine

Stop! In the Name of Focus.

Healthy boundaries are not walls. They are gates and fences that allow you to enjoy the beauty of your own garden. ~ Lydia Hall

We juggle a lot as ADHD moms, which doesn't exactly make it easy to focus. There's so much noise in our heads, our homes, and on our screens.

That's why boundaries matter. Without them, it's easy to feel like we need to be everywhere doing everything for everyone.

We may feel like we can't turn off phone notifications because we might miss something important. Or we avoid closing the door because our kids need access to us at all times.

But...what if we reframed that thinking?

Instead of "I have to be available all the time," we shift to "I'm going to communicate my availability so I can use my attention intentionally."

Instead of "My kids always have access to me," we shift to "It's healthy to teach my kids that boundaries are okay."

When our energy is fragmented, our results will be fragmented too. But when we create clear but flexible boundaries, distractions decrease and focus becomes more possible.

Put It Into Practice:

Choose one small boundary that protects your focus like silencing notifications for 30 minutes, closing the door, or letting your family know when you're in "focus time."

Distractions, Focus, Mindset

May 20

Warning: Burnout Ahead.

Sometimes the worst place you can be is in your own head.
~ Tim Ferriss

In 2023, The Ohio State University[7] surveyed 700 parents and found that 57% of them experienced burnout and that a parent's burnout can impact their children's mental health as well.

Regular check-ins can help us spot burnout early. Common mental burnout warning signs include decreased joy or accomplishment, overwhelm, racing thoughts, decision fatigue, distractibility, difficulty focusing, and heightened emotional reactions.

While many of these sound similar to ADHD symptoms, true burnout tends to show up when several symptoms hit at once, feel more intense than usual, and linger over time. It's often a slow build where tasks feel harder, emotions run higher, and productivity drops.

As the school year ends, burnout can sneak up quickly. But by lowering stress and increasing recovery through rest, movement, self-care, and lighter expectations, we can reduce its impact and protect our energy.

Put It Into Practice:

Pause and do a burnout check-in. If you're running on empty, choose one supportive step today...rest, simplify your to-do list, ask for help, or schedule recovery time.

Burnout, Self-Care, Mom Life

Simple But Impossible.

Doing nothing is very hard. You never know
when you are finished. ~ Leslie Nielsen

I've been driving around with a screw in my front left tire for almost three months. There are so many easy ways to fix it. I could take it to a tire store where they patch it for free. Or I could take it to the auto shop that is roughly 1,000 feet from my house.

And yet, I choose to put my energy into putting air into my tire every couple of days rather than fixing it. But why?

This is a perfect example of situational variability or the way our ability to follow through can change depending on context. How we feel physically or emotionally, whether we're interested in the task, and what else is happening in our environment can all affect motivation and task initiation.

When a task is interesting, we can tap into hyperfocus. But boring tasks can lead to low dopamine and hypofocus, making even "simple" ones feel impossible to start.

The solution isn't more willpower. It's changing the conditions. If we can improve our mood, interest, or environment, we can lower the barrier to entry and finally follow through.

Put It Into Practice:

Ask yourself, "How can I make this task more interesting?" when you're stuck. Try listening to music, gamifying the task, or adding rewards to spark motivation.

Taking Action, Procrastination

May 22

Summer Bucket List.

There's a hundred and four days of summer vacation 'til school comes along just to end it. So the annual problem for our generation is finding a good way to spend it. ~ Phineas and Ferb

The weather is warming up, the school year is ending, and we'll find ourselves in the hustle and bustle of summer before we know it.

To avoid waking up on August 3rd thinking, "Wait... we haven't done _____ yet," let's plan a family summer bucket list now and get a few things scheduled before we (a) forget and (b) run out of summer.

Keep in mind that not all the planning needs to fall squarely on our shoulders. Part of the joy in creating a summer bucket list is inviting ideas from our family because they may find fun in places we wouldn't think to look. When we started this a few years back, I was thinking about amusement parks, and my kids just wanted to walk and get ice cream.

Sometimes the best memories are the simplest ones, especially when we make time for them on purpose.

Put It Into Practice:

Ask your family for summer bucket list ideas. Once you choose the what, schedule the when so the fun doesn't get lost in the chaos.

Mom Life, Planning

Know Your Summer Flow.

Summer used to last forever. Now it's twelve weeks.
~ John Goodman

Even though many ADHDers hate to admit it, most of us do thrive on the structure that the school year provides. And then summer comes along and blows up our whole harmonious, structured vibe.

Ok, maybe it wasn't all harmonious, but it was structured.

Summer starts. Schedules change. Nights are later. Routines disappear. And once-a-year opportunities for fun and frivolity present themselves at every turn. There are times I swear the summer might be as busy, if not busier than, the school year.

And when we lose the built-in structure that school provides, the transition to summer schedules can create a whole lot of chaos in our ADHD mom lives.

That's why it helps to plan ahead and create a little structure on purpose. When we know who's going where, when, and with whom, we're far less likely to feel overwhelmed once summer is in full swing.

Put It Into Practice:

Add summer camps, activities, appointments, and events to your calendar now so you have built-in daily and weekly structure before the season gets busy.

Time Management, Planning, Mom Life

May 24

Work With Your Energy.

Contrary to what you might have heard, there is a
perfect time to do just about anything. ~ Dr. Michael Breus

Are there certain times during the day when motivation is easier, especially for tasks we really don't want to do? This may be influenced by our chronotype, the body's biological inclination to sleep or wake.

Unlike circadian rhythms, which can shift based on routine and lifestyle, chronotypes are strongly influenced by genetics.

When we understand our chronotype, we can work with our energy instead of fighting it. Scheduling tasks that require focus or tasks we tend to avoid during our peak energy windows can make follow-through much easier.

For example, I used to feel major mom guilt for not finishing the dishes after dinner. Every night, I struggled to get them done because I had nothing left. But once I learned I'm a "Lion" chronotype (aka a morning person), I moved dishes to the morning, when my energy and motivation were naturally higher. The dishes still get done... just not right after dinner. And that's okay.

Knowing our chronotype can reduce guilt and increase consistency by helping us match tasks to our energy instead of forcing productivity at our lowest points.

Put It Into Practice:

Take Dr. Michael Breus's chronotype quiz on SleepDoctor.com to identify your peak energy times, then schedule one challenging task during your peak energy times.

Energy Management

Flexible But Functional.

Balance is not something you find, it's something you create. ~ Jana Kingsford

ADHDers love the benefits of structure, but we don't always love implementing it. That's why the built-in rhythm of the school year works so well for many of us. Summer is a different story.

That's why it helps to create a simple structure for our days and weeks, ideally before school is officially out.

We start by adding any non-negotiable commitments we already have…practices, camps, vacations, appointments, and so on. Seeing everything in one place helps us identify which days will be busier than others.

Once the must-dos are on the calendar, it becomes much easier to see what time is actually available for errands, work, rest, and fun. It also helps prevent overcommitting because we can spot schedule overload before it happens.

Keep this weekly overview somewhere the whole family can reference it. This helps everyone stay aware of who needs to be where and when. And which days would be best for an impromptu trip to the zoo or a drive-in movie night.

Put It Into Practice:

Add your summer commitments and activities to your calendar now so you have a clear weekly structure to work from.

Time Management, Planning, Mom Life

May 26

The Power of Persistence.

In one world, effort is a bad thing. It, like failure, means you're not smart or talented. If you were, you wouldn't need effort. In the other world, effort is what makes you smart or talented. ~ Carol Dweck

A growth mindset, coined by Stanford psychologist Carol Dweck, is the belief that abilities develop through effort and learning from mistakes. Its opposite, a fixed mindset, assumes our abilities are unalterable qualities.

Many ADHDers default to a fixed mindset, often fueled by perfectionism and fear of failure rooted in Rejection Sensitive Dysphoria (RSD) and the intense emotions we feel when we perceive negativity. Because if we're faultless, no one can judge us...right?

But when we only do what we're sure we'll succeed at, we miss out on opportunities and experiences that could enrich our lives.

Shifting from a fixed "I can't do that" mindset to a growth "Look how far I've come" mindset takes time. I've been working on this for years and still slip. But when we look for lessons in mistakes, accept feedback without spiraling, and replace perfection with progress...we expand what's possible for us.

Put It Into Practice:

Focus on effort and progress when trying something new rather than the outcome. Then praise yourself for stepping outside your comfort zone.

Mindset, RSD, Productivity

Stopping the Scroll.

Social media isn't a bad thing if you use it with intention and boundaries. ~ Jay Shetty

I've found myself in far too many scroll holes since social media entered my life. And it makes sense why ADHD brains are drawn to our phones...they provide hits of dopamine we carry in our pockets.

The downside is that scrolling quietly steals our time, focus, and energy from our family, work, and sleep.

If we're looking for a scrolling solution, app blockers can make a massive impact on changing our phone habits and reclaiming our time.

I started using an app blocker because I hated spending my mornings sucked into scrolling social media and struggling to put my phone down in the evenings so I could go to sleep at a reasonable time.

I tried using the built-in app limits on my phone but quickly realized I could bypass them. I needed a tool to block access on a schedule without relying on my willpower. Like hiring a babysitter for my phone use.

There are several app blockers that are difficult to circumvent and allow you to schedule automatic app blocks. I personally use the Digital Detox app for Android, but I also recommend Freedom, which works for iPhone/Android and Mac/Windows.

Put It Into Practice:

Choose an app blocker that's hard to bypass and lets you schedule times when the apps are automatically blocked, so limiting your scrolling doesn't depend on remembering or self-control.

Distractions, Productivity, Self-Care

May 28

Processing Post-Its.

I admit that Post-it note sheets that adhere to virtually any surface are now my substitute of choice for retention. ~ Candice Bergen

Post-Its are a great way for ADHDers to create external reminders and support working memory. They come in a variety of colors and styles to help us visualize and organize our thoughts and to-dos.

Because working memory is an executive function many ADHDers struggle with, it's important to capture critical information in a place where it isn't forgotten. But if our Post-It process ends when we write something down, those iconic little squares risk becoming nothing more than visual clutter.

That's why I recommend blocking specific time to process Post-Its on a regular basis. Make it a habit to clear them from the computer screen at the end of a work session. Or color code different types of information (green for bills to pay, pink for urgent tasks, etc.) and set aside specific time to follow through with that color. Maybe create a "Post-Its parking lot" to gather all the notes, then clear the space when it becomes full.

We can keep using Post-Its…we just need to make sure they lead to action.

Put It Into Practice:

Schedule time to process the reminders and tasks on your Post-Its so they don't become clutter or get forgotten.

Memory Support, Productivity

The Procrastivity Trap.

A day can really slip by when you're deliberately avoiding what you're supposed to do. ~ Bill Watterson

Is it still procrastinating if you're being productive? Well, technically yes. Procrastination isn't just scrolling through TikTok instead of checking whether our kids have everything they need for summer camp. It's also doing the dishes to avoid checking whether our kids have everything they need for summer camp.

Yes, the dishes need to be done. But if we do the dishes to avoid some other task that truly needs our attention, chances are we're experiencing productive procrastination or "procrastivity," a term coined by ADHD expert Dr. Russell Ramsay.

Procrastivity happens when we combine procrastination with a productive but non-essential task. And I'd be willing to bet dollars to donuts that most ADHDers have procrastivated a time or 763.

Most of us will recognize when this happens. If so, ask, "Is this what I need to be doing right now?" If the answer is no, identify one small next step for the task that actually needs attention and pivot. If distractions are high, an accountability buddy can help by checking in to make sure we're on track.

Put It Into Practice:

Pause and ask, "Is this what I need to be doing right now?" when you notice yourself procrastivating. Then take one small step on the task you're avoiding.

Procrastivity, Procrastination, Productivity

May 30

A Successful Summer.

Summer is the annual permission slip to be lazy. To do nothing and have it count for something. ~ Regina Brett

Nearly every summer since becoming a mom, I've made these grand plans for what our family will do during our summer "downtime."

But, alas, what I seem to forget every summer since becoming a mom is that there is no downtime. There is always something happening. Each summer feels busier and busier and shorter and shorter. And yet I still picture fitting in far more than three months can hold.

When those plans inevitably don't happen, it's easy for ADHD moms to slip into guilt or feel like we've "failed" summer. That's why it helps to define a range of what success looks like.

Instead of labeling summer as either "amazing" or "a total flop," decide what a good summer would include for the family. Then identify what would make it even better...and what would make it a bonus best-case scenario.

Even if we don't reach "best," we can still have a really good one and that's worth celebrating.

Put It Into Practice:

Write down what a good, better, and best summer would look like as you finalize your summer plans.

Planning, Mindset, Mom Life

Your Brain Runs on REM.

Your future depends on your dreams, so go to sleep.
~ Mesut Barazany

Rapid Eye Movement sleep (REM), the fourth stage of the sleep cycle, is known for its vivid, memorable dreams. REM is vital for mental restoration like emotional processing, memory consolidation, and problem-solving. Think of it like a software update for the brain, pruning old neural connections and strengthening new ones.

When it comes to ADHD and REM sleep, some research suggests we may experience differences in REM, such as getting less total REM sleep, waking more frequently during this stage, or reaching REM later due to delayed sleep cycles.

If we don't update our software through REM sleep, we may experience increased challenges with emotional regulation, focus, and memory. When these issues impact us while we're awake, it makes falling asleep more difficult, perpetuating the cycle and leading to increased anxiety, difficulty with memory recall, and a shorter temper.

Simple steps like consistent bedtimes, reducing light exposure in the evening, and regular exercise can significantly improve overall sleep quality and our chances of reaching the crucial REM stage.

Put It Into Practice:

Choose one small sleep-supporting habit like a consistent bedtime, less screen time at night, or daily movement to help improve your sleep quality and support REM.

Sleep, Self-Care

June

Protect Your Summer Vibe.

The more you value yourself, the healthier your boundaries are. ~ Lorraine Nilon

Summer break is prime FOMO season for ADHD moms. As the weather warms, there are so many spontaneous temptations to throw our time, energy, and budget off track.

And I totally get wanting to do all the things while the kids are out of school. I nearly have a panic attack whenever I see the "you only get 18 summers…" memes.

But when we run ourselves ragged doing all the things for everyone else, we end up stressed, overwhelmed, and with no time for ourselves. And darn it…we want to enjoy the summer too!

Which is why it's important to set a few boundaries and create a bit of structure as summer break starts. Clear boundaries help us know where the line is, how much we can handle, and when we have reached our capacity. Because going over capacity puts us on the fast track to resentment, frustration, and burnout.

Protecting our energy = protecting our vibe.

Put It Into Practice:

Decide your summer non-negotiables for self-care, family, and work. Block time for them first, so you can set boundaries before committing to anything else.

Self-Care, Mom Life, Time Management

June 2

Get Productive in Public.

Alone we can do so little, together we can do so much.
~ Helen Keller

Body doubling or working alongside others helps kick-start our motivation by providing a sense of accountability. There's just something about stating what we're working on to a partner that energizes our brain to follow through so we can report our progress at the end of the session.

But it is possible to experience the benefits of body doubling even if we don't have a specifically scheduled time with a specific partner.

Taking our laptop to a coffee shop to pay bills, studying at a library, or going into the office to work with co-workers can trigger the same "public pressure" that improves task initiation and focus.

For example, when I started my podcast, I wrote nearly every episode while sitting at my son's swim practice. When I stopped staying for the practices, the motivation and follow-through to write my episodes became much harder.

So if we're struggling to start and follow through this summer, try adding a little productivity in public.

Put It Into Practice:

Head to your local coffee shop, library, or other public place to help trigger your workflow the next time you're stuck at home staring at a screen.

Body Doubling, Accountability, Productivity

June 3

Soft Structure.

You don't get time. You create time.
~ Sanhita Baruah

We still need some structure in the summer. But ADHDers often resist time blocking because it feels rigid and inflexible.

We're not going to let that stupid calendar tell us what to do between 1–4 p.m. on Tuesday!!

It is possible to time block in a way that feels flexible. Instead of scheduling specific tasks at specific times, we can create generalized blocks that protect time for what matters without micromanaging our day. Let's call it "time blocking for people who dislike time blocking."

This might look like a "work" block early in the morning before the kids are up. Or a "housework" block after dinner to make time for dishes and laundry. Maybe a "family" block on Sunday afternoons for special dinners or activities.

Think flexibility. You can decide what happens inside the block based on urgency, energy, or priorities that day. It's not about the perfectly blocked schedule…it's making sure the important stuff doesn't fall through the cracks while you're trying to enjoy summer.

Put It Into Practice:

Create a few generalized time blocks on your calendar to protect time for work, home tasks, or family activities, especially if strict schedules make you feel resistant or boxed in.

Time Management, Planning, Mom Life

June 4

One Space at a Time.

The shorter way to do many things is to only do one thing at a time.
~ Wolfgang Amadeus Mozart

ADHD ambition will say things like "Let's get the whole house organized this summer." But ADHD motivation will be like "Um...that sounds like a completely overwhelming task that I'm not sure how to start so I vote we do literally anything else."

Because planning and organizing require executive function, broad and undefined tasks can feel impossible to initiate and kill productivity for ADHD brains.

Reducing the scope and clarifying the steps of any project makes taking action easier. And for organizing projects specifically, this may mean committing to only one space or part of a space at a time.

Instead of "organize the house," think "organize the kitchen." If that still feels too big, think "organize this cupboard." As a bonus, every space we complete gives us a dopamine hit to motivate us to keep going.

Once we choose a space, make a simple checklist of steps (or find one online) so it's easier to start and easier to jump back in if we have to step away.

Put It Into Practice:

Pick one room or one small space and focus only on that. Create a checklist so you know what to do next.

Cleaning and Organizing

June 5

Don't Sweat It Alone.

A buddy will keep you honest and add a dimension of fun to your workout. ~ Bill Toomey

Tackling tasks with other people typically makes them easier. And a bit more fun. The same is true with exercise, which is one of the best ways to support ADHD symptoms.

A workout buddy can act as a body double, meaning their presence alone helps us follow through and stay focused. They don't even have to do the same workout (think going to the gym). Simply moving alongside someone else can boost motivation and consistency.

Workout buddies also add accountability. When a workout is scheduled with someone else, it's harder to bail when motivation dips.

And there are lots of workout buddy options...Ask someone to go on a walk before the kids wake up. Invite friends to go out dancing or to a yoga class. Join a softball or bowling league.

We can also hire a personal trainer as our workout buddy. Because paying for accountability is a powerful way to motivate us to follow through.

Put It Into Practice:

Choose one way to add a workout buddy to your routine this summer...someone to walk with, a group class, a league, or a trainer. Then schedule your first session.

Exercise, Accountability, Body Doubling, Self-Care

June 6

Automate. Outsource. Delegate.

Don't try and do everything yourself because you can't.
~ Anthea Turner

ADHDers are often described as "driven by a motor." It's hard for us to slow down or sit still. We want to do it all. And many times, that's perfectly OK.

The friction comes when doing all the things keeps us from being present with our family and friends. Or we run ourselves ragged and end up burned out.

So before summer is in full swing, it's helpful to brainstorm ways to automate, outsource, or delegate tasks so we can keep life running without carrying it all ourselves.

For example, if bill-paying slips when we're spending time poolside, set up automatic payments.

If the dog spends too much time in the crate because we're out and about, hire the neighbor kid to walk him.

And if we cannot spend one more evening sitting in a parking lot waiting for open gym to end, consider asking another family to trade off carpooling duties.

Doing it all doesn't have to mean doing it all ourselves.

Put It Into Practice:

Choose one task to automate, outsource, or delegate this summer so your time and energy can go toward what matters most.

Productivity, Mom Life

June 7

A Vacation from Vacation.

Traveling with kids is like being in a frat party. Nobody
sleeps, everything's broken, and there's a lot
of throwing up. ~ Ray Romano

Ever feel like taking a vacation from vacation while on vacation? Even though our ADHD brains love new, exciting, and different, we can burn out if we're overstimulated for too long...even when overstimulation is fun.

When we're excited about our adventures, we often forget our ADHD brains run better with some regular structure. Instead of routine, we pack the schedule from sunup to sundown. Because it's vacation and we may never get another chance to bungee jump into a shark pit at the bottom of a waterfall ever again.

But travel means additional decision-making and constant transitions, which drain executive function. Add time shifts, disrupted sleep, and a change in eating habits and suddenly we have a full-blown executive-function meltdown on our hands.

So as we plan summer travel, build in some unscheduled, unplanned time each day. It gives everyone, neurodivergent or not, a chance to rest, reset, and actually enjoy the trip.

Put It Into Practice:

Plan for unstructured time on vacation so your ADHD brain has space to recharge and reset.

Travel, Overstimulation, Mom Life

June 8

Beat Birthday Busts.

It is lovely, when I forget all birthdays, including my own,
to find that somebody remembers me.
~ Ellen Glasgow

Today is my birthday. And while I would love to spend it regaling you with stories of birthdays past (like the time I dressed up as Lady Gaga for my 40th birthday lip sync battle party), I think this space is better used for a gift-giving tip.

I am the queen of grabbing a gift on the way to a birthday party. Stop at the store. Grab a gift card. Then spend an absurd amount on a greeting card to go with it.

One day I had the idea to order boxes of birthday and assorted cards to keep on hand for emergencies.

Now when we're rushing out the door for a birthday party (or I want to send a thank you card), I can do it more easily, more affordably, and when I am thinking about it…instead of waiting until I have time to run to the store and inevitably forgetting.

Put It Into Practice:

Order a box of birthday and assorted greeting cards to keep on hand. Bonus points if you also keep stamps around so sending your cards doesn't require an extra errand.

Time Investments, Mom Life

The Not 5 a.m. Club.

*Morning is wonderful. Its only drawback is that it comes at
such an inconvenient time of day.*
~ Glen Cook

Just because it's a morning routine doesn't mean it happens before the sun rises.

A morning routine, at its core, is about the ritual of starting your day, not the time of day that we start.

And along with the start time, we get to choose what works best for us. There are a lot of opinions about morning routines, but when it comes to ADHD brains, flexibility and choice matter. If a routine feels too rigid or unrealistic, it won't stick.

Our morning routine may start off with just a few things to fill our cup. Over time, it may evolve. It may change with the season, our schedule, or our energy levels.

Just remember…it's not about the when. It's about setting up the brain and body for the day ahead.

Put It Into Practice:

Choose 2–3 things you'd like to do to start your day. If you need a little more time, set your alarm a few minutes earlier, but don't feel like you have to wake up before dawn… unless you want to.

Morning Routine, Self-Care

June 10

When Sips Set You Back.

You leave old habits behind by starting out with the thought, "I release the need for this in my life." ~ Dr. Wayne Dyer

Summer is in full swing…patios are open and cocktails are flowing. And far be it from me to judge anyone for enjoying an adult beverage. But like most indulgences, from desserts to shopping, too much of something we enjoy can come with consequences.

Many ADHDers notice a short-term boost from alcohol, whether it's a temporary lift in mood or a brief sense of relief from anxiety. But over time, regular drinking can worsen ADHD symptoms like inattention, impulsivity, and emotional dysregulation. And because impulse control can already be a struggle for ADHD brains, it may be harder to stop at "just one."

Alcohol can also impact brain chemistry in a way that increases the likelihood and severity of depression and anxiety. In fact, a 2019 study[8] found that people with ADHD have a higher risk of both depression and binge drinking.

If alcohol tends to make symptoms worse, it may help to explore other ways to boost dopamine and reduce stress like movement, time outdoors, music, social connection, or creative hobbies. And if cutting back feels harder than swapping a hard seltzer for soda water, reaching out to a professional for support is a strong next step.

Put It Into Practice:

Pay attention to how alcohol affects your mood, sleep, and ADHD symptoms. If the downsides outweigh the upsides, try an alcohol-free alternative and find another way to recharge.

Mental Health, Anxiety, Self-Care

June 11

You're Not Lazy.

Give us the tools, and we will finish the job.
~ Winston Churchill

No matter what we've heard from parents, teachers, co-workers, or spouses, feeling less than motivated to start less than exciting tasks as an ADHDer is not laziness More often than not, it's a dopamine issue.

Dopamine helps drive motivation and action. But because ADHD brains struggle to regulate dopamine, we won't always have enough of it available to fire up executive function and get moving.

Laziness, on the other hand, is defined as "having or showing an unwillingness to work." And I can confidently say, every ADHDer I've worked with has a willingness to work.

Where we tend to struggle is with executive function...deciding where to start, breaking tasks into actionable steps, and following through to the finish line.

We can support motivation by boosting dopamine and working with our natural energy patterns. Step outside for sunlight. Move our bodies. Take a cold shower. Try a quick meditation. Laugh at cat videos (just not for too long).

Put It Into Practice:

Pick a quick dopamine booster when you're struggling to start. Then use that momentum to take one small step.

Dopamine, Taking Action, Executive Function

June 12

Suitcase or Storage Unit?

*No, I didn't "overpack." I just wanted all of my clothes to feel
like they took a vacation. ~ David Blue*

It took me several years to break my chronic overpacking habit. And I still have my moments (like when I brought a suitcase just for shoes to my sister's wedding). Whether it's procrastination, fatigue, or fear of forgetting something, packing can be a real challenge for ADHD brains. But with a few simple hacks, we can streamline our suitcase.

Start by choosing the bag before the clothes. If we have limited trunk space or plan to carry on, seeing how much space we actually have makes it easier to gauge how much to bring.

Next, choose shoes first. They're likely our bulkiest item, so paring down our pairs can free up space.

Then, think about outfits, not options. Choose mix-and-match pieces that create multiple looks instead of tossing in "just in case" items. Bonus points if your outfits coordinate with your minimal shoes. And don't forget…most hotels, resorts, and rentals have laundry, so we may not need multiples if we can wash and re-wear.

Put It Into Practice:

Prevent overpacking by limiting the space you have to fill, choosing only the shoes you need, and coordinating your clothes to mix and match.

Travel, Decision-Making

Distractions Derail Your Day.

You will never reach your destination if you stop and throw stones at every dog that barks. ~ Winston Churchill

Is there a Pavlovian urge to grab your phone the second it makes a noise? Is it difficult to pay bills in the kitchen while the kids argue over who gets the last bowl of Cocoa Puffs?

Distractions come in all sorts of shapes, sizes, and varieties. And for ADHD brains, they can become black holes for our attention. While we can't eliminate every distraction, we can reduce many of them with a few simple strategies:

- Turn off unnecessary phone and computer notifications
- Limit access to distracting apps with app blockers or focus mode
- Wear noise-cancelling headphones with white noise
- Close the door or create a "do not disturb" signal
- Move to a quieter or less distracting space
- Clear visual clutter from our work area

Limiting distractions makes it easier to focus and follow through on the task at hand.

Put It Into Practice:

Choose one distraction-limiting strategy from above when you're struggling to focus.

Focus, Distractions, Productivity

June 14

Feed Your Focus.

Your brain is hungry for the right fuel. Feed it wisely.
~ Dr. Daniel Amen

L-tyrosine is an amino acid the body uses to help produce dopamine and norepinephrine, two neurotransmitters involved in focus, motivation, and executive function. And a 1999 study[9] found it may support working memory and cognitive flexibility when under stress.

While we can't "eat our way" out of ADHD, choosing foods that support brain chemistry is an easy way to help our body do its job. Lucky for us, L-tyrosine shows up in many everyday, healthy foods we may want to incorporate into our diet anyway. They include:

- Almonds
- Apples
- Avocados
- Bananas
- Beets
- Chicken & poultry
- Chocolate
- Dairy
- Green leafy vegetables
- Green tea
- Lima beans
- Oatmeal
- Oranges
- Peas
- Sesame & pumpkin seeds
- Soy
- Tomatoes
- Watermelon
- Wheat germ

Put It Into Practice:

Add one L-tyrosine-rich food to your day as a simple way to support focus and dopamine production.

Eating and Meal Planning, Dopamine, Self-Care

Quieting Your Busy Brain.

Anxiety's like a rocking chair. It gives you something to do, but it doesn't get you very far. ~ Jodi Picoult

Studies suggest that 25–50% of people diagnosed with ADHD also have an anxiety disorder. And that doesn't even account for those of us who aren't diagnosed but regularly experience situational anxiety or the anxiety that shows up in response to new, unfamiliar, or stressful situations.

Regular mindfulness practices help reduce anxiety by interrupting negative thinking, bringing us back to the present moment, and reducing spirals into rumination about the past or worry about the future.

Many ADHDers also find mindfulness supports focus and emotional regulation, which helps to calm our busy, overworked brains.

Some mindful practices we can easily incorporate into our daily routine include deep breathing exercises, body scans, meditation, and a journaling or gratitude practice. The best part…the practice doesn't need to take a long time to be effective.

Put It Into Practice:

Choose one simple mindfulness practice to try today like deep breathing, a body scan, or journaling. Make it part of your routine to help reduce stress and anxiety.

Anxiety, Self-Care, Mental Health

June 16

The 97%-ers.

Work is the greatest thing in the world,
so we should always save some of it for tomorrow. ~ Don Herold

My husband and I have an ongoing joke that I am the president of the "97% Club" because so many projects I start get so close to the finish...only for me to fizzle out right before it's complete. For instance:

- I lined my linen closet shelves except for the top one because I needed to grab a ladder. And I never did.
- I built a clubhouse for my kids when they were little and stopped before I put a roof on. By the time I finally finished it, the inside was already rotting.

Why does this happen more often in ADHD brains than neurotypical ones? Because ADHD motivation is often driven by interest, while neurotypical motivation is more driven by importance. Once something stops feeling exciting, our brain starts scanning for something new, shiny, and stimulating.

We can breathe life back into an unfinished project by adding interest. Change the environment. Switch locations. Add a reward. Ask someone to work alongside us. Or recruit an accountability buddy to check in on our progress.

Put It Into Practice:

Pick one almost-finished project that still matters and choose a way to make it more interesting so you can finally cross the finish line.

Taking Action, Productivity, ADHD Symptoms

The Beverage Goblin.

A beverage goblin needs at least 3 drinks at a time. She needs them while she's working for her body and mind. One to hydrate, one to energize and one just for fun. A beverage goblin needs beverages to make the brain run.
~ Kristen West

Depending on the time of day, I usually have two to four beverages within arm's reach. I've been this way for as long as I can remember. Typically water, green tea, and bubbly water…all at once.

Beverage collecting is one of those oddly specific ADHD traits I only learned about after my diagnosis. After hearing the term beverage goblin on TikTok from The Centered Life Co., I fell down a Reddit rabbit hole reading about others' thirst to quench their thirst.

While there's no official research explaining the beverage goblin phenomenon, a few theories make sense. Drinks with different temperatures, textures, and flavors may offer sensory stimulation that helps us focus. And sometimes each drink has a job like coffee for energy, water for hydration, and apple juice because we love it.

Whatever the reason, staying hydrated supports our brain and body, so drink up!

Put It Into Practice:

Grab a drink. Or three.

Eating and Meal Planning, Self-Care

June 18

You Shall Not Pass.

Walls keep everybody out. Boundaries teach them where the door is.
~ Mark Groves

ADHDers love to say "yes." We love being helpful and involved. We don't want to let people down and we definitely don't want to miss out on the fun. But in our rush to say yes to everyone else, we often end up saying no to ourselves...and that's a fast track to burnout.

Boundaries protect our energy and emotional regulation by preventing overcommitment before it happens. This is particularly important for ADHD introverts who are more prone to overstimulation in social situations.

But between people-pleasing, time management struggles, and a dash of mom guilt, many ADHD moms find themselves stuck in a boundaryless burnout spiral.

Clear boundaries help us identify and communicate where we draw the line, how much we can handle, and when we're nearing capacity. They give us back control of our time and energy so we can focus on what we truly value.

Put It Into Practice:

Identify where you need a boundary to protect your time and energy. Then communicate your boundary with the people it impacts.

Burnout, Introverts, People-Pleasing

June 19
The Doorway Effect.

I regularly find myself walking into a room and wondering why I'm there. I return to where I was before and still have no idea why I left in the first place. ~ Dr. Ira Hyman

When we walk into a room, only to forget why we're there, we've experienced what is known as "the doorway effect." Also known as the "location updating effect," researchers theorize we forget things of recent significance when we cross a boundary, like moving from one room to another.

A 2011 study from the University of Notre Dame[10] found that the simple act of walking through a doorway can trigger memory lapses. The doorway acts as an "event boundary" for the brain, signaling that one moment is over and it's time to move on. Our brains say, "We're moving on. Don't think about that previous thing anymore."

Because ADHD impacts working memory and increases distractibility, many ADHDers experience the doorway effect more often. If so, try pausing before walking through the door and saying the reason out loud. Yes, even if that reason was just "to get scissors." Or jot the reason down on a slip of paper as a quick visual reminder.

It can also help to slow down and move more mindfully through your space, because rushing tends to make these lapses more likely.

Put It Into Practice:

Pause to focus on why you're moving from one space to another so you don't forget what you came for.

Memory Support

June 20

Connecting the Dots.

*The ability to recognize patterns is the foundation
of all great ideas. ~ Oprah Winfrey*

We may have heard someone say "ADHD is a superpower." And while that can feel like a BS line of toxic positivity, many ADHD brains do tend to have one strength that looks a lot like a superpower: pattern recognition.

ADHDers often notice connections others miss. We might predict a movie plot early, spot word patterns quickly, or sense that a friend's relationship is on shaky ground long before anyone else sees it. That's pattern recognition at work.

Many ADHDers are also strong visual thinkers. We tend to process information better when we can see it (writing things down, mapping it out, or laying it all out in front of us). Some researchers theorize this preference for visual processing may be a way the ADHD brain compensates for working memory challenges...using external visuals to "hold" information that might otherwise slip away.

These heightened observation skills can be a gift. They fuel creativity, big-picture thinking, and problem solving. But the downside is that our brains may stay "switched on," constantly scanning for patterns, leading to overanalyzing, worry, and rumination.

Put It Into Practice:

Acknowledge the next time your ADHD brain recognizes a pattern someone else may have missed. Your brain is doing what it does best.

ADHD Symptoms

June 21

First Day of Summer.

Spring flew swiftly by, and summer came.
~ Charles Dickens

Welcome to summer...officially! Time for fun, sun, and a quick seasonal reset for us and our home. These small maintenance tasks can help us avoid the ADHD tax later, like higher utilities from dirty filters, extra time from missed car maintenance, or losing files when a computer crashes.

For your home and property, remember to:

- Check and replace smoke detector batteries
- Change the furnace and refrigerator water filter
- Change the oil in the car
- Clean out the dryer vent

For you and your family:

- Replace toothbrushes
- Wash makeup brushes
- Delete unwanted digital photos
- Back up the computer's hard drive
- Drop off the donations that have been living in the back of the car

Put It Into Practice:

Schedule time this week for some seasonal household maintenance tasks for your home and your family.

Time Investments, Cleaning and Organizing

June 22

So Shiny.

Focus is a matter of deciding what things you're not going to do. ~ John Carmack

In our constant quest for dopamine, ADHDers, with our impulse- and reward-driven brains, often flit from project to project, leaving a trail of unfinished work in our wake. This is known as Shiny Object Syndrome.

Our tendency to follow the shiny rabbit down their hole may come from boredom or fear of missing out. And while trying new things and getting the dopamine we need can be great, giving too much energy to "new and shiny" can slow our momentum on what actually matters.

Instead of chasing every rabbit, try slowing down long enough to evaluate it. Ask yourself, "Does this align with my goals or values right now?" A small delay can help us decide what to commit to and what can be delayed, delegated, or deleted.

It can also help to create an "idea parking lot" for the thoughts that pop into our head. We often pivot because we're afraid we'll forget the new idea. But writing it down creates external memory and gives our brain permission to stay on task.

Put It Into Practice:

Pause and ask yourself, "Is this a priority right now?" before you pivot to a new, shiny idea. If not, park it somewhere you'll remember.

Productivity, Focus, Goal Setting

Take Charge of Recharge.

*O time, thou must untangle this, not I. It is too hard a knot for me t'untie. ~
William Shakespeare*

Most of us have approximately 5,268 charging cords and blocks scattered around the house. And somehow, we can never find the right one when we need it.

At last count, we had 72 cords and blocks in our home. Eeek! Even with four family members and a whole lineup of devices that feels excessive.

A periodic cord purge can help us take back control. When we gather everything in one place, we can see what we actually have, toss what we don't need, and assign a "home" to what remains so we can find the right cord when the battery is at 2%. And a pro tip…a little piece of masking tape as a label for unique cords goes a long way in helping us remember what they belong to.

And don't just throw old cords away. Many can be recycled, which helps reduce waste and supports electronics recycling programs.

Put It Into Practice:

Gather all your cords and charging blocks in one place. Keep only what you use, recycle the rest, and assign a home to what remains.

Cleaning and Organizing, Mom Life

June 24

Stack and Go.

This is a golden rule: Never run a single errand at a time. You'll save time, gas, energy and stress hormones by grouping your errands into batches. ~ George Miata

Humans naturally seek the path of least resistance, trying to conserve energy and get the most out of the least effort. And ADHDers can save time, energy, and mental bandwidth by errand stacking, or grouping errands into one trip instead of making multiple runs.

How we stack errands depends on personal preference. We can group them geographically like dropping an Amazon return at the UPS store near our kid's piano lesson. Or by combining stops like picking up a prescription at the grocery store pharmacy instead of driving to a standalone location.

It helps to keep a running errand list on our phone or on paper. We can also keep a short "nearby list" of what's close to places we visit regularly like school, work, the gym, or our favorite coffee shop so planning a multi-stop mission takes less brainpower. We can also designate a reusable bag for returns and drop-offs, so we don't forget about or lose them. Then make it a habit to check the errand list and bag before heading out.

Put It Into Practice:

Create a running errand list and try stacking two errands into one trip this week.

Productivity, Time Management

Fidget to Focus.

Rather than trying to suppress fidgeting tendencies, individuals can embrace its positive aspects through appropriate sensory resources. ~ Allanah Bazzard

"Why are you wiggling?"

"Can't you just sit still?"

"Do you see anyone else moving right now?"

Many of us heard phrases like these frequently throughout our lives. It wasn't that we wanted to be disruptive…we just needed to move.

And now, research suggests fidgeting may actually be the brain's way of trying to regulate attention. In other words, a mindless fidget that doesn't interfere with the task at hand can help improve focus.

A 2021 study from the University of Auckland[11] asked adults with ADHD to undergo an MRI while researchers captured brain images as participants fidgeted. The results showed increased blood flow to the prefrontal cortex, the area responsible for executive function.

So go ahead and tap into the benefits of fidgeting, as long as it's automatic, doesn't pull our attention away from the task at hand, and doesn't distract the people around us.

Put It Into Practice:

Find a mindless fidget that helps you focus like doodling, a quiet fidget toy, chewing gum, tapping your foot, or using an exercise ball.

Fidgets and Stimming, Productivity

June 26

Active Rest.

*Rest is not idleness, and to lie sometimes on the grass
under trees on a summer's day...
is by no means a waste of time. ~ John Lubbock*

For as long as I can remember, my family has joked that I'm the Energizer Bunny (I keep going and going). My mom even has the "Flight of the Bumblebee" as my ringtone.

Even though I know rest is essential for energy management, I've always struggled with resting in the traditional sense. Sitting still can feel stressful and uncomfortable, so I used to assume I was doing rest "wrong."

Then I reframed my definition of rest.

I no longer force myself to stop moving. Instead, I choose activities that genuinely recharge me, even if they're active. That might look like brunch with friends, a date night with my husband, baking cookies, crafting, or cheering on the sidelines at my kids' games.

So don't get hung up on what rest should look like. If it helps us recharge, it can be active and still be rest.

Put It Into Practice:

Schedule one activity this week that will recharge you, whether it's quiet rest or active rest.

Energy Management, Self-Care

Time for You.

Taking care of yourself doesn't mean me first,
it means me too. ~ L.R. Knost

It's very easy to allow summer fun to revolve around what our kids want to do and neglect ourselves in the process.

Which is why summer self-care may be even more important than during the school year for an ADHD mom. When we lose the structure that supports our executive function, time management becomes harder without school bells to anchor the day. Decision fatigue multiplies from constant choices, and dopamine runs low by evening, making mood and emotional regulation more difficult.

Self-care doesn't have to mean a solo vacation or a day at the spa. Instead, we can look for small ways to refuel through simple activities like reading, working out, baking, listening to music, or anything that feels restorative. We can upgrade routines we already have by buying a shower gel we love, refreshing our skincare, or using a mug or water bottle that makes us smile.

If it makes you think, "this is nice," it counts.

Put It Into Practice:

Schedule a little self-care time for yourself today. It doesn't have to be long to be effective.

Self-Care

June 28

RSD Redirect.

Negativity is cannibalistic. The more you feed it,
the bigger and stronger it grows. ~ Bobby Darnell

Rejection Sensitive Dysphoria (RSD) happens when those of us with ADHD experience intense emotional pain from criticism, perceived failure, or rejection. Many of us feel our feelings waaaay deeper than our neurotypical counterparts.

And while it's important to experience and process these emotions rather than ignore them, our struggles with emotional regulation can make the situation spiral, especially when we ruminate on it for days, weeks, or even years afterward.

But when we can recognize RSD in the moment and catch ourselves before we spiral, we can practice redirecting our energy into something that supports us. That might look like movement, journaling, talking it out with someone safe, or doing something small that restores our confidence. It's not about pretending it doesn't hurt...it's about keeping one hard moment from hijacking the whole day.

Put It Into Practice:

Choose one positive place to redirect your RSD energy the next time it shows up. Then come back to process the situation later when your nervous system has calmed down.

RSD, Emotional Regulation, Mindset

Can You See Time?

One thing that seems true for the vast majority of ADHD adults is that they experience the passage of it in a fashion different from that of "normal" individuals. ~ Thom Hartman

Time perception, or the ability to feel time passing, is a challenge for many ADHDers. Neurological differences in the prefrontal cortex (where executive function lives) and disruptions in dopamine signaling can make it harder to estimate time, plan ahead, and connect our time decisions to future consequences. This is one reason we often wait until the last minute.

For ADHD brains, time can feel invisible unless we make it visible.

That's why it's helpful to use external cues to signal the passage of time. This might be as simple as keeping analog clocks around the house or using a visual timer like the Time Timer, particularly during activities where we tend to hyperfocus.

We can also use a timer to shut off our TV when it's time to go to bed, Wi-Fi-enabled light bulbs to turn the lights on when we want to wake up, or app timers and app blockers to signal "you've spent enough time on social media today." We can also create music playlists of specific length to help track time without watching the clock.

Put It Into Practice:

Use analog clocks, visual timers, and external cues (like alarms, playlists, or app limits) to help you feel time passing.

Time Blindness, Time Management

June 30

At an Appropriate Hour.

*Sorry I didn't text you back. I was pretending I didn't see it
and I ended up actually forgetting. ~ Joydeep Ruidas*

I always seem to remember I need to text someone when it's a completely inappropriate time…usually when I'm up at 5 a.m. and I'm pretty sure nobody wants to hear from me then.

But instead of adding "Text Sara back" to my to-do list with the other 50 billion tasks, I can simply write the text when I think of it and schedule it to go out at a more reasonable time.

Scheduling texts also works great when we don't want to forget to say "Happy birthday," "Congratulations," or "Thinking of you," but we know our life and faulty memory may get in the way.

Here's how to schedule texts on the two most popular apps:

- Google Messages: Type the message → tap the + → select Schedule send → follow the prompts.
- iPhone: Type the message → press and hold the blue send arrow → select Send Later → follow the prompts.

Put It Into Practice:

Schedule a text today so you know how to do it the next time you need it.

Memory Support, Time Investments

July

Taming Your Digital Tiger.

The constant dilemma of the information age is that our ability to gather a sea of data greatly exceeds the tools and techniques available to sort, extract, and apply the information we've collected. ~ Jeff Davidson

Just because we can't see our digital clutter doesn't mean it isn't there. In fact, the photos on our phones and the files on our computers may be more chaotic than the mess we can see in our homes.

And just like physical clutter, digital clutter can cause distractions, make it harder to find what we need, and eat up valuable storage space.

That's why taking a little time to sort our digital files can make everything easier in the future. And this can be a perfect summertime poolside or backyard productive task.

Start by creating folders with broad categories like Family, Kids, Work, School, and Photos. Then drag and drop files into those folders and delete anything that's duplicated, outdated, or no longer needed.

Keep it simple on the first pass. Our mission is sorting not perfection. Done is better than detailed for this first round. We can always come back later to create subfolders if we need them.

Put It Into Practice:

Spend a few minutes clearing digital clutter today. Create broad folders, sort your files, and delete duplicates, unused apps, and old photos to free up space.

Cleaning and Organizing, Productivity

July 2

Sun, Fun, and Yum.

*Summer cooking implies a sense of immediacy, a capacity
to capture the essence of the fleeting moment. ~ Elizabeth David*

For most of us, there are about 42 billion things we'd rather do than meal planning during the summer. But alas… we all must eat. Which is why it helps to keep meal planning and prep as streamlined as possible during these FOMO-filled months.

Summer is a great time to:

- Explore meal delivery services to reduce decision fatigue, prep time, and the energy it takes to stop at the store.
- Outsource part of the meal-prep process by using pre-cut veggies, salad kits, rotisserie chicken, or heat-and-eat frozen options.
- Consider click-and-pickup or delivery to keep food on hand and avoid the drive-thru scramble.

As an added bonus, many grocery apps save past orders and shopping lists, making future shopping even easier.

And remember, summer doesn't have to be the season of perfect meals. Sometimes "good enough" is the best plan. If meal kits or grocery delivery feel like a luxury, summer may be the perfect time to treat ourselves so we can stay present and enjoy time with our family.

Put It Into Practice:

Pick one way to streamline meals this week like meal kits, grocery pickup, pre-prepped ingredients, or simple repeat meals so feeding your family takes less brainpower.

Eating and Meal Planning, Time Investments, Mom Life

Stuck in Study Mode.

*He who learns and makes no use of his learning
is a beast of burden with a load of books. ~ Anton Chekhov*

We live in a society plagued by information overload. Couple that with ADHDers' tendency to chase learning for the instant dopamine boost, and it's no wonder it can feel hard to stop researching long enough to make a decision or take action.

Sometimes the learning loop isn't just about curiosity...it's also about fear. Fear of making the wrong decision. Fear of failing. Fear of regret. So we keep learning and learning and learning because learning feels productive, even when it's really just avoiding the next step.

When we find ourselves stuck in study mode, one of the best ways to shift into action is to set limits. We can set a time limit on research, a deadline for making a decision, or a cap on the number of sources we consult before moving forward.

It may also help to enlist an accountability buddy...someone we can share what we've learned with and then say, "OK, what's my next step?"

Keep this mantra on repeat to help break the cycle, "I don't need more information, I need a next step."

Put It Into Practice:

Pick one decision or project you've been over-researching. Set a limit (time, sources, or a decision deadline), then take one small step forward.

Taking Action, Productivity

July 4

When It All Goes Boom.

Energy and persistence conquer all things.
~ Benjamin Franklin

The Fourth of July often feels like the halfway point of summer. And it's also when many ADHD moms start to notice the gap between what we planned to do and what we've actually followed through on.

Even with the best intentions, plans go off track. And because ADHD brains often overestimate what we can accomplish (or underestimate how much energy it will take), we can hit this midpoint feeling defeated, behind, or overwhelmed.

But all is not lost! There is still time to make progress on our plans (if those goals still matter).

A great place to start is by prioritizing what's on the list. Whether it's a household project or a fun family day out, some things are more important than others. Once you know what matters most, get it on the schedule ASAP. And if something feels too big, schedule smaller steps so starting doesn't feel overwhelming.

And remember, even if we aren't as "productive" as we hoped, spending time with our family enjoying spontaneous summer fun is producing memories that will live on beyond any unfinished projects.

Put It Into Practice:

Revisit your summer plans. Choose what still matters, schedule it, and let go of what doesn't.

Consistency, Taking Action

The Perfection Connection.

At its root, perfectionism isn't really about a deep love of being meticulous. It's about fear. Fear of making a mistake. Fear of disappointing others. Fear of failure. Fear of success. ~ Michael Law

ADHDers often find ourselves stuck on a hamster wheel of perfectionism. This may be due to a fear of failure mixed with hyperfocus and a splash of trying to control outcomes. Because if we create the perfect report at work or decorate the perfect cake for our kid's birthday, we're clearly dedicated, motivated, and responsible…right?

But perfectionism doesn't just cause stress. It can also lead to procrastination.

We may not start a project if we can't do it perfectly or the "right way." Or if we struggled with a similar task in the past. Maybe we pour all our time and effort into something we know we're good at and avoid projects that don't have a guaranteed successful outcome.

But as with so many ADHD tendencies, once we recognize perfectionism, we can develop coping strategies to keep it from holding us back.

One way is to ask, "What's the worst thing that could happen if this is less than perfect?" When we realize the outcome won't be catastrophic, it becomes easier to move forward. And easier to stop over-polishing things that don't require perfection.

Put It Into Practice:

Pick one task you've been avoiding. Decide what "good enough" looks like, then take the next step forward.

Perfectionism, Taking Action, Productivity

July 6
Stretch Your Thinking.

Flexibility is the key to stability.
~ John Wooden

Cognitive flexibility is a core executive function that helps us handle change, solve problems, and stay calm when we need to pivot. In other words, when life doesn't go to plan, flexible thinkers adapt and regroup.

But for ADHD brains, a change in plans can lead to stress and a spiral. Working memory challenges can make it harder to hold new information long enough to adjust. And impulsivity plus emotional dysregulation can make frustration or disappointment, even over small changes, feel bigger.

And since summer schedules are full of sun, fun, and shifting plans, building cognitive flexibility can help a surprise change not ruin the day.

One of the best ways to strengthen flexibility is to practice "new." Learning a new skill, visiting a new place, meeting new people, or trying a new activity helps our brains build the habit of adapting. Puzzles and strategy games help us see multiple solutions. And creative activities train us to look beyond the obvious and explore new possibilities.

Put It Into Practice:

Try one small "new" thing this week like taking a different route, trying a new recipe, learning a new skill, or playing a new game to strengthen your flexibility muscles.

Executive Function, Mindset, Emotional Regulation

Cool, Dark, and Dreamy.

Apparently, if you live until 75, you'll have spent 25 years in bed, so it makes sense to have a decent mattress. ~ Marc Warren

When we struggle to fall or stay asleep, our sleep solutions may stretch beyond learning to quiet our busy brains. In fact, our sleep environment plays a role in how easily we fall and stay asleep.

Clutter causes distractions and can increase anxiety. Light disrupts our circadian rhythm and suppresses melatonin, the sleep hormone. And uncomfortable bedding or clothing can irritate our skin and make restlessness worse.

That's why creating an ideal sleep space can greatly improve sleep quality for our overworked ADHD brains. Some easy, high-impact tips include making the room dark and keeping it cool to trigger deeper, more restorative sleep. We may also want to try sleep supports like:

- A white noise machine to mask sounds that may wake us
- A weighted blanket for deep pressure stimulation to calm the nervous system
- Calming scents like lavender or sandalwood to promote relaxation
- Smart bulbs that dim slowly to signal it's time to wind down

And remember…better sleep doesn't just make us less tired. It supports focus, emotional regulation, and executive function the next day.

Put It Into Practice:

Pick a step you can take to make your bedroom more ADHD sleep-friendly.

Sleep, Self-Care

July 8
Productive Procrastination.

You cannot escape the responsibility of tomorrow
by evading it today. ~ Abraham Lincoln

Productive procrastination, or procrastivity, happens when we choose a task that needs to be done but we use it to avoid another task we really don't want to do.

And why is it that we choose certain tasks over others?

It could be because the chosen task has a lower barrier to entry. Starting feels easier, the steps are clear, and we don't have to reinvent the wheel. Physical tasks like doing dishes can also feel less mentally taxing than tasks that require focus, decisions, or emotional effort.

It may be because the task has a clear endpoint. When we mow the lawn, we can see it's done. But when we send an email, we may need follow-up later, which makes it feel unfinished.

Or maybe the task offers a stronger sense of reward. Completing something releases dopamine but it's harder to feel "done" with tasks like paying bills because they seem to never end.

Whatever the reason for our procrastivity, the first step to overcoming it is recognizing when it's happening.

Put It Into Practice:

The next time you catch yourself procrastivating, ask: "What need is this task meeting?" (easy start, quick win, clear finish, dopamine). Then find a way to bring that same benefit to the task you're avoiding.

Procrastivity, Procrastination, Taking Action, Productivity

Summer Sensory Overload.

My brain is sun-bleached, all rule and thought boiled away, leaving only sensory steam. ~ Linda Rodriguez

If the ADHD brain is known for being busy, one would think the slower pace of summer would help. But...one would be wrong. Between the loss of school-year structure and the increase in heat, crowds, noise, and stimulating activities, summer is full of overstimulation opportunities.

The ADHD brain is easily overwhelmed by sensory input from sights, sounds, smells, tastes, touch, body position, and sensations. And because focus relies on executive function, it's challenging to determine what deserves our attention because everything feels equally important or urgent.

When we combine our lack of structure with an exhausted brain trying to process all the extra summertime information, we may feel more restless, irritable, fidgety, and anxious.

To overcome our overwhelm, try strategies like taking sensory breaks in a cool, quiet space, building flexible routines that support our day, and setting boundaries so we're not doing all the things for everyone at all times.

It's important to remember that we don't have to push through when our nervous system is running on empty. These small resets can help prevent full meltdowns.

Put It Into Practice:

Pay attention to what triggers your sensory overload. Choose one go-to reset like a quiet break, cooling down, noise canceling headphones, or a dark room and make it easy to access when needed.

Overstimulation, Self-Care

July 10

The Trip-Over Trick.

Out of sight, out of mind.
~ Homer

Our ADHD brains crave visual cues and reminders to make information easier to access and remember. It's why we're often afraid to put things away because "out of sight" can feel like "lost forever."

And while too many visual cues can become clutter, reminders that double as annoying obstacles can be incredibly helpful for supporting our working memory.

We can create an effective visual reminder by using a picture, object, or note that holds a specific meaning and placing it in a strategic location for a short time like:

- Placing the trash can or recycling bin by the door so it's difficult to leave without taking it out.
- Leaving a bill that needs to be paid on the keyboard or taped to the screen.
- Moving the donation bag from the trunk to the passenger seat (and ideally all the way to the drop-off).
- Sticking a Post-It over the car's ignition that says, "Don't forget to get gas."

Just remember, if the reminder isn't removed, it risks losing its power and becoming background clutter. Use this strategy for tasks with a deadline or for tasks that are truly time-sensitive.

Put It Into Practice:

Pick one task you keep forgetting and create a "trip-over" reminder that makes it hard to ignore. Then remove it as soon as the task is done.

Memory Support, Productivity

The Silence of the Ding.

Concentrate all your thoughts upon the work in hand.
The sun's rays do not burn until brought to
a focus. ~ Alexander Graham Bell

As if the apps on our phones aren't distracting enough, our ADHD brains also have to deal with constant nudges like "Check out the latest video…" or "Time to practice Spanish today!"

And as moms, we often feel like we need to keep our ringer on, just in case our kids, school, or daycare needs us.

But there's plenty of wiggle room between being interrupted every 42 seconds by non-essential updates and completely shutting off the outside world.

- On iPhone, we can disable notifications by going to Settings > Notifications. Scroll to the app we'd like to silence and toggle off notifications.
- On Android, we can adjust settings through Settings > Notifications, or long-press a notification when it pops up and choose our preferred notification options.

And to save time in the future, say "no" to notifications when downloading new apps. Most of them don't need to interrupt the day to be useful.

Put It Into Practice:

Turn off notifications for non-essential apps to protect your focus. Start with the ones that pull you in the most.

Distractions, Focus

July 12
Work to the Music.

Where words fail, music speaks.
~ Hans Christian Andersen

Music is a powerful tool in our ADHD toolbox. And you might think that listening to music would be distracting when you're trying to focus. But a 2020 study in Psychiatry Research[12] found that reading comprehension improved for a group of preadolescents with ADHD while it deteriorated among typically developing peers.

For many ADHD brains, music works best when it's predictable and low-distraction. Instrumental music, lo-fi beats, movie soundtracks, or even familiar songs we already know can help stimulate our brain without pulling us away with new lyrics.

Along with supporting focus, music can lower cortisol (the stress hormone), reduce anxiety, and boost dopamine, oxytocin, and endorphins, helping us feel calmer and more motivated.

Music can also provide structure for time management. A playlist of a certain length can train our brain to fit an activity, like getting ready in the morning, into a specific time frame. It can also make boring tasks easier to start when we know we only have to do them until the music ends.

And a "launch sequence" playlist made up of a short, familiar set of songs can help cue transitions like leaving the house, starting work, or winding down for bed.

Put It Into Practice:

Use music during your day to help you focus, improve mood, and create external structure to keep track of time.

Focus, Time Management, Anxiety

It's the One You'll Do.

*Fitness needs to be perceived as fun and games
or we subconsciously avoid it. ~ Alan Thicke*

Is there a particular type of exercise that's best for someone with ADHD to get those dopamine-boosting benefits? Short answer...no.

What matters most is elevating our heart rate for about 10–20 minutes enough that we're breathing harder and our body feels worked.

This could be dancing in our living room or taking a CrossFit class. It could be taking a walk in a park or walking up and down the stairs at work. We could join a sports team at our local rec center or start a pickleball league with our friends. If it gets our heart rate up, it counts.

And don't forget...interest fuels consistency. ADHD brains love new, fresh, and exciting. Changing up our movement regularly can make it easier to stay motivated and keep coming back.

Another easy way to stay consistent is by lowering the barrier to start. Keep shoes by the door, leave a yoga mat out, or choose a workout that doesn't require driving anywhere or finding childcare first. The less setup needed, the more likely it is we'll follow through.

Put It Into Practice:

Pick a form of movement you can do today for 10–20 minutes to boost dopamine. Bonus points if you choose a second option for tomorrow so you're not relying on willpower in the moment.

Exercise, Self-Care, Dopamine

July 14
When Your Brain Won't Go.

If I'm overwhelmed, I slow down. It's more effective.
~ Kirsten Gillibrand

When we're overwhelmed by thoughts, emotions, or information, we may experience ADHD mental paralysis, a brain crash that makes it hard to figure out what to do or say next.

It often happens when our executive function struggles to filter out irrelevant input or slow down long enough to process what's happening. Instead of moving forward, we get stuck replaying the same scenario on loop...overthinking, ruminating, and feeling frozen.

But now that we have a name for this brain-stuck feeling, we can create an action plan to help when it hits again.

We start by noticing the times and triggers that tend to lead to overthinking so we can prepare for similar situations. Then give the brain a place to offload what it's holding. Write it in a journal, record a voice memo, or talk it out with someone safe. It can also help to keep a short list of "happy distractions" to reset the brain when we feel stuck. These strategies form the basis for a mental paralysis toolkit.

Our toolkit doesn't need to be complicated. Think of it as having:

- One way to offload thoughts
- One way to process them
- One way to reset our nervous system

It's not about solving everything in the moment. It's about helping our brain unstick so we can move forward.

Put It Into Practice:

Build a mental-paralysis toolkit to use when your brain won't move forward.

Paralysis, Taking Action

The Decluttering Dilemma.

People with ADHD have trouble organizing things. They have trouble organizing time, their thoughts, and data. ~ Dr. Ned Hallowell

Many ADHD coping strategies suggest we take what's happening (or not happening) inside our brains and externalize it. We can do this through reminders, lists, calendars, bins, or systems to support executive functions like memory and time management. The downside is that externalizing often creates more stuff around us.

On top of surrounding ourselves with extra stuff, organizing our stuff requires motivation, prioritization, and decision-making. And those executive functions may not always be ready to fire when needed.

Most of us know that creating systems and keeping only what we truly need within reach helps prevent overwhelm. But darn it...decluttering takes brain power, energy, and follow-through, which can feel impossible when we're already tapped out.

Organizing as an ADHD mom starts with scaling back to the basics. We're not aiming for Pinterest perfection. Just simple ways to reduce visual noise and find what we need when we need it.

Think using clear bins so items are contained but still visible. Paring down closets to see what we have and put laundry away more easily. Or processing mail immediately instead of piling it up on the counter.

Not sure where to start? Try starting where success is most likely. Quick wins give our brain a dopamine boost and build momentum to keep going.

Put It Into Practice:

Pick one small, simple step you can take today to reduce clutter and make your space feel more manageable.

Cleaning and Organizing, Mom Life

July 16

The Original Hard Drive.

Paper is to write things down that we need to remember.
~ Albert Einstein

Working memory is an executive function that temporarily holds information long enough for our brain to decide what to do with it.

If someone tells us a list of tasks and we forget it 60 seconds later, that's working memory in action (or not in action).

When our working memory is overloaded with too much input and too many things going on, it can be difficult to remember things and focus on the task at hand.

Which is why writing things down can be helpful for ADHDers. I'm talking pen and paper, not typing. Because the physical act of writing requires us to process and organize information as we write, helping us to file the information away for later retrieval.

A 2024 article in Frontiers in Psychology[13] found that students taking notes by hand showed higher levels of brain activity in the regions related to movement, vision, sensory processing, and memory than those that typed their notes.

Writing also helps to reduce mental fatigue because we don't have to actively remember the information we're taking in. This frees up cognitive resources to use in other mental processes.

Put It Into Practice:

Grab a pen and paper the next time you receive information you need to recall later.

Memory Support, Executive Function

Quiet Your Brain for a Boost.

The quieter you become, the more you can hear.
~ Ram Dass

Can we slow down to speed up? As in taking a few minutes to meditate so our dopamine and productivity can kick in?

Along with the traditional meditation benefits like lowering blood pressure, reducing heart rate, and strengthening our immune system, there are also ADHD-specific benefits when we meditate.

Meditation has been linked to increases in gray matter, which supports memory and emotional regulation. It can improve attention because we're training our brain to focus on one thing at a time. Some research even suggests that frequent meditators may develop higher baseline levels of dopamine.[14]

Over time, meditation may also increase the thickness and strength of the prefrontal cortex, which is where executive function takes place.

If the thought of settling your busy brain down to meditate feels impossible, let me share what a coach once told me when I rejected their meditation suggestion…"It isn't about sitting perfectly still and clearing your brain. It's about training your brain to return when it wanders."

Put It Into Practice:

Find a short meditation and try it for a week. Use a free trial on apps like Calm or Headspace, or search for options on YouTube, Spotify, or Apple Podcasts.

Focus, Executive Function, Dopamine, Self-Care

July 18

The 1-3-5 Rule.

By being intentional about our work, and reflecting on how we use our time, it's possible to buck nature and get results in the process. ~ Alex Cavoulacos

My to-do list has been rolling over day after day for around 34 years. Some days I add more to it than others, but one thing stays constant...there's always too much on it.

When it comes to following through, our brains rely heavily on working memory to temporarily hold information so we can execute tasks. The more tasks we try to manage at once, the more working memory we need to juggle details without dropping anything.

And since working memory is a core executive function, its capacity is already limited for those of us with ADHD. That's why we often struggle to juggle tasks, remember instructions, or keep track of the steps we need to take.

What we really need to do is lower our cognitive load, so task management feels more doable.

Enter the 1-3-5 Rule, created by Alex Cavoulacos. We choose one large task, three medium tasks, and five small tasks or quick wins. This creates a more realistic daily list for our ADHD brain while keeping us motivated through quick wins (and dopamine hits). Anything else goes on a "later list," just not today's list.

Put It Into Practice:

Use the 1-3-5 Rule to create a realistic snapshot of what you can actually complete today.

Productivity, Taking Action

Vent Before You Burst.

When we're brave enough to risk a conversation, we have the chance to rediscover what it means to be human. ~ Margaret Wheatley

It's hard enough to manage executive function challenges with ADHD. Couple that with the societal pressures of motherhood and the extra executive function required to manage a household and family, and it's no wonder many ADHD moms hover on the edge of burnout.

But we don't have to accept a life of chronic irritability, brain fog, and exhaustion. There are simple tools we can use to prevent burnout and recover from it when it hits. And one of the most powerful is to talk it out.

Sharing our struggles with a friend or family member validates our emotions, reduces feelings of isolation, and keeps stress from building up and taking over.

And if it seems like a simple conversation couldn't make much of a difference, research suggests otherwise. A 2023 study of healthcare specialists in Romania[15] found that higher social support was linked to lower emotional exhaustion, improved well-being, and a stronger sense of personal accomplishment.

Burnout isn't a sudden explosion…it's pressure that builds. Talking it out helps release that pressure little by little. Because we don't have to wait until things go south to share.

Put It Into Practice:

Schedule regular time to talk with someone you care about, especially if you notice increased overwhelm, anxiety, or exhaustion.

Burnout, Self-Care, Relationships

July 20

Know Before You Go.

*He who is best prepared can best serve his
moment of inspiration. ~ Samuel Taylor Coleridge*

Awareness is half the battle with ADHD. When we know what we need, we can make a plan. And plans make follow-through easier.

That's why it helps to start thinking about the back-to-school transition before it's suddenly on top of us.

Between school supplies, registrations, schedule changes, closets to clean out, and a million little details, it can feel overwhelming just deciding where to put our time, energy, and money. So start by asking:

- What do we need to buy or restock?
- What do we need to register for?
- What are the most important upcoming dates?
- When do we need to start acting on these things?
- What stressed us out last year that we want to prevent this year?
- What else do we need to remember?

This first step isn't about action...yet. We're simply creating a jumping-off point for all the other back-to-school tasks we need to tackle.

Put It Into Practice:

Make a list of the back-to-school-related tasks you want to or need to accomplish.

Back-to-School, Mom Life

Delegation is a Superpower.

*You must focus on the most important, mission-critical tasks
each day and night, and then share,
delegate, delay or skip the rest. ~ Jessica Jackley*

Just because we can do something doesn't mean we should. Or that we personally must do it.

But many ADHD moms get stuck in a loop of doing all the things. No wonder we're tired, our dopamine is shot, and our executive function is hanging by a thread. That's a lot to juggle!

If this sounds familiar, consider where to ask for help or hire help to reduce the burden and free up bandwidth for what truly needs our focus.

Delegating might be as simple as asking your family to pitch in with childcare, housework, laundry, or meal planning. Or it might look like hiring support for dog walking, home repairs, lawn care, errands, or home organization. And don't forget…some people genuinely love things we dread, like planning travel or shopping for gifts. If it needs to be done, there's likely someone we can ask or hire to help get it off our plate.

If we're going to conquer the mom juggle struggle, it's important to view delegation as a strategy, not a weakness.

Put It Into Practice:

Delegate a task you've been putting off or don't have the bandwidth for by asking someone at home or hiring help.

Productivity, Mom Life, Time Management

July 22

The Curse of Options.

Over analysis leads to paralysis.
~ Rebecca Jane

Does this sound familiar? We want to buy something, so we start researching the best option... but there are so many choices. We research more. And more. We worry that if we choose now, a better solution might appear. So we delay. And delay. And delay.

This decision-making spiral is called analysis paralysis, or the inability to make a choice and take action due to overanalyzing, too many options, or fear of making the wrong decision.

If we're stuck in this spin cycle, we can try a few tactics to move forward:

- Limit the number of choices we research before deciding
- Set a deadline so the decision can't drag on forever
- Take a break and come back with fresh eyes

And watch out for perfectionism. Sometimes "good enough" is exactly what gets us unstuck. Try a mantra like, "This option is better than no option."

Put It Into Practice:

The next time you feel stuck in analysis paralysis, limit yourself to three options, set a 10-minute timer, and pick one.

Decision-Making, Taking Action, Productivity

School Supply Scramble.

Buying school supplies six weeks before your kids' first day of school doesn't make the school year arrive any faster like I hoped it would. ~ Hollie Harris

Some years I am so on it with school supplies. And some (or maybe most) years, I'm the mom at the 24-hour grocery store trying to fill the list at 10 p.m. the night before the first day.

But trust me (the mom on her hands and knees digging through pencils in an empty back-to-school supply aisle)…the sooner we cross school supplies off our list, the better.

Since buying supplies is a multi-step task, here are some steps to make it easier:

- Find the school supply list. Check the school website, your email, or ask another parent.
- Add the extras….Clothes, backpacks, lunch boxes, headphones, etc.
- Check for a sales tax holiday and put it on your calendar so you don't forget.
- Decide where supplies will "live" so they don't wander off before school starts.

Put It Into Practice:

Create a plan for purchasing and storing back-to-school supplies now so you're not panic-shopping the night before.

Back-to-School, Mom Life

July 24

Don't Ignore the Warning Lights.

I was the perfect person to have a burnout because
I was not listening to my body at all. ~ Robin Söderling

Burnout doesn't happen suddenly. It's a slow build in our brain and body due to constant demands and stress. And unfortunately, we often don't realize we're crashing until it's too late.

That may be because many ADHDers operate like a speeding car, going and going until we run out of gas. We ignore the warning lights flashing on the dashboard and end up stuck in the burnout desert waiting for enough energy to start the cycle again.

But those warning lights are there for a reason. And learning to recognize what triggers our stress and burnout is key for both prevention and recovery. When we know what pushes us toward burnout, we can create coping strategies to reduce the impact or avoid the crash altogether.

For example, if vacation prep always leaves us spent, try reducing other commitments in the days leading up to it. Or if conversations with that certain uncle at the family reunion leave us angry and ruminating, plan ahead to limit interaction or shorten the time there.

Put It Into Practice:

Identify the stressors that trigger your burnout so you can plan for stress reduction before they hit.

Burnout, Self-Care

I Can't Help Falling...

Don't be offended, but you seem to be one of those people who just attract accidents like a magnet. ~ Stephenie Meyer

I feel like I have spent my life covered in random bruises I can't account for. I manage to regularly run into door frames or doorknobs in the home where I've lived since 2009. And I know for sure we haven't moved any doorways.

While clumsiness isn't directly related to executive function, motor skills and sensory processing rely on some of the same brain systems and both rely on dopamine. So if we're low on dopamine... well, that could explain why our spatial awareness sometimes feels a little glitchy.

Clumsiness can also be linked to reduced focus and impulse control, which makes small details, like an object on the stairs, easier to miss. It's not that we're careless... our brains are just juggling a lot.

There are ways to improve spatial awareness and reduce unnecessary bumps and bruises. Balance exercises or yoga can support the proprioceptive system, which tells the brain where the body is in space. Regular gross motor movement (like walking or strength training) helps too, as do fine motor activities like knitting, puzzles, or crafts that improve coordination.

Put It Into Practice:

Try one coordination boost today like balancing for 60 seconds, taking a quick walk, or doing something with your hands (puzzles, crafts, knitting) to build body awareness.

ADHD Symptoms

July 26

A Family Huddle.

Coming together is a beginning, staying together is progress, and working together is success. ~ Henry Ford

Transitions are hard for us ADHDers. Whether it's from task to task or summer break to the school year, it takes a truckload of energy for our ADHD brains to stop one activity and shift to a new one.

These shifts often leave us feeling fatigued, irritated, scattered, and overwhelmed. And it can feel even harder if we're an ADHD mom raising an ADHD child.

This is why we're bringing the whole family into the planning process. When everyone is in the loop, the transition into the school year gets a whole lot easier. A back-to-school family meeting agenda might include:

- What should morning, after-school, and bedtime routines look like? (Wake-up time, homework time, bedtime, etc.)
- What will a typical week look like with school, work, lessons, sports, and activities?
- What are some go-to breakfast, lunch, and dinner ideas? (So Mom doesn't make every decision.)
- What support does each family member need during this transition?

When expectations are clear, the transition feels less chaotic for everyone.

Put It Into Practice:

Block time on the calendar for a back-to-school family meeting.

Back-to-School, Mom Life

Return on Investment.

The key is in not spending time, but in investing it.
~ Stephen R. Covey

An ADHD time investment is something we do with the expectation of a positive return in terms of our time, energy, or effort. Just like a monetary investment, the idea is if we put in time up front, it will pay dividends on the back-end.

Time investments are particularly helpful for ADHD moms because they reduce future decision fatigue, last-minute scrambling, and the amount of ADHD tax we pay.

Time investments might include lifestyle investments like scheduling doctor's appointments or going to the gym. Or creating a family chore chart so we aren't solely responsible for keeping the house in order. Maybe we spring for click-and-pickup or grocery delivery to streamline feeding the family.

We can also make time investments in creating systems like:

- Setting up automatic bill pay to avoid missing payments
- Decluttering our closet to make getting dressed easier
- Making checklists for regular tasks and routines to reduce missing important steps
- Setting up a "launch pad" for backpacks, shoes, and keys to save time and chaos every morning

Time investments aren't about overhauling our whole life. It's choosing a small investment that makes future-you's day a little easier.

Put It Into Practice:

Find one place where you can invest time to improve your ADHD mom life. Ask, "If I spend time now, what will save me time later?"

Time Investments, Time Management, Productivity

July 28

Mornings Minus Meltdowns.

Good morning is a contradiction of terms. ~ Jim Davis

Mornings + motherhood + ADHD can equal a rough start to the day. And that's not how any of us want to begin. Which is why it helps to create and write down a solid morning routine for ourselves and our kids.

There's no right or wrong way to build a morning routine. It can be a few simple steps or very detailed. And just like everything else in mom life, it may shift and adjust as our needs change.

Create a family morning routine and checklist by:

- Making a list of the regular morning tasks you do before leaving the house
- Turning it into a checklist and posting it where everyone can see it
- Practicing the routine for a few days before school starts so the flow feels familiar
- Setting alarms or reminders on your phone or digital assistant to help everyone stay on track

A simple morning routine and checklist reduces the decisions our brains have to make so we can have more energy for the rest of the day.

Put It Into Practice:

Plan your school morning routine and create a checklist so you and your family can follow the steps with fewer surprises (and fewer meltdowns).

Back-to-School, Morning Routine, Mom Life

Snack. Unpack. Relax?

My hobbies include driving my kids around
to their hobbies. ~ Tara Rondinelli

If I dwell too long on our current after-school schedule, I break out in hives. Sometimes I think it would be easier to just hang on for dear life.

For years, we kept things simple. Each kid could choose one activity per season, and most weeks included one practice and one game. Low commitment. Manageable.

But now my boys have found their things (which I love) and our after-school schedule has ramped up big time. That means we need a routine that keeps everyone moving, even when we're tired, hungry, and overstimulated.

This is where an after-school checklist can be a lifesaver. Discuss it with the kids, then post a printed copy somewhere they can see it. This is especially helpful for a child with ADHD, since executive function challenges can make it easy to forget steps or lose momentum.

Checklists also help when we aren't home when our kids walk in the door. They create structure, clarify expectations, and reduce the number of reminders we have to give.

Put It Into Practice:

Create an after-school checklist for your kids. Include basics like emptying lunchboxes and backpacks, along with expectations like chores and homework.

Back-to-School, Mom Life

July 30

School Night Snooze Plan.

Happiness consists of getting enough sleep. Just that, nothing more.
~ Robert A. Heinlein, Starship Troopers

Sleep is one of the most important supports for an ADHD brain. And as I'm sure many of us have experienced, a stressful bedtime does not lend itself to a good night's sleep.

While an evening wind-down routine may not solve every sleep struggle, it can go a long way in lowering stress, supporting emotional regulation, and helping everyone in the house get the rest they need. Create an evening routine and checklist by:

- Making a list of low-energy tasks that help the family wind down
- Asking the kids what helps them relax
- Creating a checklist and posting it where everyone can see it
- Practicing the routine and shifting bedtime earlier in increments several days before school starts
- Setting a sleep timer or app blocker on devices to signal it's time to wind down

Getting consistent, quality sleep helps ADHD brains function better during waking hours. Which is why developing a routine helps us wind down to get some shut-eye.

Put It Into Practice:

Create an evening wind-down routine and checklist for your family.

Back-to-School, Sleep, Mom Life

Overcoming Your Trough.

Discomfort is the price of admission to a meaningful life.
~ Susan David

If we eat ice cream and drink a Coke, we'll typically experience an energy spike then a crash that leaves us lower than where we started. And it can take a while to feel "normal" again.

Dopamine works in a similar way. We may ride a dopamine high during vacation because we're having fun and experiencing new things. But when we return home, we may find it harder than normal to motivate ourselves. That's because our dopamine levels can dip below baseline after a big "high," creating a temporary motivation trough.

So, how can we overcome this dopamine trough?

Stanford neurobiologist Dr. Andrew Huberman explains that when we're feeling especially unmotivated, doing something mildly uncomfortable can help jump-start our system again. In other words…do something hard on purpose.

It might be a cold shower, a tough workout, really sour food, or even tackling a dreaded chore (I'm looking at you, dishes).

Put It Into Practice:

Choose one small "uncomfortable" activity (something you usually avoid) to help your dopamine rebound the next time you're struggling to focus or take action.

Dopamine, Taking Action

August

You Need a Routine, Too.

An early-morning walk is a blessing for the whole day.
~ Henry David Thoreau

A morning routine doesn't have to include waking up before college students get home from the previous night. In fact, a mom morning routine is simply a pattern of activities we do to set up our day and prioritize our needs before attending to the needs of others.

It's kind of amazing how starting the day with something like reading, journaling, taking a walk, or working out helps us begin on a positive foot.

A mom morning routine should be simple to start. Pick just one or two things so it doesn't feel time-consuming or overwhelming.

And a morning routine is much easier to follow through on when we set ourselves up the night before. Pick out our workout clothes. Set up the coffee pot or tea strainer. Put our journal and favorite pen somewhere we'll actually see them.

There is no right or wrong way to do a morning routine. We can do as little or as much as our time and energy allow. Even as little as 5 minutes can make a difference. The main takeaway is to start our day our way, by focusing on something that fills our cup...so we can fill the cups of those we love.

Put It Into Practice:

Create a simple mom morning routine to help care for yourself and start your day in a positive way.

Morning Routine, Self-Care, Mom Life

August 2

Pick a Style. Any Style.

A proper family diary with everyone's events and parties in it really helps organise the household. ~ Anthea Turner

The only wrong option when it comes to managing our family's calendar is not using one. And if we aren't currently using a calendar or don't like the one we're using, now is a great time to explore a different option.

Maybe we love the variety of paper planners but struggle to keep everyone in the loop because there's only one copy. Maybe we like a giant wall calendar in the kitchen, but we don't update it because we can't take it with us. Or maybe we prefer the convenience of a shared digital calendar, but we don't use it consistently because there are too many steps.

By choosing a style and using it before the school year is in full swing, we give ourselves time to practice and work out the kinks. We could:

- Plan a weekly schedule review on Sunday so everyone is aligned
- Block time each month to update our wall calendar at our favorite coffee shop
- Use Alexa to add events by voice prompt

Remember…it's not about what we use to track our family's comings and goings. It's about finding a way to know when those comings and goings are happening.

Put It Into Practice:

Choose a family calendar style and schedule regular time to update it because the best calendar is the one you'll actually use.

Back-to-School, Time Management, Mom Life

The Taming of the School.

Planning is bringing the future into the present
so that you can do something about it now. ~ Alan Lakein

We know when the first day of school is because it feels urgent…it's now (or soon). But things like teacher in-service days in February or early dismissals the Friday before spring break don't feel important yet because they're not now.

Then February rolls around and we forget to schedule a sitter. Or we get a call from the school secretary because we're late for pickup.

That's why taking a little time now to add school-year dates to our calendar can save us a lot of stress later. Add the full-year district calendar as soon as it's released. That way, there are no surprise days off, like realizing in November that the kids have the entire week of Thanksgiving break when we were only planning for Wednesday.

And don't stop there. Be sure to add classroom-specific dates, too. Field trips, project due dates, concerts, early dismissals…if it comes home in a folder or hits the email inbox, it belongs on the calendar.

Put It Into Practice:

Find the full school-year calendar (days off, vacations, early dismissals) on your district website or in school communications and add it to your calendar. Then add teacher/classroom events as soon as you receive them.

Back-to-School, Time Blindness, Time Management, Mom Life

August 4

Going Every Which Way.

Being a mom has made me so tired. And so happy.
~ Tina Fey

I once heard a mom on a podcast say that her biggest surprise in motherhood was the amount of time she spent in her car. I don't know if I've ever felt more seen.

Once after-school activities start, getting everyone everywhere becomes a full-time juggling act. Which is why it's crucial to add every activity to the calendar before the school year really gets rolling.

I'm talking the sports and musical instrument lessons. The art, gymnastics, and dance classes. The performances, meetings, and clubs. Anything that requires someone to be somewhere at a specific time.

And even if the activity happens the same day and time every week and we swear we'll never forget it...put it on the calendar anyway.

Because when we can see what our days actually look like, we can plan smarter. We can group errands, adjust meals and prep, plan carpools, and recognize ahead of time when we need to say "no" so our schedule doesn't become a daily sprint.

Put It Into Practice:

Add all your family's extracurricular activities to your calendar, even the ones you're sure you won't forget.

Back-to-School, Time Management, Mom Life

Your Weekly Game Plan.

Details create the big picture.
~ Sanford I. Weill

Many ADHDers see patterns and connections more easily when we step back and get a bird's eye view. Which is why it can be helpful to take a snapshot of what our overall week looks like as we head into the school year.

This overview isn't about getting super detailed…it's about seeing who is going where, when the busy blocks stack up, and what needs adjusting. The key is to zoom out before we burn out.

For example, we might notice multiple kids have activities on the same night, meaning it's a great time to plan easier dinner options for those evenings. Or maybe Fridays are the only nights everyone is home, so we want to protect that time for family game night.

A simple way to do this is to grab our schedule and a piece of paper. Divide it into the days of the week, with morning, afternoon, and evening blocks. Then add our recurring events. Remember, this is a broad overview, not a minute-by-minute breakdown.

There will be a bit of variation week to week. And it's also a good idea to repeat this exercise anytime there's a big schedule shift like the end of a sports season or a change in activities.

Put It Into Practice:

Create a weekly overview of your schedule so you can plan meals, errands, and responsibilities around the real rhythm of your week.

Back-to-School, Time Management, Mom Life

August 6

Fewer Facepalms.

*A mistake is only an error. It becomes a mistake
when you fail to correct it. ~ John Lennon*

Mistakes are a part of life. There are times when we're going to forget a step, miss a detail, or do something the hard way.

And when we toss ADHD executive function challenges into the mix, mistakes can start to feel like a regular part of our day.

But when we're a busy ADHD mom juggling all the things, mistakes can cost us time (and sometimes money) that we don't really have. This simple equation explains the impact really well:

Task time + Time spent fixing mistakes + Cost of mistakes = Slowdown

And I definitely don't have time in my day to slow down. This is why creating and using checklists is important for helping us avoid costly mistakes.

Checklists help us see all the steps so we can check them off as we go along, remember where we left off if we have to step away, and avoid missing important steps...meaning we make fewer mistakes (most days).

Put It Into Practice:

Create checklists for regular routines and activities like what you need to do to get out the door in the morning, expectations for cleaning a room, or what you need to bring to volleyball practice.

Checklists, Productivity

Expect the Expected.

Expectations are like fine pottery. The harder you held them, the more likely they were to crack. ~ Brandon Sanderson

ADHDers dream big and set lofty goals. And then the reality of our task initiation, follow-through, and time management challenges rear their ugly little heads…and suddenly we feel like we're struggling just to keep our heads above water, let alone make progress.

At the start of the school year, we're also presented with new opportunities and time we may not have had during summer break. It's very tempting to overcommit.

And believe me, I want moms to use that "found time" when kids go back to school to tackle a project, start a hobby, or follow a whim.

But before we go all-in on whim-following, it helps to take a beat and consider everything else changing right now before committing to something new. Are there additional expenses we might encounter? Is there actually space for this commitment when we account for other non-negotiable tasks and activities? Do we realistically have the time, effort, energy, and money to take this on?

When we create awareness around what we'd like to do and what we actually have capacity for, we set more realistic expectations. And that can help stave off those familiar ADHD feelings of failure or inadequacy that can set us back later.

Put It Into Practice:

Review current commitments and goals before adding new obligations to your schedule.

Goal Setting, Time Management, Mom Life

August 8

We'll Have Fun! Fun! Fun!

Never, ever underestimate the importance
of having fun. ~ Randy Pausch

As the summer winds down, we may feel inclined to cram in as much fun as possible. And honestly? This isn't necessarily a bad thing.

In fact, fun is necessary for ADHDers because of its vital role in triggering the release of dopamine, a key neurotransmitter involved in motivation and executive function.

But the benefits of fun extend beyond dopamine. Fun can lower stress levels and boost our mood by increasing serotonin, the feel-good chemical that helps us feel calmer and more emotionally steady.

It can also improve motivation and productivity when we pair it with tasks or activities we find less enjoyable.

And of course, fun strengthens connection, helping us build and protect our relationships with family and friends.

One more important ADHD note...if we notice we aren't getting the same boost from our "usual" fun, we may be experiencing diminishing returns and possibly a dopamine deficit.

That doesn't mean anything is wrong. It just means our brain needs novelty. Switching up our fun can help "reset" the reward system, so we feel that dopamine boost again.

Remember...fun isn't a reward we earn, it's a fuel we need.

Put It Into Practice:

Schedule regular fun for yourself and with your family. Don't be afraid to change it up if it starts to feel stale.

Dopamine, Mom Life

Practice = Productivity.

Simply having someone else present...creates a sense of accountability that's helped me stay on task. ~ Alice Lang

Body doubling is one of my favorite productivity strategies. When we work alongside someone else, it may be easier to complete a task we would otherwise struggle to start or finish. Just having another person nearby helps us stay focused, engaged, and motivated.

But here's the thing…the other person doesn't have to be working on the same thing we're working on.

If we've ever found it easier to make a grocery list while out to lunch than we can at home, we've already experienced the benefits of body doubling.

When my oldest started club swimming a few years back, I decided to experiment. Would his work in the pool inspire my work on the deck?

Turns out…yes!

I've written podcast episodes, created meal plans and grocery lists, and caught up on email correspondence while my son was swimming laps.

So as the fall activity sessions start, here's a reminder that time on the sidelines doesn't have to be "dead time." It can be the perfect moment to tackle the things we struggle to motivate ourselves to do when we're home alone.

Put It Into Practice:

Bring your "work" along when you're sitting on the sidelines during practices, rehearsals, or lessons.

Body Doubling, Accountability, Productivity

August 10

Reset the Mess.

*Everybody wants to build and nobody wants
to do maintenance. ~ Kurt Vonnegut*

It's much easier to keep up than to catch up. Picking up a bedroom, doing the dishes, or putting away laundry goes much quicker when we do it on a regular basis.

But alas, ADHDers often struggle with both consistency and motivation.

That's why implementing a regular reset block can be so helpful. It brings the house back to a manageable baseline. Rooms get picked up, laundry baskets get emptied, backpacks and lunchboxes get cleared out, and all the "wanderers" around the house get put back where they belong.

This reset is not a deep clean, and it shouldn't take hours. We're simply restoring rooms and zones to their ideal state.

Reset blocks help us feel like our home is less out of control during a busy week. And if we start to feel overwhelmed as the week goes on, we can remind ourselves that we've built in time to reset and reclaim our space.

Put It Into Practice:

Schedule regular reset blocks for you and your family. Consider creating a checklist of what you want to cover during your block.

Cleaning and Organizing, Mom Life

The House Won't Clean Itself.

Cleaning your house while your kids are still growing is like shoveling the walk before it stops snowing. ~ Phyllis Diller

I can think of about 95,000 things I would rather do than clean my house. And I know I'm not alone.

But another part of me knows that when my house looks cluttered and less-than-clean, my motivation is lower, and my distractions are higher.

Now, I also realize not everyone has the utter disdain for cleaning that I do. Some people even find cleaning relaxing. But as busy moms, most of us still struggle to find the time and energy to keep up with it.

Which is why we need a plan for keeping up with our homes when we're pulled in twenty different directions, whether we're team "cleaning is awesome" or team "cleaning sucks."

And like so many other regular tasks in a busy schedule, we're much more likely to follow through if we choose a specific time to clean instead of waiting for motivation to show up.

Depending on the family, it may be easier to schedule one longer session on the weekend or several shorter sessions throughout the week. And don't forget to assign age-appropriate chores so the burden doesn't fall entirely on mom. Creating a checklist helps everyone know what needs to be done and what the steps are to do it.

Put It Into Practice:

Schedule regular cleaning blocks so your family can keep the house in order.

Cleaning and Organizing, Mom Life

251

August 12

Make Time for Management.

You will never find time for anything. If you want time,
you must make it. ~ Charles Buxton

There's a whole host of administrative tasks involved with managing our family life:

- Bills to pay and bank accounts to balance
- Parties and holiday events to plan and gifts to purchase
- Meals to plan and grocery lists to write
- Appointments to book from doctors to hair and nails
- Register the kid for classes, lessons, teams, and camps

Short of hiring a house manager to make sure all the "i's" are dotted and "t's" are crossed, scheduling a specific block of time for life-admin tasks can go a long way. It helps ensure bills get paid on time, there's food in the cupboards, and our kid doesn't miss out on that soccer camp with their friends...again.

It also helps to create a checklist of the regular tasks we want to cover during our life-admin block, like paying bills, making appointments, updating the family schedule, and registering for activities. And consider keeping a running list (on paper or in the Notes app) for one-off tasks we don't want to forget.

Put It Into Practice:

Block time each week to handle the administrative tasks for your family.

Mom Life

Capacity for Care.

When you take time to replenish your spirit, it allows you to serve others from the overflow. You cannot serve from an empty vessel. ~ Eleanor Brownn

As moms, we're the brains, the problem-solvers, and the engine that keeps our family running. But when we're already at (or over) capacity, even small things can push us into overwhelm. And we won't have much left for what matters most.

That's why it's important to look at our schedule and figure out where we can include something that's just for us. Because when we take care of ourselves, we're better able to care for our kids as they transition back to school and beyond.

And self-care doesn't have to be elaborate to "count." It just needs to be specifically for us.

It could be something quick and easy, like 10 minutes a day learning a foreign language or walking on the treadmill. It could be a regular lunch date with friends or a date night with our spouse. We could take an art class at the rec center or a bread-baking class at a local bakery.

For ADHD moms, self-care isn't indulgent...it's regulation. It helps us protect our energy, lower overwhelm, and come back to our people with more patience and capacity.

We deserve (and more importantly need) time to fill our cup.

Put It Into Practice:

Make a list of activities you enjoy, then look over your schedule to decide when you can fit them in on a daily, weekly, or monthly basis.

Self-Care, Mom Life

August 14

How Burnout Feels.

Sometimes, the most productive thing you can do is rest. ~ Sam Keen

Mom life can sometimes feel like we're the Energizer Bunny… we have to just keep going and going and going.

But unlike a battery-powered bunny, we don't have the luxury of swapping out our power source and jumping right back in. If we continually deplete our energy without caring for ourselves and making time to rest, we will eventually encounter burnout.

Burnout is more than stress. It can show up in our bodies as frequent headaches, sleeplessness, and tense muscles. We may feel constantly fatigued or like we lack the energy for even small tasks. And we might feel like we're teetering on the edge of an illness, or we can't seem to shake one.

Those physical symptoms are signals that we need to step back and recover. And by no means does that mean we've done something wrong. It's just our body asking for support. And if rest doesn't seem to ease our symptoms, it's important to consult a doctor or therapist to assess any additional physical or mental health concerns that may be contributing.

Put It Into Practice:

Prioritize rest and recovery if you start noticing these physical burnout symptoms and keep doing so until they subside.

Burnout, Self-Care, Mental Health

What Was I Going to Do?

I never knew a time would come when I would struggle to remember what I said I was going to do 5 minutes ago. ~ Rita Chidinma

As I'm sitting at my desk writing this section, there are no less than three bright yellow sticky notes on my screen reminding me to put air in my tire, switch my laundry, and contact a client. Sure, I could have added these tasks to my to-do list… but I knew I needed something in my field of vision to remind me, or I might forget.

It's not that we don't try to remember things. It's our working memory deficits that delete information before we have time to act on it. Or our prioritization challenges that make it difficult to filter distracting information until our brain feels overwhelmed.

But rather than surrendering to forgetfulness, we can incorporate external prompts, visual cues, and alarms to support our memory and help us take action.

It may take some practice to actually follow through when we encounter these reminders. And we may need to change things up if they start to blend into the background. But switching the color of a sticky note or changing the song used as an alarm can be a simple fix when our reminders stop reminding.

Put It Into Practice:

Create visual or audible reminders for tasks you want to remember to act on.

Memory Support, Productivity

August 16

Prepping Your Wallet.

Beware of little expenses; a small leak will
sink a great ship. ~ Benjamin Franklin

There's no way around it... kids cost money. A lot of money. And that's just for the day-in, day-out basics of feeding, clothing, and caring for them. Add in activities, and it can start to feel like all we do is work, just to turn around and spend it on our kids.

For a variety of executive function reasons, many ADHDers struggle with finances. It might be impulsive spending. Or it might be that motivating ourselves to pay bills is hard because it isn't interesting or urgent. Maybe we forget to check bank balances and lose track of what we actually have.

And much like managing our time, managing finances as an ADHD mom gets easier when we create awareness around what we'll need our sweet moolah for and when we'll need it. That awareness can go a long way in helping us stay on top of things as the school year starts (and the expenses start stacking up).

It's helpful to make a list of regular family expenses like music lessons, club dues, and sports leagues. Then brainstorm any additional upcoming expenses by month like field trips, memberships, camps, vacations, birthdays, and holidays.

Put It Into Practice:

Forecast your expenses for the upcoming school year so there are fewer financial surprises.

Money Management, Back-to-School, Mom Life

Get Help, Not Guilt.

Asking for help isn't giving up. It's refusing to give up.
~ Charlie Mackesy

Time is the great equalizer... it moves exactly the same for everyone. It's how we use that time (and how much support we have) that makes the difference between an "I don't know how she juggles it all" mom and an "I'm really worried about her stress levels" mom.

And when we're feeling overworked and overwhelmed, it may be time to find some help. That help can come from our family, a swap with a friend, or hiring someone.

Start by identifying the areas where we'd benefit most from support, then decide what makes sense: ask vs. hire. And if we want to pay someone, what budget feels realistic?

Swapping tasks can be a great option because it benefits both people. For instance, you could watch a friend's kids for a morning each week if they help you fold laundry. (Or trade carpooling, meal prep, errand runs...whatever actually helps.)

And look, I know asking for help can be hard. I'm still working on it too. For some reason, we're conditioned to believe it's weakness or that there's some kind of bonus prize for running ourselves ragged doing everything alone.

But in the end, what's more important: that things get done or that we do them ourselves?

Put It Into Practice:

Ask a friend or family member to help you with a task you haven't had time to do. Or hire someone to get it off your list.

Mom Life, Productivity

August 18

Becky – Jack's Mom.

*The adult with ADHD can be forgetful with a full night's sleep,
a full breakfast, and a full checklist in their hands...
ADHD is forgetfulness with style. ~ Douglas Cootey*

Memory is one of my biggest struggles as an ADHD mom. And I am really terrible at remembering my kids' friends' parents' names the first time I meet them... or the tenth time, if we're being honest.

It's not that I don't care. My brain just doesn't always store names in a way I can easily retrieve later, especially when I'm juggling a million other details.

That's why several years ago I started saving contacts for my kids' friends' parents with both the parent's first name and the kid's name. Having both names in the contact means I can search for "Jack" even if I can't remember Jack's mom or dad's name.

I also started using this method for service providers I don't use often, like plumbers and electricians, so I can find the person or company we used in the past even if I can't remember their name.

Put It Into Practice:

Save contacts for your kids' friends' parents and service providers using both their name and extra identifying info (like the kid's name, service type, neighborhood, or company name) so you can easily search for them later. Future-you will be so grateful.

Mom Life, Memory Support, Time Investments

Calendar Clarity.

A schedule defends from chaos and whim.
~ Annie Dillard

Part of the reason I struggled to use planners (besides forgetting I had them in the first place) came down to my need for more information than they could realistically give me on a single page.

Our ADHD brains can only hold a small amount of information in working memory. Add in time blindness, which makes it harder to register events that aren't in the immediate future, and it makes sense why we might need multiple "views" to stay on top of busy mom life.

My personal planning process starts with maintaining a Google Calendar so I can easily see a monthly view and share it with my family. Then I use that digital calendar to create a weekly overview, a quick snapshot of who is going where, when, and which days are likely to be more hectic than others. From there, I use that weekly overview to get a realistic sense of my daily capacity...what I can take on and what I can't.

And I know our ADHD brains will try to tell us that multiple calendar views are "unnecessary." But if we're consistently making the same overscheduled, energy-draining mistakes, a few extra minutes of awareness up front is better than missing events or ending the week completely exhausted.

Put It Into Practice:

Review your schedule from a monthly, weekly, and daily view so you can spot busier seasons, tight turnarounds, and potential overload before it hits.

Time Management, Mom Life

August 20

Grace on the Off Days.

The very skills with which I struggle are the ones I supposedly need to be a "good mother."...In these moments of immense pressure and overwhelm, I am learning to give myself grace, probably the most important coping tool I have. ~ Jennifer Childs, M.A.

Before my ADHD diagnosis, I experienced intense anxiety and shame around my forgetfulness and lack of motivation. There are still times when I feel those emotions creeping in, but I'm learning to notice them, analyze them, and let them go, instead of letting them fester into a pit of guilt and shame.

Am I great at giving myself grace? No.

Am I better than I used to be? Yes.

And as another school year begins, with more obligations, more things to remember, and more balls to juggle, it's important to practice giving ourselves grace. It reduces the anxiety, guilt, and shame that can come with being a busy mom with ADHD.

Undoing years of negative self-talk and guilt around our ADHD symptoms won't happen overnight. But we can start to loosen the grip of that negativity and frustration, so it doesn't keep holding us back.

Put It Into Practice:

Pause and reframe situations when you feel shame or guilt. Can you learn a lesson, adjust your plan, or make a different choice next time without turning it into a judgment of your character?

Mindset, Mom Life

Save This for Next Summer.

Everything good, everything magical happens
between the months of June and August. ~ Jenny Han

Tell me if this sounds familiar…we see a Facebook post of a friend's kid at camp and think, "Oh, I bet my kid would love that, too." Or we hear about a local street festival on the news and wish we'd known about it earlier.

Then next summer rolls around…and we've forgotten all about that camp or that festival. And we miss it again. Bummer!

This is exactly why doing a quick summer review and jotting down a few notes for next year is so helpful while the memories are still fresh.

Because trusting our ADHD brains to remember all the super cool things we want to do for ourselves or our family 300 days from now is risky. But when we write it down, we create external memory and we're less likely to forget.

And honestly? This doesn't have to be a big project or a five-hour journaling session. Keep it short and simple. Even five minutes of notes can save hours of regret next year.

Put It Into Practice:

Review your summer and brainstorm ideas for next year. Jot down favorite memories. Make a list of camps or activities you want to research, festivals you wish you'd made time for, things you want to schedule, and ways you'd like to improve next summer.

Mom Life, Memory Support

August 22

Shift Happens.

Look on every exit as being an entrance somewhere else.
~ Tom Stoppard

ADHD can feel like a walking contradiction. Take transitions, for example. Some days we can't muster the energy to start a task, even one we really want to do. But once we do, it can feel nearly impossible to stop.

Transition struggles can happen physically (getting up and into the shower), cognitively (answering a question when our mind is elsewhere), and seasonally (shifting from summer break to the school year).

Stopping something we enjoy can feel like slamming on the brakes. It's hard to pull away because we're getting dopamine hits. And hyperfocus makes switching even harder because it takes so much effort to get started in the first place.

To reduce friction around transitions, try:

- Creating external cues to signal an approaching change
- Following routines so the brain recognizes when something is nearing its end
- Using hard stops (like a school pickup) to help pull us away

These strategies won't make every transition easy, but they can reduce the energy needed for daily shifts, so we have more bandwidth for the ones that matter most.

Put It Into Practice:

Find a way to incorporate external cues, routines, or hard stops to reduce the energy needed for everyday switches.

ADHD Symptoms

Outgrown and Outta Here.

If you want to improve your life immediately, clean out a closet.
~ Cheryl Richardson

Clothes, like food, are a necessary evil for our families. They need to be washed, put away, and replaced because our kids just won't stop growing. But there's an often-overlooked step in this buying-wearing-washing-putting away cycle...organizing.

Not Pinterest-perfect organizing with labeled drawers, dividers, file folds, or color-coordinated closets, but regular closet and drawer maintenance.

Paring down clothes is particularly helpful for ADHD moms (and ADHD kids). Too many options can lead to decision fatigue when we're trying to get dressed. Overstuffed drawers make it harder to put laundry away. And a lack of structure means more time spent hunting down that favorite shirt or pair of socks.

The basic steps for organizing clothes are:

- Pull everything out
- Set aside what's damaged, too small, or unloved
- Group like items together
- Put away what remains

In the end, closet organizing is about making it easier to get dressed, put laundry away, and find what we need when we need it.

Put It Into Practice:

Schedule time to clean out your kids' closets and drawers. If possible, involve the kids so they can build their decluttering muscles too.

Cleaning and Organizing, Back-to-School, Mom Life

August 24

Favorites Over Frenzy.

Part of the secret of a success in life is to eat what you like and let the food fight it out inside. ~ Mark Twain

Since decision-making is an executive function, and ADHD impacts executive function, it makes sense that deciding what to eat or what to make for meals can feel extra hard…especially when we're tapped out at the end of a long weekday.

But meal planning and grocery lists get *so* much easier when we create a go-to list of family favorites. Think:

- Favorite quick dinners
- Favorite dinners for nights with more time
- Favorite snacks for kids
- Favorite snacks for adults
- Favorite grab-and-go breakfasts
- Favorite lunch options

Choosing what to add to the grocery list is much easier when we're picking from a list of pre-chosen favorites instead of scrolling through every recipe and kid-friendly snack option on the internet. And when kids help choose the favorites list, it may prevent some mealtime arguing…at least most days.

Put It Into Practice:

Create lists of family favorites by asking everyone to contribute their options for meals and snacks. Bonus points if you make an ingredient list for favorite recipes to make grocery shopping easier.

Eating and Meal Planning, Back-to-School, Mom Life

Plates That Match Your Pace.

Any mother could perform the jobs of several
air-traffic controllers with ease. ~ Lisa Alther

I realized early on while running this kid to soccer and that kid to swim that there were certain meals that just worked better on nights packed with activities.

To make dinner easier on those busy nights, it helps to consult the family calendar while planning to gauge how much time we realistically have to cook based on our commitments. And what kind of meal makes sense based on who will actually be home to eat it.

Think crockpot recipes, simple sandwiches, or heat-and-eat frozen meals for nights when everyone is coming and going. These options make it easier for each person to eat on their own schedule without having to reinvent dinner at 8:30 p.m.

To make planning and shopping easier, keep a list of "busy night" meals and the ingredients needed. That way, if a last-minute grocery run on the way home from practice is required, we're not starting from scratch. It also helps cut down on decision fatigue and reduces the chances of forgetting key ingredients when our executive function is tapped out.

Put It Into Practice:

Consult your calendar when planning dinners so the meal matches the time and energy you actually have available.

Eating and Meal Planning, Back-to-School, Mom Life

August 26

Let Alexa Handle That.

*I don't have the ability to smell. It's a blessing
and a curse. ~ Alexa*

When my husband gave me a first-generation Alexa Echo Dot for Christmas in 2016, I was super "meh." I thought she was just for listening to music and I'm not really much of a music person.

What I didn't realize is that she would turn out to be an awesome ADHD support tool.

Some of Alexa's ADHD-friendly features include:

- Alarms to break hyperfocus or signal when to leave
- Timers to limit the amount of time spent on an activity
- Reminders for one-off or regular activities
- Routines featuring a series of reminders
- Finding a lost cell phone (if the ringer is on)
- Adding events to calendars
- Adding items to shopping, gift, chore, or grocery lists

No Alexa? No problem! Many of the features like setting alarms and timers or adding events to a calendar are also available on cell phones using Siri or Google.

Put It Into Practice:

Try using a digital assistant like Alexa to externalize executive function and help you manage time and remember more easily.

Memory Support, Productivity, Time Investments

When Your Brain Buffers.

Busy people all make the same mistake: they assume they are short on time, which of course they are. But time is not their only scarce resource. They are also short on bandwidth. ~ Sendhil Mullainathan

This idea of limited bandwidth has been very front of mind for me lately, both in the literal, data-transmission sense (since moving my computer to a different part of the house)… and in the mental capacity sense now that school and activity schedules are in full swing.

Bandwidth is essentially the amount of data we can transmit in a given amount of time. With Wi-Fi, we notice buffering when everyone is home streaming TV, playing Xbox, and scrolling social media. When more devices need a piece of the bandwidth pie, there's simply less available for everything connected.

And there's a very good chance our ADHD brains can hit that same overloaded point.

When several demands pull at our limited executive function, it becomes harder to decide what to focus on and harder to follow through on everything competing for our attention.

That's why it's so important to take some commitments offline temporarily (or permanently) when our bandwidth is maxed out.

Put It Into Practice:

Reduce your mental load and commitments when you notice your energy waning and your executive function struggling more than usual.

Energy Management

August 28

Smart Snacking Made Easy.

Everyone I know is looking for solace, hope and a tasty snack.
~ Maira Kalman

Snacking has had its fair share of ups and downs when it comes to reputation. For the longest time, "they" said snacking would ruin our meals, so we should avoid it. Then "they" shifted and said we should eat several small, snack-like meals throughout the day.

To be honest, I'm not exactly sure where society stands on snacking at the moment. But I do know this…when it comes to food and ADHD, what and when we eat can have a major impact on our symptoms. And keeping healthy snacks on hand makes it much easier to stay consistent with fueling our brain throughout the day.

Snacks can also help reduce hyperactivity and irritability by keeping blood sugar more stable, which supports focus, mood, and follow-through.

Stock the pantry with protein-packed, ADHD-friendly snack options like:

- Nuts, seeds, and nut butters
- Protein bars and shakes
- Cheese sticks, Greek yogurt, and cottage cheese
- Jerky, lunch meat, and canned tuna
- Edamame and hummus

Put It Into Practice:

Add a few ADHD-friendly snack options to your grocery list and keep them stocked for quick brain boosts.

Eating and Meal Planning, Back-to-School

Vertical. Visible. Visual.

You likely don't forget things because you lack object permanence...you forget things because your brain struggles to keep items in active memory, especially when new stimuli interrupt your attention. ~ Sara Makin

Object permanence develops when infants begin to understand that objects continue to exist when they are no longer seen, heard, or touched. And while we may hear the term used to describe why ADHDers struggle with "out of sight, out of mind," what we're actually experiencing stems from our working memory.

An underactive executive function system and lower dopamine can make it harder to hold information in working memory long enough to act on it later. That's why we rely so heavily on visual cues to jog our memory.

But visual cues can easily become visual clutter if we aren't strategic about how we use them.

To start, try utilizing vertical space like hooks on the wall for keys, coats, and bags, or over-the-door organizers for everything from shoes and accessories to toiletries and cleaning supplies.

Next, use clear or translucent bins to keep things like craft supplies, electronics, or household utility items (like batteries) contained but still visible.

Put It Into Practice:

Find ways to store items vertically or keep them visible so they create visual cues that support your memory.

Memory Support, Cleaning and Organizing

August 30

And...I'm Spent.

The more choices we are forced to make, the more the quality of our decisions deteriorates. ~ Greg McKeown

It's often said we make around 35,000 conscious and subconscious decisions every day. And while I couldn't find an exact source to confirm that number, I can say from personal experience it feels pretty accurate.

Every one of those decisions pulls on executive function. And since ADHDers already play shorthanded when it comes to executive function, it makes sense why something like deciding what to eat for dinner or what to watch on TV can feel like a bridge too far at the end of a long day.

We're likely experiencing decision fatigue when making a choice starts to feel mentally, emotionally, and even physically exhausting. Even simple decisions can feel annoying or impossible.

Decision fatigue can show up as irritability, procrastination, or a strong urge to avoid anything that requires thinking. But it's not laziness, it's a tired brain looking for relief.

We can reduce decision fatigue by creating routines, reducing the number of choices, delegating decisions to someone else, or switching to something more automatic and decision-free to help our brain rest and reset.

Put It Into Practice:

Pick one decision-reducing tactic from above and keep it ready for the days when your decider can't decide anymore.

Decision-Making

Can ADHD Cause Anxiety?

Every day brings a choice: to practice stress or to practice peace.
~ Joan Borysenko

ADHD doesn't automatically mean anxiety… but it can absolutely fuel it. Up to 50% of people diagnosed with ADHD also have an anxiety disorder. And that doesn't even account for those of us who aren't diagnosed but regularly experience situational anxiety or anxious feelings in response to new, unfamiliar, or stressful situations.

From an ADHD standpoint, situational anxiety can show up in a lot of familiar ways. Maybe we set high expectations for what we can accomplish in a certain amount of time but due to time blindness, we can't realistically deliver. Or we spend impulsively, then avoid our credit card bills or struggle to tell our spouse what happened. Or we look at our kids' toys knowing we need to declutter, but decision-making challenges make it hard to figure out where to start.

In many cases, this kind of anxiety is a response to executive function challenges…not a personal failure.

By developing support strategies for executive function like creating routines, practicing mindfulness, exercising regularly, and getting enough sleep, we can often reduce situational anxiety.

But if what we're feeling isn't temporary or situational, it's important to speak with a mental health professional to help us address the root causes of our anxiety.

Put It Into Practice:

Incorporate executive function support strategies into your daily routine to help minimize situational anxiety.

Anxiety, Mental Health

September

The Multitasking Myth.

*Be like a postage stamp, stick to one thing until
you get there. ~ Josh Billings*

The word multitask didn't exist before 1965. It was developed to describe computer functions, originally meaning "the use of a single CPU for the simultaneous processing of two or more jobs."

As hustle culture gained popularity, multitasking became a badge of honor. The problem is… our brains aren't a CPU. We can't truly do two tasks at once. What we're usually doing is task switching and that constant switching is dopamine-draining. It costs us productive time, focus, and energy.

In addition, multitasking impacts the gray matter volume in our brain, which plays a role in processing information, memory, attention span, and emotional regulation. In fact, a 2014 study[16] shows it leads to a decrease in gray matter. And with 3–5% less gray matter to start[17], ADHDers don't have gray matter to spare!

Which is why, believe it or not, uni-tasking, or finishing one task at a time, can help ADHDers get more done, with fewer errors, and less burnout.

Put It Into Practice:

Practice uni-tasking by scheduling time to do one specific task. Limit distractions during that block to help you stay focused on the task at hand.

Focus, Productivity

September 2

Stop Shoulding on Yourself.

I've learned to replace the word "should" with "could"
as "could" implies that we have a choice.
We ALWAYS have a choice. ~ Hannah Braime

"Should" is a dangerous word for us ADHDers. It implies that we're somehow failing to meet a standard one imposed by ourselves or someone else.

And "shoulding" ourselves doesn't help. It reduces motivation, piles on shame and guilt, and makes hard tasks feel impossible.

One simple trick for quieting our inner critic is to replace "should" with "could":

- "Should" assumes there is only one way to reach an outcome. "Could" implies it is one option and we can continue to seek a better fit for a way forward.
- "Should" has an expectation or ideal outcome in mind. "Could" means there are multiple means to an end.
- "Should" implies that we adhere to a norm someone somewhere at some time made up. "Could" bucks the norm and allows us to chart our own path.

When we shift from "should" to "could," we create a path forward instead of a pile of pressure.

Put It Into Practice:

Replace "should" with "could" to shift your mindset from obligation and pressure to possibility and choice.

Mindset, Anxiety, Taking Action

5, 4, 3, 2, 1...

Rituals provide a framework for stability
when you are trying to find answers. ~ Deborah Norville

There's a specific sequence NASA follows when it launches a rocket to let everyone involved know when it's go time.

And since structure and routine are calming for ADHD brains, creating our own "launch sequence" can be incredibly helpful when we're struggling to start.

Just like a rocket launch sequence signals that it's time to lift off, our launch sequence signals that it's time to do a specific thing.

This task-initiation sequence should include a few short, easy, pre-determined steps you repeat consistently to get ready to go. For example, a work launch sequence might be: eat a quick snack, fill your water bottle, and go to the bathroom...small cues that signal, "It's time to sit down and work."

A bedtime launch sequence might look like brushing your teeth, washing your face, and putting on pajamas to tell your brain, "It's time to wind down and sleep."

Keep it short, simple, and repeatable. And yes...consistency can be hard for ADHDers, which is exactly why the sequence needs to stay simple.

Put It Into Practice:

Create a 2–3 step launch sequence for a task or project you regularly struggle to start.

Taking Action, Productivity

September 4

Space for Your Stuff.

Your home is a living space, not a storage space.
~ Francine Jay

In the decade I spent as a professional organizer, there is one fact I learned that is true for every household on every block in every neighborhood...stuff will not magically disappear when it is no longer needed or used.

Clearing out basements, garages, attics, and closets takes a ton of executive function skills like task initiation, planning, and decision-making. Add in a busy mom schedule, and it makes perfect sense why storage spaces become drop zones we avoid as quickly as possible.

But there are a few strategies that can help when we're tired of wasting time looking for items we know we own or wasting money replacing items we can't find.

Start small. Choose one shelf, one bin, or one corner instead of the entire space. This lowers task initiation overwhelm and helps get the decluttering momentum going.

Next, set a specific time to work so it doesn't become something we "mean to get around to." Bonus points for asking a friend or family member to serve as a body double.

And finally, be ruthless. More options create more decision fatigue and more clutter. If we truly don't have a use for something, it's better to send it to a home where it can live out its purpose.

Put It Into Practice:

Schedule time to tackle one small part of a storage space so you can find what you need, when you need it.

Cleaning and Organizing

From Chaos to Cozy.

Sometimes, all you can do is lie in bed, and hope to fall asleep before you fall apart. ~ William C. Hannan

It's like clockwork. I lie down to sleep…and my brain revs up its engine to review my day, plan next week's meals, and ruminate on that dumb thing I said in high school.

Sleep challenges often start with brain biology. Lower daytime dopamine can delay the release of melatonin, the hormone that regulates our sleep-wake cycle, making it harder to fall asleep at a "normal" time. That late melatonin release can also mess with dopamine production, making it harder to wake up and maintain typical circadian rhythms. Add in racing thoughts and restlessness, and it's a wonder we ever get any sleep at all!

Sleep stories can help by providing a calm distraction for a busy brain, a gentle focus point that promotes relaxation without sparking new thoughts. They give our mind something soothing to follow while lowering stress and reducing stimulating input.

There are tons of sleep story options on Spotify or YouTube and in apps like Calm or Headspace. Look for stories that focus on relaxation. It can also help to listen to the same story repeatedly, so your brain starts to associate it with falling asleep.

Put It Into Practice:

Try a sleep story to help wind down your busy brain and fall asleep.

Sleep, Self-Care

September 6

The Short List.

The reason your to-do list will always be bigger than the amount of time you have to accomplish it is because your imagination is bigger than your calendar. ~ Denise Nyenhuis

I'd venture to guess most of us have a very long list of things we must do, should do, and would like to do as an ADHD mom. I'd also guess that looking at that endless list often makes us want to do absolutely nothing on it. (I speak from experience.)

Instead of relying on one big, aspirational list to track what needs "to-done" today, try creating a shorter, more approachable list. A concise list reduces decision fatigue because we decide once what we'll focus on. It also reduces task switching, which drains executive function, and helps us set realistic expectations for what we can actually accomplish.

We can keep the longer list as a master list to pull from. Then choose 3–6 tasks from that master list that we want to complete today. It helps to use a small notepad or a Post-it so we don't feel pressure to fill the page with everything we "should" do.

Think of this short list like a container…it doesn't hold everything we could do, it holds what we have the capacity to do today.

Put It Into Practice:

Pare your long to-do list down to a shorter daily list so it feels approachable and actionable.

Taking Action, Productivity

Rotisserie Chicken FTW.

Simplicity is the ultimate sophistication.
~ Leonardo da Vinci

The term "ADHD tax" typically refers to extra money we pay because of our ADHD, like late fees on bills or paying more when we wait too long to book flights.

But there are also times when paying a little more can reduce stress and anxiety. I like to think of these as "ADHD investments." And now that we're back in the hustle and bustle of the school year, it's a great time to make a few time-saving investments that make feeding our families easier.

For example, if it's easier to eat fruit and vegetables when they're already prepped, invest in pre-cut fruit and veggies.

Or if we need a nearly zero-prep healthy dinner option, grab a rotisserie chicken from the deli along with a salad kit from the produce department.

We can also invest in grocery delivery to save time and reduce the overwhelm of shopping in a busy store.

If an "investment" makes meal planning and meal prep easier (and our ADHD mom life feel less stressful), I'd say that's a pretty good return on investment.

Put It Into Practice:

Look for one place where you can invest a little time or money to make feeding your family easier this week.

Eating and Meal Planning, Mom Life

September 8

Inside Out.

Accountability is a statement of personal promise, both to yourself and to the people around you, to deliver specific defined results. ~ Brian Dive

I regularly need the dopamine rush of a deadline, people coming over, or a client expecting something from me to get things done. These external motivators give me structure and a reason to act, especially for tasks I don't want to do.

Struggles with internal motivation are common for ADHDers. The satisfaction of completing a task for our own benefit often isn't enough for a dopamine reward. Time blindness can make future rewards feel distant. And completing tasks just because we "should" feels boring, routine, and unrewarding.

But when we have external motivation like due dates, obligations, or real consequences, our internal motivation can kick into gear. And one of the best external motivators is accountability.

Sharing what we'd like to do with a friend or family member can help boost self-regulation and kick our executive function into gear so we can follow through and do what we need to do.

A quick text to an accountability buddy like "I'm starting now" and "I'm done" can make a big motivational difference.

Put It Into Practice:

Ask a friend or family member to follow up or check on you when you're struggling to work on a task or project.

Accountability, Taking Action

205 Times a Day.

It is okay to own a technology, what is not okay
is to be owned by technology. ~ Abhijit Naskar

A 2024 survey of cell phone habits by Reviews.org[18] found the average American checks their phone 205 times a day or roughly every five minutes.

Add in our ADHD tendencies toward impulsiveness and instant gratification, plus a sprinkle of dopamine dysregulation, and I'd guess that stat is pretty accurate for us ADHDers.

And while scrolling can give us a quick dopamine hit, our time blindness can waste that boosted focus on "just one more" TikTok or one more round of crushing candies.

On the flip side, playing games, scrolling social media, or falling down rabbit holes researching defunct Disney projects (one of my personal favorites) isn't always bad. It's all about timing.

That's why creating small roadblocks can help. Like a lock screen reminder that asks, "Is this what you should be doing right now?" It's a simple way to curb distractions and train our brain to pause and step away when needed.

A pause is often the space our brain needs to make a different choice.

Put It Into Practice:

Create reminders to put the phone down so you don't waste too much time on distractions. Change the reminder when you start to ignore the message.

Distractions, Productivity

September 10

For Your Reconsideration.

Once you replace negative thoughts with positive ones,
you'll start having positive results. ~ Willie Nelson

The ADHD brain is heavily motivated by interest. It's why we're drawn to tasks and projects that feel new, fun, or different… and why we resist the ones that feel boring or dull.

Our brains also listen to the messages we send them like "I hate doing the dishes" or "making dinner is the absolute worst part of the day." And when we flood ourselves with negative thoughts about things we need to do, our nervous system can treat that task like something to avoid. It's not logical. It's protective. It's our brain trying to steer us away from something it expects to feel unpleasant.

That's why reframing can reduce friction and make task initiation easier.

For example, instead of saying, "I hate doing the dishes," try, "I love when my sink doesn't smell like last night's dinner the next day." Or replace, "Making dinner is the absolute worst part of the day," with "I love the time we spend catching up as a family when we eat dinner."

This tiny reframe can be the difference between procrastinating and starting.

Put It Into Practice:

Practice reframing one task you dread into a statement that highlights the benefit or outcome you actually care about.

Procrastination, Mindset, Taking Action

Never Forget.

We cannot selectively numb emotions, when we numb the painful emotions, we also numb the positive emotions. ~ Brené Brown

On September 11, 2001, at 8:46 a.m., I was just beginning to teach a water aerobics class on the 24th floor of a building in downtown Chicago when the front desk attendant told us we were evacuating. The hours and days that followed were filled with fear, anxiety, and a deep sadness.

Big emotions can be extra hard for ADHDers. An overreactive amygdala can hijack our emotional response, making feelings more intense and harder to regulate.

Working memory challenges can make it harder to pause, suppress emotional outbursts, and gauge an appropriate response (especially in the moment). And for those of us who experience Rejection Sensitive Dysphoria (RSD), emotional spirals can feel nearly impossible to escape.

But there are strategies that can help soften the impact of intense emotions and support regulation. Practicing grounding techniques like deep breathing, regular movement, getting enough sleep, and approaches like Cognitive Behavioral Therapy (CBT) have all been shown to help with emotional regulation.

Feeling deeply doesn't mean we're flawed; it means we're human.

Put It Into Practice:

Create an emotional response toolkit to help you process and respond when big emotions strike.

Emotional Regulation, RSD, Anxiety

September 12

TRIM to Prevent Burnout.

When we stop long enough to think about it, we realize that our dilemma goes deeper than shortage of time; it is basically a problem of priorities. ~ Charles E. Hummel

Prioritization is choosing one thing over another. That may sound simple in theory. But when we combine an overwhelming to-do list with decision fatigue and time blindness that makes it hard to estimate how long things will take, we can end up on the fast track to task paralysis and burnout.

While it may not come naturally, prioritization is a skill we can practice and improve. And when we practice it, we get better at focusing our time and energy where it matters most without spreading ourselves too thin.

To make choosing easier, I created a series of simple yes-or-no questions to TRIM your to-do list and determine whether a task is a priority or if it can wait. Ask whether the task is:

- Time Sensitive – Does it have a due date?
- Required – Does it need to be completed to move on?
- Impactful – Will it make a positive impact if completed?
- Money Related – Will it make you money or cost you money?

If you answer yes to any of these, the task is a priority. And when we focus our energy on our priority tasks, we reduce the possibility of burnout.

Put It Into Practice:

Prioritize your to-do list using the TRIM method above to help avoid feeling overwhelmed or spreading yourself too thin.

Burnout, Paralysis, Productivity

Avoiding Demand Avoidance.

You are far too smart to be the only thing standing in your way.
~ Emma Kate Dawson

Demand avoidance is a persistent pattern of resisting demands from ourselves or others, even when we want to do the thing. We just feel a strong urge to push back.

For ADHDers, this can happen because of what researchers call a positively valenced cognitive avoidance cycle. In this cycle, we avoid a task, then send ourselves comforting messages like, "It's no big deal if I don't do it right now." Those thoughts justify the avoidance and help us feel better in the moment.

The problem is that those positive feelings create a reward loop. Over time, our brain starts building neural pathways around resistance, which can make it harder to take action in the future.

But we can train our brain to disrupt that cycle by noticing and celebrating the times we do get our executive function in gear to do the thing we're avoiding. Celebrating small victories reinforces new, positive pathways around follow-through and can boost motivation over time.

Put It Into Practice:

Celebrate any and every time you do something you really don't want to do. Eventually your brain starts to notice, "Hey, I like how we feel when we follow through. Let's do that again."

Taking Action, Productivity

September 14

Skip the Drawers.

Be as tough as your mothers. They show up all the time.
~ Coach Mike Krzyzewski

When my son started club soccer, the coaches would always say "bring the other jersey just in case." And of course, one game the "just in case" happened. The other team wore a similar color and guess whose other jersey was at home in his drawer. Whomp whomp.

That's when I decided to keep his full uniform...shorts, jerseys, socks...in his soccer bag rather than putting them away in his drawer and repacking his bag for each game.

It worked so well I started doing a similar thing for my swimmer son after too many towel-less practices. Now the swim towels go straight into the swim bag when they're folded instead of being packed right before practice.

Since many rehearsals, practices, and games happen at the end of a long day, our executive function may be running on empty when we need to remember all the items for our kids' activities. Keeping what you need where you need it doesn't just reduce steps, it also reduces the chances you'll forget something important.

Put It Into Practice:

Pack or store what your kids need for activities in their activity bags so you're less likely to leave something behind.

Mom Life, Memory Support

Tune In to Tune In.

Music creates order out of chaos.
~ Yehudi Menuhin

Until recently, I thought I needed absolute quiet to focus…no music, TV, or even white noise. That changed when I was introduced to binaural beats, which work by playing two tones at slightly different frequencies, one in each ear. The brain perceives the difference between the tones as a third, "phantom" beat, and the idea is that this can influence brainwave activity.

If this all sounds a little too woo-woo, there is a bit of science behind it. A 2025 study[19] found that binaural beats can impact brainwave activity and improve performance on tasks involving attention and memory, though the research is evolving and more is needed.

It's important to choose the right frequency range based on the desired activity:

- Delta waves (1-4 Hz) for deep sleep
- Theta waves (4-8 Hz) for relaxation and creativity
- Alpha waves (8-14 Hz) for relaxed focus
- Beta waves (14-30 Hz) for focused attention
- Gamma waves (30-100 Hz) for deep concentration

And be sure to listen through headphones, since binaural beats require separate tones in each ear.

Put It Into Practice:

Grab your headphones and search for binaural beats playlists on the internet, in a music app, or YouTube the next time you're struggling to focus.

Focus, Productivity

September 16

Mindfulness Builds Memory.

Researchers theorize that mindfulness meditation promotes metacognitive awareness, decreases rumination...and enhances attentional capacities through gains in working memory. ~ Daphne M. Davis

For several years, mindfulness has been a buzzword around mom communities...and for good reason. Mindfulness practices can help reduce stress and anxiety while improving mood and emotional regulation.

Along with those benefits, mindfulness may also support ADHD-related challenges like working memory, organizing thoughts, impulsivity, and emotional dysregulation. (The research is ongoing, but the trend is promising.)

One well-known study[20] found that after an eight-week Mindfulness-Based Stress Reduction (MBSR) program, participants showed increases in gray matter concentration compared to a control group. And gray matter plays a role in things like memory, attention, learning, and reasoning, just to name a few.

From body scans and breathing exercises to mindful walking and meditation, there are many options to try to find a mindful practice that works best for our ADHD brain.

Put It Into Practice:

Start a short, regular mindfulness practice to help boost your brain and executive function.

Memory Support, Executive Function, Self-Care

Perfection Paralysis.

Perfectionism is a twenty-ton shield we lug around thinking it will protect us when, in fact, it's the thing that's really preventing us from taking flight. ~ Brené Brown

As a recovering perfectionist, I know how hard it is to let go of perfectionistic tendencies. I've abandoned far too many tasks and projects because I couldn't make them exactly the way I thought they should be.

Along with those abandoned ambitions, perfectionism can contribute to procrastination and paralysis. We consciously put off a task because we feel scared, stuck, or overwhelmed. It's like all progress comes to a screeching halt, and we freeze.

This shutdown happens when our amygdala, the part of the brain responsible for processing fear, treats imperfection like a threat. Because at its core, perfectionism often isn't about striving for excellence… it's about fear of judgment.

To overcome perfectionism, we need to rewire our brain's response to imperfection. We can take messy action and choose some progress over none. We can analyze perceived failures for lessons learned and ways to improve. And we can track what we did do during the day so we celebrate small victories instead of obsessing over how perfectly we did them.

Put It Into Practice:

Practice imperfection if perfectionism is holding you back or causing you to freeze.

Perfectionism, Paralysis, Taking Action

September 18

A Focus Friend.

Agreeing to do something with someone else...adds a social element to the task that makes it much more likely an adult with ADHD will follow through, show up, and thereby engage in a desired task. ~ Dr. Russell Ramsay

When we don't have enough in the tank to tackle a task or project we've been avoiding, it can help to ask a friend or family member to body double (work alongside us) for the motivational push we need to get started and follow through.

The tasks we choose don't have to match. One person can fold laundry while the other updates the family calendar. The key is choosing a partner who helps us stay on track, not someone who pulls us into distraction. A body doubling session (whether in person or online) isn't really a time to catch up or socialize... it's a time to get things done.

It can help to keep it short and structured. Even 20–30 minutes is enough to build momentum. Start by sharing what you'll work on, do the work quietly, then check in at the end to celebrate what you finished.

A willing body doubling partner is a great resource for tackling tasks we feel less than enthusiastic about.

Pick a time, pick a task, pick a partner, and go!

Put It Into Practice:

Schedule a body doubling session with a friend or family member to help you take action on a task or project you've been avoiding.

Body Doubling, Accountability, Taking Action, Productivity

The Confidence Conundrum.

You, yourself, as much as anybody in the entire universe, deserve your love and affection. ~ Sharon Salzberg

From a young age, many ADHDers hear messages like "sit still," "be quiet," "pay attention," or "try harder." The problem is, we want to sit still, be quiet, and pay attention. We are trying hard. Our ADHD brains just aren't responding to those expectations in the same way.

A lifetime of negative messaging about our behavior can take a toll. Over time, it can contribute to a poor self-image and increase the risk of co-occurring conditions like anxiety and depression. Add in underdiagnosis, mental health stigma, and widespread misunderstandings about what ADHD is and how it affects the brain, and it's easier to see why so many ADHD adults end up stuck in cycles of shame and low self-esteem.

A 2024 review of studies analyzing self-esteem in ADHD adults by American Professional Society of ADHD and Related Disorders[21] found a "robust association between ADHD and low self-esteem in adults."

But just as awareness helps us better manage our time and productivity, recognizing negative thought patterns and practicing coping strategies can help us rebuild self-esteem and reduce the impact of negative self-talk over time. Working with a Cognitive Behavioral Therapist (CBT) is also helpful for breaking these cycles and building supportive skills.

Put It Into Practice:

Take back control of your mindset by developing coping strategies that reduce negative self-talk and support healthier self-esteem.

Mindset, Mental Health

September 20

Connect the Thoughts.

Mind maps are the reflection of your brain's natural, image-filled thinking processes and abilities. ~ Kapil Goel

Mind mapping uses visual diagrams to organize information around a central idea so it's easier to see connections between related thoughts. For ADHDers, creating these visual connections helps us move what's in our head into an external format we can actually process.

Mind maps are great for breaking down complex ideas, brainstorming, planning project steps, or organizing information that feels tangled. And for ADHD brains, mind maps can be a more vibrant, creative way to organize thoughts than a traditional list.

They can also be helpful for goal setting when a goal feels big or vague. A mind map helps us break a big, scary goal into smaller steps and recognize the support we may need.

To create a mind map, simply place a central idea or theme in the middle of a page (either on paper or digitally), then create branches of related ideas or information extending from the center.

For example, to plan a vacation, start by placing "Vacation" at the center of the page. Then add branches for "Transportation," "Accommodations," and "Excursions." From there, you can subdivide the branches by adding "scuba diving," "fishing," or "rent a boat" under Excursions.

Put It Into Practice:

Create a mind map the next time you need to break down a task, plan a project, organize a lot of related information, or map out a goal.

Taking Action, Goal Setting

First Day of Fall.

Life starts all over again when it gets crisp in the fall.
~ F. Scott Fitzgerald

It's officially the season of pumpkin patches, apple picking, and snack-sized candy bars. It's also time for another round of quarterly maintenance for our home and our family.

Because the change of season happens at the same time every year, it serves as a built-in reminder to check in on those maintenance tasks we might otherwise overlook.

For your home and property, remember to:

- Check and replace smoke detector batteries
- Change the furnace and refrigerator water filter
- Change the oil in the car
- Clean out the dryer vent

For you and your family:

- Replace toothbrushes
- Wash makeup brushes
- Delete unwanted digital photos
- Back up the computer's hard drive
- Drop off the donations in the back of the car

Put It Into Practice:

Schedule time this week for a few seasonal maintenance tasks for your home and family.

Time Investments, Cleaning and Organizing

September 22

Let the List Decide.

No matter how expert you may be, well-designed checklists can improve outcomes. ~ Steven Levitt

Any time we can offload the act of remembering, we reduce mental stress. And since we have to remember so much information to make thousands of decisions every day, it makes sense that we'd benefit from anything that reduces that load.

Enter the checklist.

Checklists make it easier to initiate tasks because we don't have to burn precious executive function trying to remember what comes first or decide what our next move should be. Since decision-making and prioritization are both energy-draining executive functions, having the steps already laid out makes starting and continuing much easier.

And when we free up mental energy from remembering and deciding, we have more energy to actually do the thing.

To make a checklist useful, keep it clean and simple. Focus on the key steps...not every possible detail. A short checklist we actually use is better than a long checklist we ignore. And keep it somewhere visible or easy to access so it doesn't become "out of sight, out of mind."

Put It Into Practice:

Create a checklist for a routine or task that drains your mental energy so you can reduce decision-making and lighten your working memory load.

Checklists, Decision-Making, Productivity

Restless Legs Syndrome Day.

I'm pretty sure that my Restless Leg Syndrome is simply caused by my body just fighting the urge to RUN AWAY! ~ Tanya Masse

Today is Restless Legs Syndrome (RLS) Awareness Day. RLS, also called Willis-Ekbom disease, is a neurological condition that causes an urge to move the legs and often paired with uncomfortable sensations like tingling, crawling, or pulling, when resting or trying to sleep.

And while RLS isn't an official symptom or diagnostic criteria for ADHD, research suggests there's a notable overlap between the two. A review of published articles about ADHD and RLS in 2005[22] found that up to 44% of ADHDers have RLS or experience RLS-like symptoms.

The connection may involve our old friend dopamine. RLS has been linked to changes in dopamine signaling and brain iron levels, both of which affect movement regulation. Low iron can worsen symptoms because iron plays a role in dopamine production.

When RLS significantly impacts our sleep or quality of life, it's important to talk with a doctor or sleep specialist. We can also try lifestyle strategies like regular movement, good sleep hygiene, and limiting alcohol and caffeine to help reduce symptoms.

Put It Into Practice:

If you notice RLS symptoms, prioritize sleep support and talk with a healthcare provider, especially if it's affecting your sleep. You can also ask about checking iron levels and try simple lifestyle supports like movement and limiting caffeine or alcohol.

Sleep, Dopamine

September 24

Hey Siri, Remind Me to...

I've a grand memory for forgetting.
~ Robert Louis Stevenson

Memory is the executive function I struggle with the most. I've probably already said that in this book, but frankly...I can't remember.

Forgetfulness can plague our ADHD brains in part because of dopamine dysregulation. When dopamine is low, it can be harder for the brain to store information and hold it long enough to retrieve later.

We can give our memory a major boost by creating external memory. And one of my favorite ways is using reminders on our phones or digital assistants for routines, appointments, or tasks we tend to forget.

For instance, last winter I created a reminder on our Alexa for every school morning so I would remember to start my car remotely. Not only was the car nice and warm when we got in, we also stopped running late for school because I didn't leave time to scrape the windows... which previously happened pretty much every morning.

Some reminders an ADHD mom brain may find helpful include:

- Starting the washer or moving laundry to the dryer
- Packing lunches, signing forms, or checking the backpacks
- Prepping dinner in the morning
- Leaving for drop-offs or pickups
- Paying bills or making appointments

Put It Into Practice:

Set reminders through your phone or digital assistant (Siri, Google, Alexa, etc.) to help you stay on track with routines and recurring tasks.

Memory Support, Dopamine

September 25

Do I Need a Diagnosis?

ADHD isn't a deficit. Those who have been diagnosed with ADHD should celebrate it. ~ Jonathan Mooney

I first suspected I had ADHD in 2010. I spoke with a social worker friend about diagnosis, but never did anything with the information she gave me. Eleven years later, I brought it up to my family doctor, who shared local resources specializing in adult ADHD. And after two more years...I finally scheduled an appointment.

I put off my diagnosis because I feared the label. And because all the steps to get there felt exhausting. But I'll also say this...a huge weight lifted off my shoulders when I finally understood why my brain operated the way it did.

Now, when someone asks me if they need an official ADHD diagnosis, I ask a simple question, "Do you feel like you're struggling?"

Because if you are, it can be beneficial to talk with your doctor or a mental health professional for answers and support. Even if the diagnosis isn't ADHD, getting clarity can help you find the right tools and treatment.

And if you aren't struggling right now but you do want support with symptoms, a diagnosis can help pinpoint how ADHD affects your life so you can create coping strategies that actually fit your brain. Understanding your brain can change everything...even before you change anything else.

Put It Into Practice:

Ask your family doctor for diagnosis resources or research local providers who specialize in adult ADHD if you feel you need answers and support.

Mental Health, ADHD Symptoms

September 26

A Date with Your Must-Dos.

You get to decide where your time goes. You can either spend it moving forward, or you can spend it putting out fires, you decide. ~ Tony Morgan

One of my mottos is: "If it's on the calendar, it's more likely to get done." And this applies to everything from cleaning the house to using a coupon before it expires.

When our time blindness makes it easy to lose track of time, our motivation relies on interest, and our people-pleasing tendencies leave us overscheduled, it's no wonder we feel like we never have time for the non-negotiable tasks that keep us and our families running.

That's why it's so important to schedule our must-dos.

Whether it's time to make doctor's appointments, shop for groceries, or plan a date night with our spouse, putting specific time on the calendar makes it much more likely to happen (because there's time for it)...and much less likely to get replaced by something else (because we can't be two places at once...yet).

Treat the must-do block like a real appointment, because it's there to protect future-you from distracted-you.

Put It Into Practice:

Add a specific block of time to your schedule for one important, non-negotiable task or project you never seem to have time to do.

Time Management, Productivity, Consistency

The Why Me Mindset.

Abandon the idea that you will forever be the victim
of the things that have happened to you. Choose to be a victor.
~ Seth Adam Smith

I say over and over that ADHD is an explanation, not an excuse, for why I behave the way I do. But arriving at this conclusion took years of undoing my "Why Me" mindset.

There were definitely deep emotional wounds in my past that, in hindsight, were connected to my ADHD symptoms. But for far too long, I fixated on things like resenting others who succeeded faster than me (even though I hadn't put in the same amount of effort). Or blaming the busy schedule of my own making for why I couldn't work out or pay my bills on time.

Shifting out of that mindset put me back in the driver's seat of my life. When I handed responsibility over to other people or external circumstances, shame and blame drove the bus. But when I started recognizing my patterns and taking ownership of my decisions and actions, I could focus on the strengths that move me forward...not just the struggles that hold me back.

Put It Into Practice:

If you're ready to shift out of a "Why Me" mindset and regain more agency in your life, consider working with a mental health professional for support.

Mindset, Mental Health

September 28

What Fuels Your ADHD Brain?

The better you eat, the better you can do anything. ~ Marlon Vera

ADHD brains are needy…they need consistent fuel. Because when our blood sugar drops or we go too long without eating, focus, mood, and patience tend to drop right along with it.

Protein is especially helpful because it provides amino acids that the body uses to build neurotransmitters like dopamine for executive function and serotonin for mood.

Complex carbs help provide steadier energy and support more stable blood sugar, which can make a difference in focus and irritability. They also break down into glucose, the brain's main energy source.

It can also help to watch how much added sugar and highly processed carbs we're relying on, because big spikes and crashes in energy can make it harder to stay regulated and consistent.

And don't forget omega-3 fatty acids, which support brain health overall. Research suggests they may offer modest benefits for attention and ADHD symptoms for some people.

Sample ADHD brain-boosting foods include:

- Protein: eggs, Greek yogurt, chicken
- Complex carbs: oats, brown rice, beans
- Omega-3s: salmon, chia, flax, walnuts

When we regularly feed our brain what it needs, we're more likely to feel steady, focused, and capable.

Put It Into Practice:

Make a list of protein, complex carbs, and omega-3-rich foods you enjoy so you can keep easy brain fuel on hand.

Eating and Meal Planning, Executive Function, Self-Care

More Dopamine, More Doing.

When dopamine rises, so does your motivation to act.
~ James Clear

Many neurotypical brains use an importance-based system to prioritize and follow through on tasks based on significance, responsibility, or long-term reward.

Most ADHD brains, on the other hand, rely on an interest-based system to take action. We're motivated by novelty, challenge, and fun. And when we engage in interest-based activities, our brain releases dopamine which boosts motivation and helps us keep moving forward.

Because we're drawn to interest-based tasks, many importance-based tasks (the boring-but-important stuff) like cleaning the kitchen, going to the doctor, or taking a shower get ignored until they become urgent. Instead, we default to what feels most appealing in the moment. But as moms, we can't always spend our energy on what we want to do.

That's why finding ways to make important tasks more interesting can boost dopamine and make follow-through easier. We can turn chores into a game with rewards for completion. We can challenge ourselves to see how many appointments we can schedule in an hour. We can add novelty like buying a new vacuum, listening to a podcast, or watching a favorite show while folding laundry.

We may not need more willpower, we may just need more interest.

Put It Into Practice:

Boost your dopamine and motivation by making one importance-based task feel more interesting today.

Dopamine, Taking Action, Productivity

September 30

The Life Balance Bike.

Life is like riding a bicycle. To keep your balance,
you must keep moving. ~ Albert Einstein

There are a lot of people out there who say work-life balance is a myth or flat-out impossible. But I wholeheartedly disagree.

I just think balance looks different than we've been taught.

Instead of seeing balance as a teeter-totter, where we need perfectly equal amounts on both sides, I prefer to think of it like a bike wheel.

Think about it…we can divide a wheel into different-sized slices. And as long as all the slices are included to form a full circle, the wheel can still roll.

The same is true for the "slices" of our life. If we make sure the important areas are all represented like family, work, rest, friendships, health, faith, creativity, and whatever else matters to us, our wheel can still roll. A thin slice still counts…as long as it's there.

But when we completely remove a slice, even a small one, our wheel gets wobbly. And it becomes harder to keep our balance while we're riding.

Put It Into Practice:

List the areas of your life that need a slice of your wheel. Then choose one small way to give each slice some time on a regular basis so your life feels more balanced.

Mom Life, Time Management

October

ADHD Awareness Month.

For an adult with ADD, the key to success is to find the courage to be who you are. This means shaping your life to fit your impulsiveness, distractability, high energy, and need for stimulation. ~ Lara Honos-Webb

It's the first day of ADHD Awareness Month, so let's talk about creating awareness around our personal version of ADHD.

As a professional organizer, many clients wanted to start with buying baskets or bins. And I get it…that's the fun part. The part that feels like progress.

But when we start with changing the outside, we often skip what's actually crucial for changing behavior: Why do we need to organize in the first place?

The same is true for ADHD. We can consume books, blogs, and tips all day long. But if we don't understand our specific challenges, we won't know which solutions are actually meant for our problem.

For meaningful changes in behavior and habits, we need clarity. What are we struggling with? What are we trying to improve? What's the purpose or the why?

Because everyone's ADHD shows up differently, and different brains need different coping strategies to navigate a neurotypical world. And strategies tend to stick better when we understand why we need them.

Put It Into Practice:

Identify your ADHD strengths and challenges so you can choose strategies that fit your unique version of ADHD.

Awareness

October 2

Thinking About Thinking.

ADHD is not a deficit of attention, but a wandering of attention to the most interesting nearby stimulus. ~ Fahadh Faasil

Metacognition is the self-reflective process of thinking about how we think. It's an important skill for goal setting, critical thinking, and problem-solving.

It relies heavily on the executive functions of working memory (to hold information), organization (to track details), and sustained attention (for follow-through)...which are all areas ADHD can impact through the symptom of inattention.

While inattention is often described as a "lack of focus," for ADHDers it's usually less about choosing not to pay attention and more about struggling to stay focused long enough to avoid mistakes or forgetfulness.

Metacognition can be supported with self-management tools. Breaking tasks into smaller steps makes follow-through easier. Timers and alarms improve time awareness. And minimizing distractions reduces the interruptions that pull us off track.

It can also help to pause and ask simple metacognition questions like, "What's making this hard?" or "What do I need to make this easier?" Small check-ins like this build awareness...and awareness is the first step to better strategies.

Put It Into Practice:

Support attention and metacognition with bite-sized tasks, an up-to-date schedule, and fewer distractions.

Executive Function, Awareness, ADHD Symptoms

Planning is Not Doing.

A plan without action isn't a plan, it's a speech.
~ T. Boone Pickens

ADHDers are actually pretty awesome at planning. We are big-picture thinkers, after all. In fact, there are times I would dare say if the planning part was all that needed to happen to make our dreams a reality, we would be the most successful people on the planet.

It's those darn next steps...the follow-through, the task initiation, the motivation after the initial excitement wears off, and the implementation. That's where our executive function challenges tend to show up.

One way to bridge the gap between planning and doing is to include external accountability as part of the plan.

An accountability buddy adds a layer of obligation to tasks we're struggling to progress on. Even if the task doesn't directly impact them, knowing someone is expecting us to do something creates stakes and sometimes even a sense of consequence that helps kick our brain into gear.

So if a plan isn't happening, don't change the goal...add support.

Put It Into Practice:

Ask someone to check in on you if you're struggling to follow through or make progress on a plan you've made.

Accountability, Taking Action, Executive Function

October 4

What Feels Good.

When I did stims such as dribbling sand through my fingers,
it calmed me down. ~ Temple Grandin

Prioritization isn't just an issue for ADHDers when it comes to productivity. It also impacts our senses. When we prioritize tasks, we're filtering what matters and what can wait. Our brains do that same filtering with sensory input, too.

And because ADHD brains struggle to filter out irrelevant information, we can become agitated and overwhelmed when everything feels loud, itchy, sticky, or uncomfortable, like having too many tabs open and no way to close them.

From itchy tags and tight clothing to crunchy foods and sticky surfaces, certain textures can send the ADHD nervous system into overstimulation mode.

On the other hand, soft or silky fabrics, rough surfaces, or pressure from weighted objects or compression clothing can actually calm anxiety and help us focus.

When overstimulation triggers sensory overload, our sympathetic nervous system (SNS), the "fight or flight" response, kicks into gear, causing us to feel stressed and agitated. Engaging in calming tactile input can help stimulate dopamine release and activate the parasympathetic nervous system (PNS) to calm the body.

Put It Into Practice:

Look for calming tactile fidgets like texture tools, stress balls, or weighted objects to help calm you down when you're feeling overstimulated.

Fidgets and Stimming, Overstimulation, Anxiety

Clutter Buddy.

Asking for help with decluttering can feel like admitting we've failed, like saying "I should've been able to do this on my own." But let me tell you something... Asking for help isn't weakness, it's courage. ~ Jennifer Lebeau Gray

Decluttering projects, even the ones we want to tackle, can feel incredibly overwhelming for our ADHD executive function. That's why asking a friend or family member to help you sort, purge, and reorganize a space can make a big difference.

A clutter buddy acts as a body double, meaning just having them nearby can improve focus and follow-through. They also reduce overwhelm by dividing the workload and adding accountability. And the right clutter buddy can help us identify what we truly need to keep...without judgment.

If there isn't a friend or family member to ask, consider hiring a professional organizer. And no, I'm not just saying that as a former professional organizer. Working with a professional can make decluttering easier because your stuff doesn't mean anything to them... and I mean that in the best way.

They can sort through piles of paper and tubs of memorabilia without getting misty-eyed over the self-portrait our kid drew in preschool. They can also ask pointed questions that help us decide what to keep and what to let go.

Decluttering is easier when we don't have to do it alone.

Put It Into Practice:

Find a clutter buddy to help you tackle your next decluttering project.

Cleaning and Organizing, Body Doubling, Accountability

October 6

Get the Gunk Out.

I do a "brain dump" where everything that's in my head that needs doing gets written down. It gives your brain a rest. ~ Brigid Schulte

Being in a cluttered room surrounded by random stuff can make us feel anxious, overwhelmed, and like we need to call a junk-hauling service pronto.

Now…what if that cluttered room was actually the inside of our head?

A brain dump is like a junk remover for our thoughts. It tells our brain, "You don't have to keep holding this anymore. It's on paper. You're not going to forget."

Because ADHD brains are always on the hunt for something new and interesting to boost dopamine, we're particularly prone to getting pulled off track by random ideas, reminders, and mental clutter.

And since working memory, the place our brain holds information temporarily, isn't always reliable, we need an external place to record important thoughts so we can revisit them later. Or simply get them out of the way for now.

We can brain dump by writing things down or recording a voice memo. It can be a full mind-clearing dump, or a quick "capture this idea before I lose it" moment. There are no rules…just get it out in order to move on.

Put It Into Practice:

Declutter your thoughts with a brain dump on paper or by recording a voice memo.

Distractions, Productivity

Thinking Out Loud.

I have come to believe over and over again that what is most important to me must be spoken. ~ Audre Lorde

The need to verbally or externally process thoughts is common in neurodivergent populations. There's just something about hearing ourselves that helps us clarify what we think and feel.

Speaking our thoughts engages speech, language comprehension, and working memory systems in the brain, giving us additional ways to process information. And that's a major improvement over the "let the thoughts swirl around in my head until I'm overwhelmed" method.

Verbal processing also creates feedback loops that help our brain hear itself think. These loops can help us organize ideas, remember details, and sort out what matters because we're engaging multiple sensory systems at once.

The great thing is we don't have to have the "right person" available to do this. We can talk to ourselves or find a buddy who will listen without trying to fix or solve anything. We can also try verbal journaling using a voice memo app.

Still not sure how to start? Try a simple prompt like: "Here's what's on my mind…here's what I need to do…and here's what I'm going to do next."

Put It Into Practice:

Talk it out the next time you're stuck in your head to organize your thoughts, improve memory, and process information.

Memory Support

October 8

Out of Sight, Out of Budget.

More people should learn to tell their dollars where to go instead of asking them where they went. ~ Roger Babson

Out of sight is out of mind for many ADHDers...whether it's an event that wasn't added to the calendar, a task that never made it onto the to-do list, or a bill sitting unopened in a pile of mail on the kitchen counter.

But when we make the invisible visible by creating external reminders and visual systems, we don't have to rely on our executive function to do all the remembering.

Just like analog clocks help us see time, visual money trackers help us see where our money is going. And that awareness can make a big difference.

The trick is to make it fun so our ADHD brain will want to keep up with it. No boring spreadsheets allowed.

Try printing a thermometer to color in as we pay down debt. Fill a jar with cash to add to savings. Or create an envelope for each holiday gift recipient with a set amount of cash or gift cards to help reduce overspending.

When we can see it, we can better manage it.

Put It Into Practice:

Explore visual money tracking options that appeal to you. Look for apps that gamify budgeting or browse Etsy for printable trackers if you prefer pen and paper.

Money Management

Not Your First Rodeo.

Life doesn't get easier or more forgiving, we get stronger
and more resilient. ~ Steve Maraboli

Because ADHD brains tend to focus on now, we can forget everything we've already overcome to get to this point. That becomes important to remember when we get pulled into a cycle of rejection or failure, something many of us experience through Rejection Sensitive Dysphoria (RSD).

When RSD rears its head, it can help to recall something hard we've worked through in the past. Remembering how we've survived criticism, failure, and rejection before gives our spiraling brain evidence that we're going to be okay. We've been through hard things and we made it through.

For me, I think about how devastated I felt when my first marriage ended. I remind myself how much I love the life I've built since then with my husband and my kids. I worked hard (with the help of a therapist) to process the rejection and grief, and that work helped me get to where I am today.

RSD tells us a feeling will last forever. Our life experience proves it won't.

Put It Into Practice:

Anchor yourself in evidence when you notice an RSD shame spiral. Reflect on a time when you overcame adversity or failure. And remind yourself you can get through this, too.

RSD, Mindset

October 10

Swap Sorry with Thank You.

An apology given just to appease one's conscience is self-serving and better left unspoken. ~ Evinda Lepins

Apologies should have two parts: taking responsibility and seeking resolution. If we break something at a friend's house, we admit responsibility and offer to fix it.

But many ADHDers frequently apologize for actions tied to their symptoms, like forgetting a birthday or running late. And while we absolutely should take responsibility when negative behaviors impact someone else, we often get stuck in the apology… and skip the resolution part.

People-pleasing can make this even trickier. If we're afraid of disappointing others or being seen as "too much," apologizing can become our default way to smooth things over, even when we're already doing our best.

Saying "I'm sorry" may give us temporary relief from guilt, but it's often followed by a shame spiral when we don't address the root cause. And each time we apologize for the same behavior, our apology can lose a bit of its luster.

That's why it can be helpful to replace "I'm sorry" with "thank you." Instead of "Sorry I'm late," try "Thank you for waiting." This subtle reframe acknowledges the inconvenience in a less shame-filled way and it gently highlights areas where we might want extra support.

Put It Into Practice:

Swap your apology for gratitude when it fits. Reframe "I'm sorry" as "thank you" and notice where you might need more support or a better system.

Mindset, People-Pleasing

The 37% Rule.

The more you overthink the less you will understand. ~ Habeeb Akande

Making a decision, big or small, can quickly devolve into analysis paralysis for many ADHDers. We often delay decisions because the "wrong" choice might lead to criticism or failure and spark our RSD. So instead of making a decision, we make no decision… and no progress.

Enter the 37% Rule, also known as the "1/e rule" from optimal stopping theory. It's a mathematical framework that helps us decide when to stop researching and increase the probability of choosing the best option because, let's be honest, many of us overanalyze because we want to pick the best option.

The 37% Rule creates boundaries by defining scope and sample size. First, decide how many options you're willing to consider. Then review and reject the first 37% of them, using those options only to clarify what you like and don't like. After that, choose the next option that meets or beats the best one from your first group. Decision made.

For example, when choosing vacation accommodations, limit choice to ten options. Review the first three to clarify your preferences for location and amenities. Then select the next hotel or home that meets (or exceeds) that criteria from the remaining seven options.

Yes, good options might remain. But many choices are good enough and the only truly bad choice is not choosing at all.

Put It Into Practice:

Try using the 37% Rule when you're struggling to make a decision to help limit options and create a clear stopping point.

Decision-Making, RSD, Taking Action

October 12

Don't Wait Until It's Too Late.

*The preservation of health is easier than
the cure of disease. ~ BJ Palmer*

On October 12, 2021, I received a phone call informing me I had been diagnosed with triple HER2+ breast cancer after my first mammogram. I started chemotherapy 28 days later. And those 28 days were nothing short of a whirlwind wrapped in chaos surrounded by pandemonium.

For 4 years, my primary care doctor told me to schedule a mammogram during my annual physical. And for 3 years, I walked out of that appointment and immediately forgot.

Finally, my doctor suggested I call and make the appointment before I left the parking lot so it didn't slip away again. I did…and I'm so glad I did.

I truly believe I'm here today because my cancer was detected and treated before it progressed further. Early detection can mean earlier options, less invasive treatment, and better outcomes.

Many of us feel anxious or overwhelmed when it comes to medical appointments. But as with so many overwhelming things we face day-after-day, it's about a small step in the right direction. If making the call feels hard, it can help to have someone sit with us while we do it.

Put It Into Practice:

Schedule your mammogram if you're due. If you don't need a mammogram, schedule your physical, dentist, optometrist, or other preventive appointment.

Time Investments, Mom Life

Estrogen Rollercoaster.

The key to better outcomes for women with ADHD lies not only in better recognition of the disorder, but in the realization that in addition to their ADHD, they must cope with an ever-changing hormonal environment that can have a significant impact on their ADHD symptoms. ~ Dr. Patricia Quinn

Until fairly recently, estrogen was mostly discussed in the context of reproductive health. But estrogen also plays an important role in bone density, cholesterol, skin changes, and (yes) brain function.

And for ADHDers, this matters because estrogen and dopamine are closely connected. Research suggests estrogen can influence dopamine signaling and availability in the brain. Drops in estrogen (like the days leading into menstruation or during perimenopause and menopause) may be linked to intensifying ADHD symptoms around attention and emotional regulation.

Knowing where we are in our cycle can help us plan with more compassion and strategy. Many women notice that when estrogen is higher, tasks that require more executive function feel more doable. But motivation, focus, and emotional regulation can feel harder when estrogen dips because our brain may have less dopamine support available.

Put It Into Practice:

Track your cycle for a month or two to learn your personal "high energy" and "low bandwidth" windows. If you're in perimenopause/menopause (or no longer menstruating) and notice ADHD symptoms shifting, talk with your doctor about whether hormones could be part of the picture.

Dopamine, ADHD Symptoms

October 14

SOPs for You and Me.

*If you can't describe what you are doing as a process,
you don't know what you're doing. ~ W. Edwards Deming*

A standard operating procedure (SOP) is a set of written instructions that describes the step-by-step process for completing a routine activity. We usually hear about SOPs in the workplace, but our home life can benefit just as much from having clear, written steps for everyday routines.

These written instructions provide a plan of action that reduces the mental load of deciding what to do next. They help break down large, overwhelming tasks into smaller, manageable steps...making task initiation easier. And when the steps are written down, we're less likely to forget something important. As a bonus, written instructions make routines easier to delegate to partners or kids without repeating ourselves a thousand times.

An SOP doesn't need to be formal or complicated. It can be as simple as a checklist taped inside a cabinet, a note on our phone, or a shared document for our family. And it doesn't need to look Pinterest-perfect to act as external executive function for a tired and overwhelmed mom brain.

We won't need to remember all the steps because the steps are written down to remember for us.

Put It Into Practice:

Create an SOP for a routine in your home. List all the steps, then run through the routine using your draft to see if anything is missing. Once it works smoothly, rewrite or type it up and keep it somewhere easy to reference.

Productivity, Checklists, Memory Support

October 15

Slow Your Roll.

The faster your life is moving, the sooner your life is a blur. ~ Noah benShea

I often describe ADHD as having a "speeding train brain." We're so determined to get to the next stop that we rarely pause to notice the stations we've passed or the people we've carried along the way. It's just go, go, go!

Part of this may be because our brains crave new, exciting, and different experiences to boost dopamine, which supports motivation and focus. But that constant hunt for stimulation can also make us feel impatient and frustrated when things move slowly. It can increase impulsivity because we don't always slow down long enough to evaluate before we decide or act.

And while there are benefits to quick thinking and action, there are also times when slowing down and being present, especially as a mom, matters more than speed. (I'm looking at you, upcoming holiday season.)

It doesn't have to be all or nothing. Rather than trying to stop a runaway train all the time, Dr. Ned Hallowell suggests we "strengthen our brakes" so we can slow down when we need to. One simple way to practice is by pausing and using our senses. See the sights. Smell the smells. Hear the sounds. Feel the feels.

Building intentional "nothing time" or buffer time between activities also helps us practice slowing down. Think of it as a break that strengthens our brakes.

Put It Into Practice:

Practice using your brain brakes today: pause for 30 seconds, use your senses, and slow down before your next transition or decision.

ADHD Symptoms, Distractions

October 16

Setbacks Don't Mean Stop.

You may encounter many defeats,
but you must not be defeated. ~ Maya Angelou

Everyone experiences failure in some way, shape, or form. While it sounds cliché, it truly is a part of life. Where a neurotypical reaction might be "try, try again," ADHDers often aren't as eager to put ourselves out there again right away.

This may be due to Rejection Sensitive Dysphoria (RSD), which can make the pain of failure (or even perceived failure) feel deeper and stick around longer. And if our brains already struggle to motivate us to do things we want to do, it can feel nearly impossible to motivate ourselves when there's potential pain on the horizon.

And because RSD makes this process hard, it helps to have a simple bounce-back toolkit ready:

- Practice messy action so progress is possible, even if it isn't perfect.
- Analyze perceived failures for lessons learned instead of using them as proof you can't do it.
- Track what you've done (not how well you did it) so you can recognize effort and forward motion.

RSD will still try to convince us that trying again is too painful. But with time and practice, we can learn to reframe setbacks as information, not identity, and keep moving forward.

Put It Into Practice:

Reframe a recent setback as a learning opportunity. Ask, "What did I learn, and what's one small adjustment I can try next time?"

Mindset, RSD, Goal Setting

324

When Too Much is Too Much.

*The feeling of being overwhelmed is your invitation
to slow down. ~ Rachel Brathen*

When ADHD brains go into overdrive trying to process too much information at once, it's harder than usual to choose what to focus on.

We can't possibly take it all in or pay attention to everything but darn it...we will certainly try.

And when we do, it can overload our nervous system, leading to increased irritability, difficulty concentrating, shutdown, or even panic. Who wants that with the holiday season approaching?!

But we can often reduce the impact by identifying what triggers overstimulation before it hits.

Maybe it's tactile triggers like clothing that's too tight or a tag rubbing our skin. Maybe it's visual triggers like bright or flashing lights. Maybe it's olfactory triggers like strong smells. And crowded, busy spaces can be especially tough because they combine several triggers at once.

Once you know what sets you off, it becomes easier to prepare or even avoid those triggers when possible. Awareness gives you options.

Put It Into Practice:

Notice what triggers your overstimulation and set one small boundary to protect yourself so you can reduce the fallout and stay more regulated.

Overstimulation, Self-Care, Mental Health

October 18

Don't Drop the Ball.

To the parents who are in the whirlwind of miles spent behind the wheel after long days of work or the missed activity they so wanted to be at but couldn't, you're seen. ~ Brooke Teel

I was prepared for the commitment to practices and games when my kids joined sports teams. What I didn't prepare for was the laundry commitment.

And thanks to ADHD time blindness, there have been far too many last-minute loads washing uniforms for an after-school game because I thought, "I've got a week until the next one. I'll get around to it."

That is…until we stopped hiding uniforms in the hamper and started putting them directly into the washing machine after games. This way, I can wash the uniforms with whatever load I do next. And since I do some sort of laundry most days, the uniforms are cleaned and ready to go well in advance of the next game.

And if I'm afraid I'll forget it's waiting to be washed or buried deep in the dryer, I set a reminder on my phone or stick a Post-It to my computer as an extra reminder.

This system doesn't just work for sports moms. We can use this trick for band, work, or any uniforms our kids need regularly cleaned.

Put It Into Practice:

Put your kid's sports uniforms (or other uniforms) and equipment directly in the washing machine after a game or event so they aren't lost at the bottom of the hamper when they're needed next.

Cleaning and Organizing, Mom Life

Get Your Motor Running.

When I workout early in the morning,
the rest of the day feels so much better. ~ Robert Cheeke

I've mentioned a couple times, but exercise is truly our best non-medicated strategy for managing our ADHD. And a morning workout can compound those benefits.

Exercise at any time of day increases blood flow and the neurotransmitters dopamine and norepinephrine, which help regulate attention. Regular physical activity may help to raise the baseline levels for these neurotransmitters, making more of them available for executive functions throughout the day.

But why choose the morning for our workouts? Because exercising first thing helps us improve our ADHD symptoms before we do anything else. We'll elevate our mood from endorphins and serotonin, improve our focus with a boost of norepinephrine, and get our executive function up and firing from increased dopamine levels.

Morning movement can also support circadian rhythm for some people, particularly if it includes daylight.

We can enjoy these brain-boosting benefits in as little as 5 minutes per day. Think a brisk walk, a quick strength circuit, or stretching with music. When it comes to exercise benefits for ADHD, it's more about consistency than intensity.

Put It Into Practice:

Set your alarm a little earlier so you can get in a quick morning workout.

Exercise, Morning Routine, Dopamine

October 20

Honor Your Capacity.

Don't think of introversion as something that needs to be cured...Spend your free time the way you like, not the way you think you're supposed to. ~ Susan Cain

Normal, average, everyday life can be exhausting for ADHDers. It takes a lot of energy to focus, plan, take action, and just generally be human. And that energy demand compounds when introversion joins the party.

Because ADHD is often recognized for its outwardly visible traits like hyperactivity (I mean, it is in the name, after all), it surprises people to learn many ADHDers are introverts.

And since introverts recharge their energy in low-stimulation environments, it's even more important for ADHD introverts to manage their energy than their extroverted counterparts.

That doesn't mean introverts don't like people. It just means it's much less exhausting to be around the right people in the right environment. They might avoid crowded parties but enjoy a birthday dinner at a quiet restaurant with close friends.

Being selectively social allows ADHD introverts to build and maintain relationships on their terms without overwhelming their energy. They can choose meaningful interactions over loud, high-stimulation ones and connect over shared interests where thoughtful conversation replaces small talk.

Put It Into Practice:

Be selectively social to protect your energy and avoid burnout, especially if you're an introvert with ADHD.

Introverts, Energy Management, Burnout

Start. Fizzle. Fade.

One positive step can put an end to negative momentum.
Now is when you can take it. ~ Ralph Marston

The cycle often looks the same…something piques our interest. We invest time in learning about it, money in supplies, and energy in doing it. Then slowly but surely (despite thinking this time was different), our passion wanes. We spot something new, and the cycle starts again.

This pattern, like many ADHD behaviors, is closely tied to dopamine, specifically, the drop that happens after novelty fades. When we start something new, our brain is flush with dopamine because we're excited. That boost supports motivation and focus. But once the newness wears off, we get fewer dopamine hits, making it easier to shift our attention the moment a shiny new object crosses our path.

And I'm not suggesting we never change interests. I'm definitely looking forward to trying something new after dedicating so much time to writing this book. But when we do have a longer goal or project we want to stick with, there are ways to keep interest alive.

First, focus on tiny steps instead of the overall endgame. For example, "play the first three songs in a beginner piano book" is a much easier target than "learn piano." Crossing small thresholds gives us dopamine hits that help us keep going.

Second, build in accountability. Knowing someone is watching helps us stay engaged even when motivation dips.

Put It Into Practice:

Reignite interest in a waning goal or hobby by creating smaller steps so you can celebrate tiny victories or by asking someone to hold you accountable.

Goal Setting, Dopamine, Accountability

October 22

You Down with DPT.

Insomnia is a glamorous term for thoughts
you forgot to have in the day. ~ Alain de Botton

Deep pressure therapy (DPT) is a calming strategy that uses firm touch or pressure to help regulate the nervous system. It's often associated with a "rest and digest" response, which can help the body feel safer and more settled.

When we use a weighted blanket, gentle pressure is applied evenly across the body. This pressure can activate the vagus nerve, a critical player in the PNS, and helps counteract the sympathetic nervous system (SNS), which is responsible for our "fight or flight" response.

Letting our PNS run the show can help our heart rate slow and muscles relax while we get a dose of calming hormones like serotonin and oxytocin and along with a decrease in cortisol, the stress hormone.

In fact, a 2023 Swedish study[23] exploring children's experiences with weighted blankets during a sleep intervention reported improvements like better sleep routines, improved sleep quality, and better everyday participation for some kids with ADHD.

No weighted blanket? No problem. Other forms of deep pressure input include firm hugs, compression clothing, squeezing stress balls or playdough, or "heavy work" like lifting weights or intense cleaning.

Put It Into Practice:

Consider deep pressure therapy like a weighted blanket or another calming pressure-based strategy.

Sleep

Safety note: Weighted sleep products are not recommended for infants, and caregivers should follow age/weight guidance and consult a clinician if they're unsure.

Slow Down to Speed Up.

If you get tired, learn to rest, not to quit.
~ Banksy

Sometimes the best thing we can do for an overworked ADHD brain is take a break. Just like our cell phone provider might throttle data once we hit our limit, our brain slows down and struggles to process information when its energy is low.

But all breaks are not created equal. To keep breaks effective, they need to be time-bound or task-bound so they don't turn into a distraction.

Choose a short, specific amount of time, around 10 minutes, or choose a task with a clear finish line, like doing the dishes or walking around the block.

It also helps to schedule breaks ahead of time and set a reminder for when it's break time. That way, we're less likely to fall into hyperfocus and realize we burned through all our fuel, making it harder to return to the task after we finally stop.

And when it comes to what to do, match the break to what the brain needs...choose something calming if the brain is overactive, something active if we need an energy boost, or something completely different than what we were just doing to shift gears.

Sometimes the fastest way forward is a short pause.

Put It Into Practice:

Build scheduled breaks into your tasks and projects to help prevent burnout, mistakes, and mental shutdown.

Productivity, Self-Care

October 24

Don't Delay When You Pay.

The longer we delay, the more we will pay.
~ Ban Ki-moon

A well-meaning money mindset coach once told me the worst thing I could do if I wanted to get out of debt was to put my bills on autopay.

In theory, I understand the point. When our bills are in "set it and forget it" mode, we can feel less connected to what's coming in and going out each month. And awareness does matter if we're trying to get out of debt or save.

But what she didn't factor in is that ADHDers often struggle with consistency, time management, and follow-through on tasks that they don't find interesting or rewarding.

Setting up autopay helps us stay consistent with payments, worry less about missing due dates, and follow through even when we don't feel like doing it. It reduces late fees, protects credit scores, and frees up mental energy for other priorities.

And if we do have larger financial goals, like saving for retirement or paying down debt, we can automate those too. Or schedule a quick monthly "money check-in" to review what's happening and make extra payments when possible.

Using automation isn't about avoiding our finances. It's about building a system that works with our busy ADHD mom brain.

Put It Into Practice:

Set up automatic bill pay, especially for accounts where late payments can impact your credit score or come with high late fees.

Money Management

Commence or Comfort?

The fight-or-flight is often triggered in situations
where it is of little or no use to us. ~ Russ Harris

When we struggle to get started, we may have a tug-of-war happening between our limbic system and our prefrontal cortex.

Our limbic system controls behavioral response and seeks immediate gratification. It's also wired for self-preservation, which means it's quick to send messages like, "That seems hard. Let's avoid it." Or, "Let's wait until it feels easier."

Meanwhile, the prefrontal cortex handles executive functions like planning, motivation, and decision-making. So when our executive function isn't firing and our limbic system is begging us to stay comfortable...it makes for quite the motivational quandary.

There are ways to work with and hack our limbic systems to overcome frequent procrastination:

- Start small, easy steps rather than the overarching goal
- Limit the time we plan to work so there is a clear endpoint
- Add a small reward to reinforce progress

We're not lazy. Our limbic system just wants us to stay comfortable. Which means we need to make progress feel safe and doable to move forward.

Put It Into Practice:

Focus on small, easy steps and limited work time when you're struggling with procrastination.

Procrastination, Taking Action, Productivity

333

October 26

Beat the Clock.

Work expands so as to fill the time available for its completion. ~ C. Northcote Parkinson

The Pomodoro Technique is a productivity tool where we work in short intervals (typically 25 minutes) separated by brief breaks. It's about building urgency, reducing overwhelm, and making work feel more doable…unless there's ADHD involved.

Because it can take us longer to get into the groove, we might not even be fully focused by the end of 25 minutes. And expecting those of us with time blindness and distractions to return quickly after a 5-minute break can be a tall order.

We can adapt Pomodoro-style work to fit our brains by experimenting with longer work blocks or dedicating each interval to one part of a larger task. Or try my personal favorite…play Beat the Clock.

Gamifying tasks (particularly the ones we aren't jazzed about) boosts motivation and follow-through. By racing a timer, we create urgency and a rewarding feeling when we finish. This works best for short tasks with a clear endpoint like housework, routines, or decluttering.

Racing the clock also taps into Parkinson's Law, which says work expands to fill the time allowed. If we give ourselves an hour to clean the bathroom, we'll take an hour. But if we give ourselves 25 minutes, we often finish faster.

Put It Into Practice:

Play Beat the Clock today. Set a timer and see how much you can get done before it goes off.

Time Management, Productivity

G&hux$^Bnq.

Treat your password like your toothbrush. Don't let anybody else use it, and get a new one every six months. ~ Clifford Stoll

With the holiday shopping season just around the corner, many of us will log into accounts we haven't used for a while or create new accounts for sites we don't visit often. And as tempting as it is to reuse the same password because memory is a struggle, it can put our digital and financial safety at risk.

From April 2024 to April 2025, Cybernews analyzed passwords leaked in cybersecurity incidents[24] and found that a whopping 94% were reused or duplicated.

When a password is compromised on one site, hackers often try that same username and password combination across other accounts. Password reuse can create a domino effect, and one weak link can unlock a lot more than we realize.

Creating a strategy now to update and track passwords going into the online shopping season can make managing them feel less overwhelming and time-consuming.

Put It Into Practice:

Choose a method for storing passwords like paper (kept secure) or a password manager. Start with your most important accounts: email and banking. Update other accounts as you log in and enable two-factor authentication for extra protection.

Memory Support

October 28

Just One More Thing.

*I get it, it might look like laziness when I'm lying on the sofa,
doom-scrolling social media, but the truth is, I'm in a
state of decision paralysis and overwhelm. ~ Alex Partridge*

I can't count the number of times I've told myself, "I'll fit it in," only to end up in the cycle of "I forgot something else…now I'm rushing…the results aren't great…I'm mad at myself…and now I feel stuck." Cue the ADHD paralysis.

ADHD paralysis happens when we feel frozen and unable to start, even when it's a task we want to do. It isn't laziness, procrastination, or lack of motivation. It's a neurological shutdown caused by overwhelm.

Think about doing a bench press. We start with a weight we know we can lift. Then we add a little more for a challenge. But if we keep adding weight, even small amounts, the bar eventually becomes impossible to move.

That's why building awareness around the load we're already carrying matters so much before we add "just one more thing." Regularly reviewing what needs to be done, what's coming up, and what we realistically have the time and energy for helps prevent overwhelm before it hits. It also helps train our brains to slow down and evaluate before automatically committing.

That "one more thing" may be the thing that makes everything else impossible to move.

Put It Into Practice:

Review your to-do list and schedule before committing to anything new so you can protect your bandwidth and avoid overwhelm-induced ADHD paralysis.

Paralysis, Anxiety

Are You the Bottleneck?

The bottleneck is always at the top of the bottle. ~ Peter Drucker

I'm frequently the bottleneck to my own to-do list. Sometimes it's because I don't want to teach someone else how to do it. Other times it's because I'm convinced I do it best.

In fact, as I'm writing this, there's a laundry basket full of unfolded socks my kids have been digging through for a week…because I haven't folded them. And there is no good reason I can't teach them to fold socks. I just need to stop being the bottleneck.

No matter how hard we try, there is just not enough in the tank to follow through on every idea, task, project, and whim ourselves. But that doesn't stop us from trying. It's also why delegation is such an important tool for ADHDers when it comes to energy management.

Offloading tasks that don't require our specific expertise frees up bandwidth for what actually needs our attention. It also reduces bottlenecking because people aren't stuck waiting on us to get through a long list before we get to "fold the socks."

If you're new to delegating, a few reminders help:

- Focus on the outcome (the dishwasher gets loaded), not the exact method (silverware all facing down).
- Start small by delegating one step of a task instead of the whole thing.
- Give others room to do it their way so they build confidence and ownership (and so we don't feel tempted to jump back in).

Put It Into Practice:

Delegate small tasks or parts of tasks that don't need your specific expertise to help save your energy and prevent bottlenecking.

Energy Management, Productivity

October 30

A Dopamine Menu.

*From dopamine's point of view, having things is uninteresting.
It's getting things that matters. ~ Daniel Z. Lieberman*

Some days I really struggle to get my ADHD brain going. That's why I created a dopamine menu.

When we're stuck, a dopamine menu helps us choose a dopamine-boosting activity based on our interests without wasting time trying to think of something in the heat of the unmotivated moment.

Since ADHD brains are often driven more by interest than importance, we naturally lean toward stimulating tasks over necessary ones… because "necessary" sounds so boring.

But once we get dopamine flowing through something interesting and rewarding, we may be able to bring our executive function online and transition into those must-do tasks.

Here are categories to use to build a dopamine menu:

- Appetizers – Quick bites that won't suck us in
- Salads – Tasks we dread but feel good to complete
- Main Course – Takes longer but has a bigger payoff
- Side Dishes – Tasks we do alongside other tasks
- Desserts – Something we love but need to limit

Choose from the menu intentionally, so "dessert" doesn't turn into an all-day buffet.

Put It Into Practice:

Create your own dopamine menu so you can quickly choose a rewarding activity when your brain feels stuck.

Dopamine, Taking Action

Hiding Behind a Mask.

*You seem calm and capable on the outside, but inside
you feel scattered, stressed, or exhausted. ~ Tom Murfitt*

Many ADHDers spend a lot of energy trying to look "together." We work hard not to interrupt. We force ourselves to sit still when our body wants to move. We overthink our tone, our reactions, our parenting, our schedules...trying to fit in with what looks "normal."

It's not that we're trying to be rude or disruptive. We're trying to function in a world that wasn't built for our brains.

Masking isn't fake. It's a survival strategy. And sometimes it's necessary. There are situations where we do need to be more filtered, more formal, or more regulated to avoid consequences.

But if we wear the mask everywhere, all the time, it can quietly drain our mental health. Our quirky, creative brains weren't built for neurotypical expectations and keeping up with those norms can be draining.

It's not about dropping the mask completely. It's about creating a few places where we don't have to wear it...where we can exhale and be fully ourselves. Maybe it's with a trusted friend, our spouse, a therapist, or in an ADHD-friendly community. Even one safe space can make a difference.

We don't have to unmask everywhere to relieve some pressure...we just need to unmask somewhere.

Put It Into Practice:

Notice when you're masking and how it impacts you. Then choose one safe relationship or environment where you can practice being a little more honest about what you're experiencing.

Mental Health, ADHD Symptoms

November

Joy Starts Here.

When I started counting my blessings, my whole
life turned around. ~ Willie Nelson

It's officially November…and the stores and social media are filled with reminders to give thanks. And I agree. A regular gratitude practice is an easy way to support our mindset and mental health as an ADHD mom.

When we express gratitude, our brain experiences it as rewarding, which can support dopamine and serotonin activity, helping improve mood and reduce stress. Regular gratitude practices have also been linked to better sleep and overall well-being.

And we probably already have everything we need on hand. We don't need any fancy books or devices, just a pen and paper. Or maybe one of those 17 partially used journals we've got lying around.

Not a fan of writing or journaling? Try:

- Downloading a gratitude journal app
- Making a gratitude vision board
- Creating a gratitude jar and adding a slip of paper each day

It's not about how we go about expressing gratitude that's important. It is that we make the time to do it.

Put It Into Practice:

Start a simple gratitude practice to support your mindset and mental health because joy doesn't just happen, it's developed.

Gratitude, Mindset, Mental Health, Self-Care

November 2

Spark Your Serotonin.

In daily life we must see that it is not happiness that makes us grateful, but gratefulness that makes us happy. ~ David Steindl-Rast

Serotonin, often called the "happy chemical," has a lot of important jobs in our bodies. As a neurotransmitter, it helps regulate mood, anxiety, sleep, and appetite. It also plays a role in digestion and even supports functions like clotting and tissue repair.

An easy way to support serotonin activity is through a regular gratitude practice. Elevated serotonin can help with mood regulation, and may ease struggles many ADHDers experience like anxiety, irritability, low self-esteem, and depressive feelings. In fact, a 2011 four-week gratitude contemplation program[25] found that participants reported greater life satisfaction and self-esteem compared to the control group.

And the more often we practice gratitude, the stronger these positive neural pathways become thanks to neuroplasticity and Hebb's Law, which states "neurons that fire together wire together."

More gratitude. More serotonin. More balance.

Put It Into Practice:

Boost your serotonin by writing down what you're grateful for or telling someone you're grateful for them.

Gratitude, Mental Health, Self-Care

Thankful for Thought Shifts.

If you concentrate on finding whatever is good in every situation, you will discover that your life will suddenly be filled with gratitude, a feeling that nurtures the soul. ~ Rabbi Harold Kushner

Rejection Sensitive Dysphoria (RSD) is an ADHD symptom where we feel intense emotional pain and distress when we experience, or even perceive, negativity, criticism, or failure.

Most humans feel something when rejected. But for many ADHDers, the emotional sting can hit harder, last longer, and spiral faster than it might for neurotypical brains.

This is where a gratitude practice can help...not by pretending everything is fine, but by giving our brain a way to refocus when it's stuck in the worst-case story.

When we practice gratitude consistently, we build and strengthen positive pathways that make it easier to pivot away from shame and toward safety in the future. Gratitude also supports dopamine and serotonin activity, which can help with emotional and mood regulation, both of which matter when we're trying to stop the RSD spin cycle once it starts.

Practicing gratitude won't erase hard feelings. But it will give our brains a softer place to land.

Put It Into Practice:

Shift your focus to one thing you feel grateful for when you notice an RSD spiral starting. Focus on something that reminds you that you're safe, capable, and supported.

Gratitude, RSD, Mental Health

November 4

Lower Stress with Thankfulness.

The greatest weapon against stress is our ability to choose one thought over another. ~ William James

There's good stress, and there's bad stress. Eustress helps us focus and take action. Distress feels overwhelming and can contribute to long-term health problems.

A little distress means our "fight or flight" response is doing its job reacting to a perceived threat. But prolonged distress can keep cortisol elevated, draining energy from important body functions and contributing to issues like chronic headaches, tense muscles, weakened immunity, digestive problems, and mental health struggles.

To counteract a runaway stress response, we need our parasympathetic nervous system (PNS), our "rest and digest" system, to act as the brakes and help lower cortisol levels. One simple way to support the PNS is through a regular gratitude practice.

In fact, a 1998 study from Integrative Physiological and Behavioral Science[26] found that focusing on positive emotions like gratitude led to a 23% reduction in cortisol levels after just four weeks.

Gratitude doesn't just change our mindset, it helps calm our nervous system and reduce our stress levels.

Put It Into Practice:

Lower stress and support your nervous system by starting a regular gratitude practice.

Gratitude, Mental Health, Self-Care

346

Sleep Starts with Gratitude.

*Let gratitude be the pillow upon which you kneel
to say your nightly prayer. ~ Maya Angelou*

From racing thoughts and disrupted circadian rhythms to restless legs, stress, and medication side effects, there are a whole host of reasons why many ADHDers struggle to fall asleep and stay asleep.

And while it may take some trial and error to find the right mattress firmness, room temperature, or white noise to help your brain wind down, there's a simple pre-sleep ritual many of us can try to support better rest…a gratitude practice.

A 2009 study published in the Journal of Psychosomatic Research[27] found that gratitude was linked to better sleep quality, shorter sleep latency (falling asleep faster), and longer sleep duration. One reason may be that grateful thoughts can shift the brain away from worrying and rumination toward calmer, more positive thinking.

This doesn't mean gratitude will solve every sleep struggle, but it can be one easy, low-effort way to help your brain settle before bed.

Something as simple as writing three things we're grateful for or mentally listing the good things from the day can help us develop a quieter (and more grateful) brain.

Put It Into Practice:

Spend 60 seconds focusing on gratitude before you turn out the lights to help you fall asleep faster and sleep more soundly.

Gratitude, Sleep, Self-Care

November 6

Better with Friends.

Human beings are social animals. Having someone else around can make a boring or tedious task more fun. ~ Tasha Chemel

The holiday season comes with an ever-growing to-do list. Unfortunately, it doesn't come with extra motivation and energy to tackle all those extra tasks.

And when we're wrestling with festive obligations, it helps to have accountability to keep us moving. Might I suggest scheduling time to body double (working alongside another person, in person or virtually) to help you stay focused and follow through.

Holiday body doubling sessions might include shopping for gifts or groceries (online or in person), tackling cleaning or decorating tasks, decluttering before guests arrive, stuffing holiday cards, or wrapping presents.

Just remember, body doubling is not a catch-up session. Socializing is great…just not when we're trying to get things done. That's why picking a partner who understands the assignment matters.

Another benefit of body doubling is time. When we schedule a specific task for a specific window, we're more likely to follow through. And when the session has an endpoint, it's easier to start, even on tasks we dread, because we know there's a finish line.

The holidays are easier when we don't have to do them alone.

Put It Into Practice:

Schedule a body doubling session, either in-person or online, to help you start or follow through on the holiday tasks you dread.

Body Doubling, Productivity, Taking Action

Home for the Holidays.

Traveling with kids during the holiday season can feel more like surviving a marathon than strolling through a winter wonderland. ~ Rebecca Hastings

Whether it's across town or across the country, many of us will travel during the holiday season. Which means we're adding travel logistics on top of regular mom life and holiday responsibilities. That is a lot of mental load for an ADHD brain.

And if those holiday travel plans aren't nailed down yet, now is the time to start. Planning feels less overwhelming when we break it into smaller steps.

Start with when and where. Once we know our dates and destination, we can move on to booking accommodations and transportation (if needed). The sooner we do that, the more options we'll have...and the less likely the "good ones" will disappear.

But holiday travel also comes with extra layers beyond a regular trip. We may need to think through things like:

- Do we pack Grandma's special stuffing platter... or ship it?
- Do we ship gifts ahead of time... or fit them in the trunk?
- What "must-not-forget" items do we only use during the holidays? (Looking at you, Elf on the Shelf.)

When we brain dump all the small details swirling in our head, we have a better chance of turning them into to-dos and a lower chance of forgetting something important.

Put It Into Practice:

Make a holiday travel to-do list and block time to tackle the tasks, starting with the ones that require reservations, shipping, or deadlines.

Travel

349

November 8

Prioritizing Priorities.

The things that matter most should never be at the mercy of the things that matter least. ~ Johann Wolfgang von Goethe

The holiday season is filled with decisions like gifts to buy, food to make, events to attend, and more. But despite what our ADHD brains insist, most of us won't have the time, energy, or cash flow for everything on our wish list.

And since our ADHD executive function struggles with prioritization, deciding what to buy, make, or do can feel like an exhausting chore, especially when our prefrontal cortex isn't exactly dopamine-fueled or firing on all cylinders.

Simplifying and visualizing are key when it comes to deciding what deserves our bandwidth during the holidays.

We start with a brain dump of everything swirling around in our brain. Then group similar items into categories like purchases, events, or food. Finally, rank each list based on what we must do (buy a teacher gift) versus what we'd simply like to do (see three versions of *The Nutcracker*).

Focus on what rises to the top and give yourself grace. Even Type-A neurotypical moms don't finish their lists during the holidays.

We don't need to do everything…we just need to do what matters most.

Put It Into Practice:

Brain dump then categorize what you'd like to do, make, buy, or attend this holiday season. Then reorder those lists, placing what's most important at the top.

Mom Life, Time Management, Money Management

Scarcity or Abundance?

When you are grateful, fear disappears and abundance appears.
~ Tony Robbins

A scarcity mindset focuses on seeing resources like time, money, energy, or opportunities as limited. There's only one pie and only so many pieces to go around. On the flip side, an abundance mindset sees possibilities and growth...in other words, the pie can expand.

When we think about it, it's almost like the ADHD brain is pre-wired for scarcity. Time blindness can make us feel like there's never enough time. Impulsivity can make us act fast because we fear missing an opportunity. And because we know interest can fade, we may chase quick fixes over long-term goals.

Over time, living in "not enough" mode can drain our cognitive capacity and make planning harder. It can also fuel stress and anxiety because we constantly feel behind or pressured.

Developing an abundance mindset helps us reframe challenges as opportunities and focus on growth instead of lack. It helps us recognize when enough is enough (hello, perfectionism and hyperfocus). And it can reduce anxiety because we practice noticing what's going well instead of what's missing.

Shifting from scarcity to abundance starts with awareness, and gratitude is one simple way to begin.

Scarcity creates pressure. Abundance creates peace.

Put It Into Practice:

Write down 3–5 things you're grateful for today to help grow an abundance mindset. Then set a reminder to do it again tomorrow.

Mindset, Gratitude

November 10

Best Laid Plans.

The best laid plans of mice and men often go awry.
~ Robert Burns

I like to loosely time block my days and weeks to make sure I set aside time for high-priority tasks and projects. And for 10 and a half months out of the year, this system works well. Then the holiday season shows up and throws my system out of whack.

It's not like our regular mom duties disappear in mid-November to make space for extra events. Add in travel, shopping, and caring for our germ factories when they inevitably get sick, and it's no wonder we feel pressure.

Making plans takes a lot of executive function energy. Feeling disappointed when we have to shift or change them is completely understandable. The volume of obligations combined with unexpected changes can trigger ADHD paralysis and make action feel impossible. On top of that, Rejection Sensitive Dysphoria (RSD) may creep in and convince us we've failed because we couldn't follow the plan (even though life changed the plan).

While we may not be able to prevent schedule curveballs, we can build coping skills so the changes have less impact. Create a range of outcomes for what "done" looks like when perfection isn't realistic. Break tasks into smaller steps so you can still make progress. And build catch-up blocks into your week for the things you didn't get to.

Don't forget...a shifted plan isn't a failed plan. It's just mom life.

Put It Into Practice:

Don't let a change of plans derail your day. Aim for "good enough" or tackle one small part of the task so you can keep moving forward.

RSD, Executive Function

Honoring Your Opportunities.

Gratitude and opportunity create more of the same.
~ Seth Godin

There's a standard line in most award speeches where the recipient thanks the director, producer, or whoever is giving the award for the opportunity. And while we hear it so often it can feel like an obligatory throwaway line, there's a real benefit to recognizing the opportunities life tosses our way.

As ADHDers, it's easy to bounce from one moment to the next without pausing to see how everything connects. Our constant quest for dopamine often pushes us toward "what's next," instead of reflecting on what just happened and what it meant.

But when we slow down and recognize opportunities, we build something powerful...perspective.

Our good times give us confidence and a mood boost to keep moving forward. Our not-so-good times give us a chance to learn and grow. Finding gratitude in both helps us celebrate small wins, reframe challenges, strengthen self-esteem, and support our overall happiness and well-being.

This doesn't mean we have to be grateful for hard things. It just means we can look for what they taught us or how they shaped us.

Opportunities may not always feel good in the moment, but they usually lead somewhere meaningful.

Put It Into Practice:

Express gratitude for the opportunities that come your way, no matter the circumstance. Remember...even when you lose, you don't lose the lesson.

Gratitude, Mental Health

November 12

Don't Miss the Moment.

Be present in all things and thankful for all things.
~ Maya Angelou

The ADHD brain's struggle with focus often stems from thoughts and things distracting us from living in the present. Sometimes, the moment we're in isn't stimulating enough to keep dopamine flowing...so our brain impulsively searches for something else that will.

But when our thoughts frantically flit from one thing to the next, we can miss the here and now. This can be particularly hard during the holiday season, when we're so focused on doing that we don't fully enjoy the fruits of our labor.

We can put the brakes on our runaway brain with a bit of mindfulness. Simply noticing when our mind wanders and gently bringing it back to the present helps train our brain to refocus on now. (Meditation is a great way to practice this outside of real-life moments.)

We can also reduce external distractions by turning off phone notifications or clearing small clutter that might tempt us to "just handle one more thing" instead of enjoying the moment.

And since focus is an executive function that relies on dopamine, it also helps to boost dopamine before we need to be present. Easy boosts include exercise, sunlight, a cold blast at the end of a shower, or listening to a favorite song.

Put It Into Practice:

Practice staying present so you can experience and appreciate the holiday season instead of letting it speed by.

Focus, Dopamine, Mom Life

Tiny Tasks. Big Wins.

*Great things are not done by impulse, but by a series of
small things brought together. ~ Vincent Van Gogh*

The holidays are taxing for our ADHD executive function. There's a lot to do, plan, organize, and remember…and it's a lot for our dopamine-deprived brains. Add a dash of overcommitment and a splash of overstimulation, and we may find ourselves frozen.

ADHD paralysis can happen any time of year, but we're extra susceptible during the holiday season when demands on our time and energy increase. A neurotypical brain may naturally prioritize the to-do list or recognize when it's stretched too thin. But since prioritizing and time management are executive functions, the ADHD brain continues adding until it collapses under the weight of all those commitments.

And if we find ourselves unable to take action, it helps to break tasks into smaller, more accessible steps. Instead of writing "plan Thanksgiving meal" on your list, break it down into:

- Brainstorm dishes
- Ask guests what they'd like to bring
- Write a grocery list
- Shop for groceries

Breaking a big task into bite-sized chunks helps us make incremental progress and reduces the overwhelm caused by the larger, overarching goal.

Put It Into Practice:

Break a big task into small steps to make starting and follow-through easier, especially when you're feeling frozen.

Paralysis, Taking Action, Productivity

November 14

Procrastivity Patrol.

Procrastivity is a way to gain smaller-sooner comfort by getting something done, but at the cost of the larger-later and often more important payoff from finishing the priority task. ~ Dr. Russell Ramsay

Procrastivity is productive procrastination and the love child of distraction and productivity.

During busy seasons like the holidays, when our executive function is already spread thin, our brain looks for quick wins to rebuild its dopamine stores. That's why we may gravitate toward tasks that technically need done...just not the big executive-function-sapping tasks on our list. That is procrastivity.

And it makes sense why we're drawn to it. These tasks usually have a low barrier to entry and aren't cognitively demanding. We already know all the steps. There's a clear endpoint. And because they're easy to start and finish, it's easier to earn a dopamine reward.

We can retrain our brains away from procrastivity by making overwhelming tasks feel less overwhelming:

- Create a checklist so we know the steps
- Set a stop time so there's a clear endpoint
- Break big tasks into smaller pieces for quick wins

Procrastivity isn't lack of motivation. It's just our brain hunting for dopamine and quick wins.

Put It Into Practice:

Notice when you're procrastivating and take one step to make the "bigger" task easier to start.

Procrastivity, Procrastination, Distractions, Taking Action

Clean Out Your Fridge Day.

*Cooking Tip: Wrap turkey leftovers in aluminum foil
and throw them out. ~ Nicole Hollander*

In 1999, Whirlpool declared November 15th "National Clean Out Your Refrigerator Day" to encourage people to clean out their fridges in advance of the holiday season.

Since ADHD brains struggle with "out of sight, out of mind," our refrigerators can become chock-full of forgotten items and leftovers shoved to the back or hidden in drawers. Which is why we may need a different approach than those aesthetically pleasing Pinterest fridge photos may suggest.

To start, things don't need to go where they're "supposed" to go. If we need to use the fridge door for leftovers or produce instead of condiments, do it. We're much less likely to forget about what we can see.

On the flip side, use drawers for things we know we'll regularly look for like lunch supplies for our kids or our favorite after-dinner chocolate treat.

If the fridge cleaning feels overwhelming, set a 10–15 minute timer and focus on one category at a time like expired items, leftovers, produce, or condiments. We don't have to make it perfect...we just need it functional.

Put It Into Practice:

Schedule time to declutter and organize your refrigerator to make room for holiday food and stop buying things you already have.

Cleaning and Organizing, Eating and Meal Planning

Calendar Your Chaos.

Calendars and clocks exist to measure time, but that signifies little because we all know that an hour can seem as eternity or pass in a flash, according to how we spend it. ~ Michael Ende

Many ADHDers are visual, big-picture thinkers. Seeing information through mind maps, drawings, or color-coding helps us organize thoughts and solve problems. Which is why we often need to see our schedule to understand our busyness.

When our weeks look similar, it's easier to adjust for small changes. But the holiday season adds activities, tasks, and commitments on top of our regularly scheduled programming...and that can quickly overwhelm an ADHD brain.

That's why maintaining an up-to-date calendar is crucial during the holidays. A calendar helps us see where we do and don't have time, which reduces overcommitment. It shows us where we can block specific time for specific tasks so they actually get done. And our calendar (with the help of alarms and reminders) can help prevent hyperfocus from stealing hours on one project when there are ten other things competing for our time and energy.

Put It Into Practice:

Add non-negotiable tasks and commitments to your calendar. Then schedule time blocks for important to-dos so your priorities actually have a place to live.

Time Management, Time Blindness

Don't Go Griswold.

It's just that I know how you build things up in your mind, Sparky. You set standards that no family activity can live up to. ~ Ellen Griswold

In the holiday classic *National Lampoon's Christmas Vacation*, Clark Griswold is determined to have a good old-fashioned family Christmas surrounded by all the food, family, and fun he loves. He has a clear vision of how it should go, which of course means absolutely nothing goes to plan.

I can relate to Clark. I've made many Griswold-ian holiday plans where I build up a gift or activity so much in my mind that reality feels like a letdown.

The holiday season can also amplify Rejection Sensitive Dysphoria (RSD), our heightened emotional reactions to real or perceived negativity, criticism, or failure. Increased social pressure, sensory overload, and perfectionism can intensify emotional volatility. Where a neurotypical gift giver might not even notice a less-than-enthusiastic reaction, an ADHD brain may immediately spiral and ruminate.

And since RSD isn't something we can just turn off, a bit of preparation goes a long way. We can aim for a range of positive outcomes instead of "perfect or ruined." We can keep plans simple so they're easier to execute and harder to find fault in. And we can protect our energy so we aren't running on fumes, making emotional regulation even harder.

Put It Into Practice:

Protect your mindset and energy so RSD doesn't hijack the season. Create a range of positive expectations, simplify your plans, and manage your energy so you have enough to enjoy what matters.

Mindset, RSD

November 18

The Price of a Good Deal.

ADHD impulsivity makes it especially challenging to resist quick mood boosters, like buying something on impulse...your brain is saying, "I want to feel better, and I want it now!" ~ LeighAnna Morris

Sometimes I feel like the marketing industry only caters to ADHDers. Advertisers know exactly how to trigger our FOMO and encourage impulse purchases. Add the dopamine rush of an easy "Add to Cart," and suddenly boxes show up while we're thinking, "Wait... what did I buy?"

As with many ADHD coping skills, awareness is our first line of defense against impulse spending. It helps to know what triggers us to buy (certain brands, websites, emails, or wording in ads). Once we know what starts the shopping spiral, we can strategize ways to reduce overbuying and overspending.

One option is the 24-hour rule. Add the item to your cart, then set a reminder to decide later. We can also increase purchasing friction by deleting saved credit cards or disabling one-click purchases. Even small barriers create a pause point before we buy.

When our brain brakes aren't reliable, impulsive spending can put us in financial hot water. Consider keeping a separate "fun money" account for shopping or ask an accountability buddy to talk through purchases before they happen.

We don't have to stop shopping entirely, but it helps to stop buying on autopilot.

Put It Into Practice:

Create a purchase plan to reduce impulse spending and protect your budget during the holiday shopping season.

ADHD Symptoms, Money Management

The Thank You Effect.

Feeling gratitude and not expressing it is like wrapping a present and not giving it. ~ William Arthur Ward

Dr. Robert A. Emmons is a professor of psychology at the University of California, Davis, and one of the world's leading scientific experts on gratitude. According to Dr. Emmons, gratitude has two components…recognizing something good and acknowledging where it came from. And while there is definitely good we generate for ourselves, much of the good we experience comes from the effort of others.

Expressing gratitude releases dopamine (yes, that dopamine!) and serotonin to help improve our mood and focus while lowering stress and negativity. When we notice what others do for us, we also deepen bonds of trust, friendship, and love, depending on the relationship.

But recognizing what others contribute can take practice if we're used to speeding through life. That's why ADHD-friendly strategies can help us follow through. For example, snap a photo of what inspired the appreciation. This not only helps us remember to say thank you later, but also strengthens the gratitude connection in our brain, since we're visual processors.

And if possible, send the thank you right away. The longer we wait, the more likely it is to disappear into the ADHD void.

Think. Thank. Send.

Put It Into Practice:

Thank someone for something good they've added to your life.

Gratitude, Relationships, Mindset, Mental Health

November 20

When the Going Gets Tough.

It's your reaction to adversity, not adversity itself that determines how your life's story will develop. ~ Dieter F. Uchtdorf

My breast cancer treatment included intense chemotherapy, a mastectomy, and various other infusions and surgeries over the course of 18 months. Stressful doesn't even begin to describe what I was feeling, especially since my kids were only ten and eight at the time.

For ADHDers, highly stressful situations are ripe for emotional volatility, catastrophizing, and paralysis, making it difficult to start or complete anything. And while we can't prevent all the hardships life has in store, we can build tools that help us cope and respond when hard times hit.

A vital piece of my cancer-coping toolkit was a regular gratitude practice. I looked for ways to focus on what I still had (friends who brought my family dinner) instead of what I didn't (my eyebrows and eyelashes).

Practicing gratitude helps calm our stress response and boost dopamine, which supports emotional regulation. It builds resilience by shifting our thoughts away from doom spirals and helps move the brain from anxiety-driven "fight or flight" into "rest and digest."

This doesn't mean we have to be grateful for what hurts. It just means we can look for something steady to hold onto while we walk through it.

Put It Into Practice:

Practice finding gratitude when you experience difficult situations. It can be as easy as saying "thank you" to your support system or noticing the small things you enjoy each day.

Gratitude, Mindset, Mental Health

November 21
Gratitude in Real Time.

*I don't have to chase extraordinary moments to find happiness,
it's right in front of me if I'm paying attention and
practicing gratitude. - Brené Brown*

This past summer, a friend invited me to watch her neighbor's quintet in her backyard. It was a beautiful summer day. The musicians were incredibly talented. It was a wonderful experience. And I made sure to note, in the moment, how grateful I was for it.

When our ADHD brains speed through life, jumping from one stimulation to another, we often miss the chance to pause and acknowledge the moments that make our lives great. The perfect balance of cream and sugar in our morning coffee. How great our skin looks when we actually follow our skincare routine. The relief we feel when we walk in after a busy day and there's takeout on the counter.

Pausing to notice what we're thankful for in real time helps build an abundance mindset that focuses on what we have instead of a scarcity mindset that's always chasing what's next. That pause also helps our ADHD brain stay present, particularly during the holiday season when we're making memories.

And when we recognize a moment as it's happening, we're more likely to remember it later.

Put It Into Practice:

Stop and find gratitude for something right now. Then make a regular practice of pausing to notice what you're grateful for in the moment.

Gratitude, Mindset

November 22

Stopping the Spiral.

ADHD brains process emotions differently. They often "turn up the volume" on feelings, making even small rejections feel crushing. ~ Dr. Sharon Saline

The holiday season is full of potential Rejection Sensitive Dysphoria (RSD) landmines like replaying a comment from our auntie or second-guessing a gift that didn't get the reaction we expected.

For ADHDers, perceived rejection, criticism, or failure can make emotional regulation incredibly difficult. Add in increased socializing, gift-giving pressure, and family gatherings with people who lack a filter, and RSD can quickly kick into overdrive. This year, instead of spiraling for days, we can plan ahead for how we'll cope and limit the impact on our daily life.

When that familiar sense of rejection starts to bubble up, try reframing the moment with a reminder like, "I've handled criticism before. I'll be okay." This helps shift from the emotional brain to the thinking brain and slow the spiral before it takes over. Writing our mantra down or recording a quick voice memo can make it easier to access when we need it.

It's also helpful to create space from the trigger. That might mean stepping outside, moving to another room, or giving our brain something neutral or positive to focus on until the intensity passes.

These shifts take time and practice. But we have to start somewhere…might as well be this year.

Put It Into Practice:

Create a plan to recognize and reframe perceived rejection, criticism, or failure during the holiday season.

RSD, Mental Health

Add _____ to My List.

I love to make lists. I also like to leave them on the kitchen counter and guess what's on the list while at the store. ~ Dana Trentini

At any given time, there are between three and twenty-three different lists floating around my desk and the house. It's actually a joke between me and my husband when I say, "I'll put it on the list," he responds with, "Which one?"

But there are times when an idea pops into my head, an ingredient needs to be replaced, or I remember a gift I want to buy… and none of my lists are within writing distance.

Luckily, my home is littered with digital assistants. I can shout, "Alexa, add strawberry jelly to my grocery list" from anywhere, and the item appears instantly. And as a bonus, those lists sync to an app on my phone so I can see them at the store even if I forget the paper list at home (assuming I remember my phone).

Digital assistants like Alexa, Siri, and Google can help us capture tasks, gift ideas, and random reminders the moment we think of them. From books to read and shows to watch, to chore lists, guest lists, and grocery lists…there are endless ways to use voice-to-list tools to externalize our memory.

It may take a small time investment to set up the lists or learn how to access them through an app. But once we're rolling, the list making possibilities are endless.

Put It Into Practice:

Use your digital assistant or phone to create lists and add items the moment you think of them.

Memory Support, Time Investments, Mom Life

November 24

Thankful for ADHD?

ADHD isn't a bad thing, it's a different
way of thinking. ~ David Neeleman

Part of the reason I put off my official ADHD diagnosis for over a decade was the stigma I perceived around the label. ADHDers were often seen in a certain way, and I feared being boxed in by it.

As it turns out, many traits viewed as drawbacks can also be sources of strength.

Our distractibility and impulsivity can fuel creativity and help us see connections others miss. We brainstorm outside-the-box solutions, take risks, and try new things.

When a project truly grabs our interest, our ability to hyperfocus can lead to high-quality work and incredible attention to detail.

And while not all ADHDers fall under the "hyperactive" type, many of us have an abundance of energy, whether it shows up outwardly or just in our heads. That energy often powers our creativity and action-taking. In fact, a 2019 study of adults with ADHD[28] found that an abundance of energy (and its connection to their ability to take action) was a core positive theme among participants. And our energy can create an exuberance that makes us fun to be around.

ADHD absolutely has its advantages when it comes to creativity, adaptability, and enthusiasm. It's high time we recognize and appreciate these positive traits. We don't have to love every part of ADHD to appreciate the strengths it brings.

Put It Into Practice:

Notice the positive ways your unique ADHD brain influences your life and the people around you.

Gratitude, ADHD Symptoms

Planning Prevents Pile-Ups.

*You can always change your plan, but only if
you have one. ~ Randy Pausch*

There is a 0% chance I would have finished writing this book without a plan. In fact, the first month after I decided to write it, I spent my time choosing topics for each day and mapping out when I needed to complete different tasks.

Trust me when I tell you…developing a plan was a battle with my ADHD brain. It wanted to jump in and start writing immediately. But I also knew we were heading into the busiest time of year for my kids' activities, with the holidays right around the corner. I needed a plan to reduce decision fatigue and help me remember all the moving parts.

So I made a plan. And then I altered it. Unexpected hiccups, time blindness, and a dash of waning interest meant adjustments were necessary. But I truly believe you wouldn't be reading this right now if I didn't have a solid plan in place to support taking action (and the dopamine hits that came from finishing).

As the holiday season barrels forward, taking a little time to plan what needs to happen and when can reduce cognitive load and protect our executive function.

Put It Into Practice:

Create a plan for the holiday season. Start by listing important events, travel, and purchases. Then add due dates or calendar reminders so you have time for what matters most.

Productivity, Time Management, Taking Action

November 26

Harness Your Hyperfocus.

If you don't pay appropriate attention to what has your attention, it will take more of your attention than it deserves. ~ David Allen

Lots of activities vie for our attention during the holidays. And despite ADHD standing for Attention *Deficit* Hyperactivity Disorder, there are many times when we have more attention than an activity needs.

Hyperfocus happens when something feels fun, rewarding, and stimulating. Learning something new while reading or seeing progress on a DIY project releases dopamine and fuels our focus. But hyperfocus can slide into hyperfixation when we start perfecting projects that don't need it or ignoring tasks that still need to be done.

To make hyperfocus a help and not a hindrance during the holiday season, decide what "done" looks like before the project sucks you in. Good is complete. Better has a bit more finesse. Best is perfection. Knowing it doesn't have to be perfect to be done makes it easier to step away and move on.

Next, use reminders to break the time-blind hyperfocus state. Set an alarm so we don't lose track of time, or ask someone to check in.

Our hyperfocus is a superpower when we aim it on purpose.

Put It Into Practice:

Prevent hyperfixation by deciding a range of what "done" means and using alarms to break your hyperfocus.

Time Management, ADHD Symptoms, Productivity

368

The Helpful Holiday Hustle.

A motto that I've come to live by in my fitness journey is: something is better than nothing. ~ Brett Stanavich

Next to my bank account, my workout routine takes the biggest hit during the holiday season. When I combine a shift in our normal schedule with later nights watching holiday movies and a few extra adult beverages, my movement motivation is often sorely lacking.

But since moving our bodies is so important for ADHD brains, it helps to reframe our routine during busy times instead of stopping altogether. To start, we can shorten the time we spend. We can get brain-boosting benefits from as little as 10 minutes of getting our heart rate up.

We can also build movement into seasonal activities. Try walking through neighborhoods to check out light displays or planning a night to go ice skating. We can even count deep-cleaning as movement… especially if it needs to be done anyway.

And to increase our chances of follow-through, reduce the friction it takes to start. Planning workouts in advance and setting out clothes the night before lowers resistance. Enlisting a workout buddy adds accountability so we're more likely to show up.

We don't have to move more, we just have to move in some way.

Put It Into Practice:

Keep moving your body to support your brain and dopamine levels during the holiday season. Make workouts shorter, vary your activity, and add accountability to make follow-through easier.

Exercise, Self-Care

November 28

When It All Feels So Big.

Everyone has regrets. Everyone gets sad. Everyone ruminates. But when you have ADHD, emotions set in more quickly, last longer, and require superhuman strength to escape. ~ June Silny

Impulse control is an executive function that helps us think before reacting so we can evaluate risk and consequence. For ADHDers, impulsivity can show up as interrupting others, speaking without thinking, risky behavior, impatience, and emotional dysregulation.

And during the holiday season, when structure and executive function run low while sensory overload and emotional triggers run high, we may find ourselves on the fast track to meltdown town.

Using external guardrails and internal practices can help slow emotional spirals and reduce potential fallout. Externally, maintaining a routine helps us know what to expect and protects sleep and eating habits. Scheduling downtime gives us specific time to recharge. And reducing sensory input helps take the edge off overstimulation.

Internally, it's helpful to identify what activates our emotions. Track physical cues like tense muscles, sweating, or a racing heart, along with emotional spikes like sudden irritation or anger. When we notice those early warning signs, make space to cool off...or set boundaries ahead of time to prevent overwhelm altogether. Deep breathing techniques and repeating calming phrases engage the parasympathetic nervous system (PNS), helping slow our heart rate, lower blood pressure, and relax muscles.

Put It Into Practice:

Support your emotional regulation by using both external and internal tools to reduce stress and protect your executive function.

Emotional Regulation, Overstimulation, Mental Health, Executive Function

ADHD & Insomnia.

I find the nights long, for I sleep but little,
and think much. ~ Charles Dickens

Insomnia is defined as habitual sleeplessness or the inability to sleep. Various studies report between 43–85% of adults with ADHD experience insomnia symptoms.

Our struggles with sleep may be the result of delayed sleep phases that shift our sleep-wake cycle later. Or from stimulant medications making it hard to shut down our bodies. Or from racing thoughts making it hard to shut down our minds. We may also have comorbid sleep disorders like sleep apnea, Restless Legs Syndrome (RLS), or night terrors that impact the length and quality of our sleep.

And while science isn't fully agreed on why any of us (ADHD or not) struggle with sleep, we do know what happens when we don't get enough of it. Our already-struggling executive function has even less in the tank to help us focus, prioritize, solve problems, pay attention, control impulses, regulate mood, or remember anything. Like…anything.

Since sleep is vital for brain function, addressing sleep issues is crucial for coping with ADHD. Talking to our doctor helps identify behavioral changes or underlying causes for sleeplessness. Creating a calming bedtime routine helps train our brain to relax and wind down. And avoiding stimulation from screens, sugar, caffeine, and alcohol before bed can greatly improve our ability to fall and stay asleep.

Put It Into Practice:

Talk to your doctor if you're struggling with insomnia. Implement calming bedtime rituals to help you wind down and fall asleep.

Sleep, Self-Care

November 30

Take a Break or Breakdown.

In this game, everyone needs a break to refuel, recharge,
and jump back in full throttle. ~ Helen Edwards

From changes in routines to disrupted eating habits to overstimulating events, the holiday season is chock full of potential burnout triggers, especially for us ADHD moms.

We may notice a slow build of pressure from constant stress that leads to symptoms like tense muscles, low energy, decreased joy, the feeling that we can't keep up, depression, lack of motivation, more frequent procrastination, and quitting tasks more easily. If so…welcome to burnout.

True burnout isn't waking up one morning and feeling like you didn't sleep well or procrastinating on planning what you'll bring to the school holiday party. Burnout feels debilitating. And no one wants that during the holidays.

That's why regular breaks and self-care matter. Breaks reduce stress, improve mood, and help protect sleep quality, which supports executive function. They also reduce exhaustion, making it easier to follow through on the things we need to do without feeling like we're running on fumes.

Don't think of breaks as a reward…think of them as a necessity.

Put It Into Practice:

Look for small ways you can take breaks to prevent burnout during the holiday season. Schedule recovery time after particularly exhausting, overstimulating, or emotional events so your brain and body can reset.

Burnout, Overstimulation, Mom Life

December

Passing the Baton.

Delegation is not about getting rid of tasks; it's about empowering others to help you achieve your goals. ~ Laura Stack

The holiday season is jam-packed with decisions like what to do, what to make, what to buy. It can be exhausting just to think about it. And we don't have to be the sole decider for every decision during the holidays and beyond...even though I bet we think we do.

ADHD brains often struggle with decision-making because it involves so many executive functions. And since we make thousands of decisions in everyday life before we add in all the extra holiday ones, decision fatigue can drain our mental, emotional, and even physical energy...putting a damper on our holiday spirit.

But we can reduce decision fatigue by delegating some of the day-to-day choices. This doesn't mean handing off the decisions we want to have an integral part in. But I'd venture to guess we can delegate less consequential ones, like what the kids wear or what's for dinner, so we can save our bandwidth for the special holiday decisions.

Put It Into Practice:

Delegate everyday decisions that don't need your expertise or excite you so you have extra brain power for the special holiday decisions.

Decision-Making, Mom Life

December 2

Delegate the Dusting.

This trap we've fallen into, this "you can do it all" and
"you're a great mom if you're run ragged" messaging,
is stealing our motherhoods from us. ~ Alyssa Wolf

When I was working as a professional organizer, clients would often say, "I should be able to do this myself." And honestly? I'm tired of that messaging. It's perfectly okay to not be good at something. And it's also okay to hire help...even if we are good at it.

The holidays are the perfect time to ditch the stigma around hiring house cleaners. There just isn't enough time (or executive function) in the day for everything we want to do. And the holidays make that time shortage even more obvious.

Imagine how much pressure would be relieved knowing the bathrooms are cleaned, the floors are mopped, and no one will find a three-year-old PB&J if their phone drops between the couch cushions.

Professional cleaning services can fit a variety of budgets. They can deep clean the whole house or focus only on the areas you use most. Think of it as a well-deserved mom-gift...one that saves time, executive function, and sanity.

And when we don't have to rev up our dopamine and motivation to tackle tasks like scrubbing baseboards or dusting bookshelves, we have more energy for making holiday memories.

Put It Into Practice:

Hire a cleaning service to tackle your cleaning to-dos, especially if you're hosting holiday events.

Cleaning and Organizing, Mom Life

Yuletide Wallet Watch.

I'm so poor I can't even pay attention.
~ Ron Kittle

In a season full of impulse shopping temptations, budget creep, and resistance to opening bank statements, it's no wonder many ADHD moms overspend during the holiday season.

But with a bit of awareness through regular financial check-ins, we can avoid surprises when next month's bills roll in.

We can create awareness around where our money goes and where it needs to go by:

- Checking our bank balance regularly (daily, if possible)
- Adding bill due dates to our calendar
- Scheduling a weekly money check-in

And if we're prone to impulse purchases, especially online, try implementing a 24-hour pause or "cooling off" period after adding items to the cart. This gives the brain time to evaluate whether the purchase fits our budget or if it may push us further into debt.

Creating financial awareness doesn't mean we have to stop spending. It just means pausing long enough to make sure our purchases align with the funds we actually have.

Put It Into Practice:

Spend a little time each week reviewing your bank accounts and paying bills so you don't have financial surprises in January.

Money Management

Where Will It Go?!?

The holiday season always makes me a little anxious because I know clutter will do its very best to claim a stake in our home. ~ Brooke Blazevich

Quick question…if our drawers, cupboards, and bins are currently full to the brim, where do we plan to put any new items that will descend upon our home during the holiday season? From gifts to decorations to serving platters, the holidays have a (not-so) sneaky way of increasing the amount of stuff we have in our homes.

There's a good chance our ADHD time blindness will tell us, "That's not a right-now problem." Then January arrives and our new things have nowhere to go.

But never fear! There's time to create space for what's coming in without needing the time, energy, or bandwidth of a full-on declutter.

Focus on the areas where gifts will be heading like toy rooms, closets, and dresser drawers. Make some space now so they can be easily added to the collection.

Pare down decorations while you decorate or right after decorating to make space for anything new. Because if we didn't use it this year, chances are good we won't use it next year.

Consider borrowing appliances or serving items before purchasing, especially if it is something you'll use infrequently. It is easier to give something back than find a place to store it.

Spending a little time now means we can make space and reduce potential clutter headaches when we have to put everything away.

Put It Into Practice:

Schedule time to make space for incoming gifts or holiday gear. Pare down where you can or borrow what you don't want to store.

Cleaning and Organizing

Sparkle and Stamina.

Remember that a great deal of the stress we feel
at the holidays is of our own creation. ~ Dr. Daisy Sutherland

Everyday tasks like getting the kids ready for school or doing the dishes can feel overwhelming when we add all the other commitments the holiday season brings our way. Just because we have more on our plate doesn't mean we have more energy to complete all the things.

One way to reduce exhaustion and burnout is by consciously managing our energy using The Spoon Theory, which helps us visualize how much energy we have and where it goes.

Created by Christine Miserandino, The Spoon Theory defines a set number of "spoons" you have available to start each day. Every activity costs spoons, and some activities cost more than others. To put Spoon Theory into practice, it helps to ask:

- How many spoons do I usually start the day with?
- What everyday tasks drain the most spoons?
- What holiday tasks will cost extra spoons this week?
- Where can I simplify, delegate, or ask for help when I'm out of spoons?

When we can recognize how much energy we have available and what we're spending it on, we can better allocate our energy for both everyday responsibilities and added holiday commitments.

Put It Into Practice:

Estimate your daily spoons and adjust your holiday plans if you're already running low.

Energy Management, Overstimulation, Burnout

December 6

Smart Homes Support Moms.

I can imagine that if you don't have ADHD, some of these safeguards might seem ~~absurd. Who needs a reminder to refill their dog's water bowl?~~
Me (also, technically, my dog). ~ Amanda Blum

I've fully embraced the smart home revolution...though I hate the term "smart" home. I prefer to think of it as a support home for our ADHD brains. Smart devices help us with:

- Forgetfulness: turning off lights, adjusting the thermostat, locking doors when I don't
- Task initiation: letting a robot vacuum handle the cat hair when I don't want to
- Time management: reminding me what time it is and when I need to leave

Setting up devices can take a little time and money. But since it's the season of gift-giving, here are a few smart home tools that can make ADHD mom life easier:

- Appliances to start remotely or send reminders when they're done
- Voice assistants to capture lists, set reminders, add events to schedules, and control other smart devices
- Light bulbs, plugs, or door locks to simplify everyday life
- Robots to vacuum the floors or mow the lawn

Automation reduces our cognitive load so we can save our brainpower for the other 52,000 things we need to do.

Put It Into Practice:

Identify a smart device that could help offload a daily friction point in your home or support your ADHD mom brain.

Time Investments, Memory Support

The Yes Reflex.

People pleasing pleases everyone but the pleaser. ~ Sanjo Jendayi

We are in the season of giving…which often means giving our time, energy, and money to others. And at its core, that's a beautiful thing. Making people happy often makes us happy too.

It's when that merry-making starts to feel like a chore or obligation that it begins to drain our time, mood, and energy.

Many ADHDers struggle with people-pleasing. This may be rooted in trying to avoid the pain of Rejection Sensitive Dysphoria (RSD), or it may be impulsivity and saying "yes" before our brain has a chance to think it through. Either way, we can end up overcommitted, with little room left for our own needs and obligations.

If we can train ourselves to pause before blurting out another "yes," we may save ourselves a lot of stress. Take a breath and ask:

- Do I want to do this?
- Do I have time in my schedule for this?
- Will it take time away from myself or my family?
- Is it a priority?
- Could someone else do this?
- Will there be a chance for me to do this in the future?

We may still say "yes" after answering these questions. And that's perfectly OK. That means that this "yes" is worthy of our time and energy.

Put It Into Practice:

Pause and review these questions before committing to something that might overwhelm you or your schedule.

People-Pleasing, RSD

December 8

Overstimulated. Overwhelmed.

High stimulation is both exciting and confusing for people with ADHD, because they can get overwhelmed and overstimulated easily without realizing they are approaching that point. ~ Jenara Nerenberg

Ahh, the holiday season…the lights. The sounds. The smells. The people. The sensory overload making it harder than normal to focus and manage our emotions.

Our ADHD brains struggle to filter out irrelevant information due to difficulties with the executive function of prioritization. And since there's a lot of extra input buzzing around during the holidays, it's no wonder many of us freeze.

Like many ADHD challenges, overstimulation looks a little different for everyone. We may experience increased restlessness, unease in our clothes or body, extreme or unexplainable fatigue, or even headaches and sleep issues.

And many of us may think, "Well, that pretty much sounds like my everyday mom life." Which…might be true. But we also may be overstimulated on a regular basis without realizing it because we've learned to push through.

When we're overstimulated (holidays or anytime), it's important to take a break from the chaos. Step away from the hectic environment and find a quiet space to close our eyes, take a breath, and reset before jumping back in.

Put It Into Practice:

Take a sensory break if you're feeling overstimulated. You may even want to pre-plan one by setting an alarm during activities or environments that tend to spike your sensory overload.

Overstimulation, Self-Care, Mental Health

384

Borrow a Brain.

Human working memory is able to hold no more than some four or five chunks of information at any given time. ~ Nick Bostrom

ADHDers struggle to remember when there's too much input and too many things going on. And what is the holiday season if not too much input and too many things going on?

Forgetfulness stems from the executive function of working memory, the part of our memory that holds on to information so we can process it and file it away for later use. Because working memory is powered by dopamine like all our other executive functions, it may feel extra strained when we spread our dopamine reserves too thin with increased decision-making, planning, and stress.

One way to help support our working memory during the holidays is to involve our family or friends as external memory supports. When asking, we need to be direct, specific, and explain why we need their help (although they may already know we're forgetful).

For example, we could say to our memory support person, "I have trouble remembering to buy teacher gifts until the last minute. Can you check in with me the last week of school to see if I've made progress?"

Put It Into Practice:

Enlist family or friends to help support your memory with reminders and check-ins.

Memory Support, Accountability

Make Your Phone Findable.

Home is where the heart is, but today,
the phone is where the heart is. ~ Rachitha Cabral

When I get busy, I lose things more than usual…probably because my attention is being pulled in ten directions and my working memory doesn't fully "save" where I set things down. And I don't just lose my phone in normal places. I once misplaced it for two days in my linen closet, so I'm well acquainted with ways to track a missing phone.

To start, most phones have built-in tracking tools that can make our phone play a sound even if the ringer is off, but we have to enable them *before* our phone goes missing.

For an iPhone, turn on "Find My iPhone" in Settings (menu names may vary by iOS version). You can locate it at icloud.com/find. Select your device and choose "Play Sound."

For Android phones, download Google's Find Hub app and log into the Google account associated with your phone. To locate a lost Android phone, visit google.com/android/find, select the device, and choose "Play Sound."

Other ways to track a lost phone include asking "Alexa, find my phone," and she'll call it (if the ringer is on). There are also several two-way Bluetooth trackers that will make noise or light up, which is helpful if your phone isn't on or you want to track other frequently lost things.

Put It Into Practice:

Enable "Find My" services or another method of tracking your phone in case you misplace it.

Time Investments, Mom Life

Low Battery.

*It's precisely those who are busiest who most need
to give themselves a break. ~ Pico Iyer*

If we think of the holiday season from roughly Thanksgiving to New Year's Day, we're about halfway through. And it's likely the excitement from the start of the season is beginning to wane while the pressure of what's still left on our list is mounting.

The holidays are chock full of executive function demands and sensory stimulation that chip away at our dopamine reserves. It's like when we get a new cell phone. At the beginning, 100% means 100%. But over time, even when the battery says 100%, it drains faster. It may be "full," but...how full is full?

As the season goes on, we may start to notice diminishing capacity, right when we need more focus, more motivation, and more energy. And while we may not be able to recharge like we did at the beginning, we can enlist some dopamine boosters when we need a lift. Think of it like a little power bank for your executive function.

Some easy dopamine-supporting boosts include:

- Sunlight, especially since the days are shorter
- Protein, the building blocks of dopamine
- Exercise, which boosts dopamine and helps it stick around longer
- Sleep, so your brain and body can fully recharge

Put It Into Practice:

Watch for signs your dopamine is running low during the busy holiday season and choose one small way each day to refill your tank.

Dopamine, Energy Management

December 12

Make Eating Easier.

Remember when you were a kid and your only job was to show up and eat?
Darn, I miss those days! ~ Erin Port

There's no way around it…December is a busy month. Between racing to finish school projects before winter break, end-of-year tasks at work, and the holiday rush, we're pulled in a dozen directions. And too few include the food we need to sustain our ADHD brains.

We can sometimes get by on thrown-together, carb-heavy, low-protein meals for short stretches. But over time, inconsistent nutrition plus the extra executive function demands of this season can take a toll on our brain power and energy levels.

That's why the holiday season is a great time to invest in easy ways to feed ourselves and our families. We may not need these tools as much the rest of the year, but we can make mealtimes easier by:

- Subscribing to a meal kit so ingredients are prepped and ready
- Purchasing premade meals from the deli counter or frozen aisle
- Keeping ingredients for quick family favorites on hand to reduce decision-making and extra store trips

Even if every day doesn't tick every nutritional box, making sure we're regularly eating protein, complex carbs, and produce can go a long way in keeping our mom motor running.

Put It Into Practice:

Give yourself permission to simplify meals this holiday season so you can conserve energy for everything else December demands.

Eating and Meal Planning, Time Investments

Just In Case...

When our physical energy slumps, so does the quality
of our decisions. ~ Michael Hyatt

Even with the best laid plans, life has a funny way of getting in the way. And as much as our ADHD brains love new and exciting, we prefer when it's by choice...not because of unexpected challenges.

Unfortunately, when it comes to the holidays, we can't always control store stock levels, the weather, or when our kids get sick. If we've already spent our decision-making capital on gifts, plans, and people to see, unforeseen changes can disrupt our holiday vibe.

Which is why it's helpful to pre-plan a few "default decisions" or simple backup options for when life throws us a curveball (or a snowball, given the season). Things like:

- An easy gift: gift card, candle, sweet treat
- A backup dinner: frozen lasagna, rotisserie chicken, breakfast-for-dinner
- An easy contribution: veggie tray, drinks, store-bought dessert
- A gracious no: "I can't make it, but I hope you have a great time."

Having defaults in our back pocket helps prevent decision fatigue and brain freeze when our plans don't go to plan. We can skip the mental scramble and get back to taking action.

Put It Into Practice:

Pick a few holiday defaults so you have a ready-to-go backup plan when things inevitably don't go as expected.

Decision-Making

December 14

The Com-Parent Trap.

Comparison is the thief of joy.
~ Theodore Roosevelt

Many ADHD moms struggle with comparenting (comparing ourselves to other parents). Perfectly curated highlights, perfectionism, and the desire for validation can lead to constant comparisons. And the holiday season brings that comparenting tendency out in full force.

That exhausting pressure to keep up can worsen anxiety and low self-esteem. And when we combine that with already-fried executive function from the other seasonal demands, we can end up on the fast track to burnout before the new year even starts.

With a little awareness and self-compassion, we can create a holiday season that feels good for our family without letting comparison steal the joy. To start, limit what triggers our comparisonitis. Unfollow accounts or avoid social situations that leave us feeling "less than."

On the flip side, make time for the people and activities that genuinely fill us up...our reason for the season, not the obligations we feel like we should do just because everyone else does.

And finally, remember gratitude isn't just for November. When we regularly notice what we already have, it becomes easier to focus on abundance instead of chasing what someone else has.

Put It Into Practice:

Focus on what you have and what matters most this holiday season without measuring it against anyone else's.

Mom Life, Mental Health, Gratitude

A Win for Today.

Baby steps are still steps.
~ Toni Sorenson

As we enter the final weeks of the holiday season, we may start to feel like our to-do list is stuck on "too long." Looking at everything we need to do makes us want to do nothing.

This is when it becomes important to focus on micro-steps…one thing we can do each day rather than our list as a whole. Think:

- One gift to purchase or wrap
- One room to clean or reset
- One load of laundry to wash or put away
- One recipe to look over and determine ingredients

Because one is better than none. And often, if we can knock something off our list, that little bit of dopamine we get as a reward can help power us through another task. But even if it doesn't, at least we were able to make some sort of progress.

Making a little progress each day also helps prevent falling into the time blindness trap of thinking we have plenty of time. We slowly and methodically chip away at our to-dos rather than rushing around in a panic because we waited too long.

When we're feeling overwhelmed, it helps to remember we don't have to do it all. We just have to do one thing. And that's still progress.

Put It Into Practice:

Review your to-do list and pick one holiday-related task to do each day.

Productivity, Time Management, Time Blindness

December 16
Choose Present Over Perfect.

We hope that if we put on the masks of perfection, then we will be protected from pain of not fitting in and not being good enough to be loved unconditionally during the past and in the present. ~ Debra Smouse

I am a recovering perfectionist...and there are definitely certain times of year, like the holiday season, when my old friend, the perfection gremlin, rears its ugly head.

Our ADHD propensity for perfection may come from fear of failure, hyperfocus, or an attempt to control outcomes to avoid RSD. Because if we create the perfect holiday, then we're clearly a reliable, motivated, and responsible parent...right?

Perfectionism can also lead to procrastination when we delay starting because we can't do it the "right way" or because we've struggled with a similar task in the past. Maybe instead we choose to focus our time and effort on something we do well and avoid what scares us.

But when we exhaust ourselves trying to meet our Instagram-worthy expectations, we often miss out on enjoying the moments we were working so hard to create with the people we were doing it for.

Put It Into Practice:

Focus on being present and enjoying the holiday season with your loved ones, even if it isn't perfect.

Perfectionism, Procrastination, Mom Life

Make Room for Memories.

I may not live long enough to get through
all the digital photos I own. ~ Beth Nash Bruno

Since digital clutter accumulates in the shadows, it may be shocking when our photo app shows we have 67,542 photos lurking there. And usually, we realize our storage space is running low at the most inopportune times (like when our kid is finally smiling while sitting on Santa's lap!)

Which is why, before the holiday hustle and bustle is in full swing, we need to make space for this year's memories.

To make photo decluttering less overwhelming, start with recent photos rather than older ones. It's easier to say "yay" or "nay" to bad pictures when the memory is still fresh.

Then focus on the biggest space-wasters:

- Delete duplicates and blurry photos. Find the best, delete the rest.
- Scan for screenshots. That random news article you texted your spouse three months ago doesn't need a permanent home.

To make photo decluttering easier in the future:

- Delete extras in the moment so they don't pile up
- Use the Favorites feature to mark the best photos
- Schedule quick, regular maintenance so it doesn't become overwhelming

Put It Into Practice:

Spend a little time before bed or while you're waiting in the checkout line decluttering your digital photos.

Cleaning and Organizing

December 18

Hot Mess to Dressed.

Before motherhood, women spent 41 minutes getting themselves ready for the day. After having kids, that number was trimmed to 25 minutes. ~ Julie Beer

When life gets hectic, my personal hygiene routine takes a serious hit. There was one point while writing this book, after a particularly long weekend of writing sessions, when I realized I hadn't showered since Friday. It was Tuesday.

Getting ready is a struggle for many ADHD moms because we have so many more rewarding (and less exhausting) things to do. We might forget we need to shower, wait too long to start, or rush out the door and skip steps like deodorant or brushing our teeth.

With a little planning and a few helpful products, we can streamline our routine to reduce the friction and time it takes to make ourselves public-ready:

- Decide what a good, better, or best routine looks like and pick based on our energy for the day.
- Keep quick fixes like dry shampoo, tinted moisturizer, and mouthwash for days with less time or energy.
- Store essentials like a toothbrush or deodorant in our purse or car for the times we forget.
- Schedule "get ready" time if we need a full routine. Block more time than needed and set an alarm as a start reminder.

A get-ready routine doesn't have to be all or nothing. We just need options and backups to match our time and energy.

Put It Into Practice:

Create a simple good/better/best routine and choose 2–3 quick fixes to keep stocked for the days you need a backup plan.

Mom Life

Sugar, Spice, and Side Effects.

Everybody's got their poison, and mine is sugar.
~ Derrick Rose

I love baking during the holidays. The downside is that when there is a plate of cookies on my kitchen counter, I can't help but snag one (or a few) each time I pass. Thanks, impulse control!

And while the old adage that ADHD is caused by too much sugar is long debunked, too much of it can still throw our mood and energy off. Spikes and crashes can overstimulate our taste sense and lead to irritability, low energy, and emotional overload…which I'm guessing is not how we want to show up during the holiday season.

We can enjoy sweet treats…we just need a little pre-planning so our enjoyment doesn't devolve into a sugar coma:

- Use a small plate to create a portion rather than eating directly from a platter to better see how much we consume.
- Create friction like storing cookies in a cute tin on top of the fridge rather than a platter on the counter.
- Decide in advance what is worth it when it comes to sweet treats and what can be left for others to enjoy.
- Watch out for sneaky sugar in beverages.

A little forethought can go a long way in helping us enjoy sweets while avoiding a sugar crash.

Put It Into Practice:

Notice sneaky sugar trying to steal your energy this holiday season and practice pausing before reaching for "just one more."

Eating and Meal Planning, Dopamine

December 20

Protecting Your Peace.

Even the merriest among us know that the holidays can be emotionally, physically, and psychologically taxing. ~ Hailey Magee

The holiday season comes with a lot of invisible pressure. Pressure to attend. Pressure to host. Pressure to buy the perfect gift, bake the thing, show up smiling, and prove we've got it all together.

And for ADHD moms juggling people-pleasing, impulsivity, and Rejection Sensitive Dysphoria (RSD), setting boundaries can feel especially hard. We don't want to disappoint anyone. We don't want to be judged. And sometimes we say "yes" before our brain has a chance to check the calendar, the budget, or our actual capacity.

But here's the truth…every yes costs something.

Time. Energy. Money. Patience. Peace.

And when we say yes to too much, the holiday season stops feeling joyful and starts feeling like a performance we're barely surviving.

Boundaries don't have to be dramatic. They can be simple and kind. Things like:

- "That sounds fun, but we're keeping things small this year."
- "I can't make it, but I hope you have a great time."
- "I'm not up for hosting, but I can bring something."
- "I need to leave early, but I'm glad I came."

We need to think of boundaries less like keeping people and things out and more like protecting the people and things we love.

Put It Into Practice:

Choose one small boundary to protect your time, energy, or budget this week. Practice saying it out loud before you need it.

Mindset, Mental Health, RSD

First Day of Winter.

Winter is a season of recovery and preparation.
~ Paul Theroux

Winter has officially arrived. And with it comes cozy nights under warm blankets and a gradual march toward longer days.

Since the seasons stick to a schedule better than most ADHD brains, they make a great cue to remind us to tackle regular maintenance tasks for our homes and selves that we may forget.

For your home and property, remember to:

- Check and replace smoke detector batteries
- Change the furnace and refrigerator water filters
- Change the oil in the car
- Clean out the dryer vent

For you and your family:

- Replace toothbrushes
- Wash makeup brushes
- Delete unwanted digital photos
- Back up the computer's hard drive
- Drop off the donations in the back of the car

Put It Into Practice:

Schedule time this week for seasonal household maintenance tasks for both your home and your family.

Time Investments, Cleaning and Organizing

December 22

Silent Night? Not Quite.

The average mom spends 13 days preparing for Christmas. That doesn't leave a lot of time for sleep. ~ Joe Alexander

What do we get when we combine a jam-packed schedule, a never-ending to-do list, the darkest month in the Northern Hemisphere, and ADHD? A whole bunch of sleepless nights. That's what.

Sleep can be a struggle for us any time of year, but December hits our sleep bank particularly hard. Even if we've carefully curated our routines, diet, and lifestyle to support our ADHD, the holiday season has a way of wreaking havoc on what we do the rest of the year.

Along with eating and exercise, our sleep is vital for supporting our ADHD brain, which is why the combination of dysregulation and lack of sleep can be so disruptive to our executive function. Luckily, there are ways we can help boost our sleep quality, even during busy times:

- Prioritize sleep, even if it means leaving parties early or scaling back the scope of projects
- Invest in headband headphones for sleep stories or calming music
- Take a nap. Even 20 minutes can give our brains a boost

We simply cannot function without enough sleep. So the best gift we can give ourselves this holiday season is a good night's sleep.

Put It Into Practice:

Prioritize sleep when you can during these final busy weeks of the season so your brain can reset and give you the boost you need to power through.

Sleep, Self-Care

A Decompression Session.

Sometimes the most important thing in a whole day is the rest we take between two deep breaths. ~ Etty Hillesum

We are in the final days of this holiday season…just in case your calendar and energy levels didn't already tell you. And for many of us it's been more than 5 weeks of sensory overload, increased cognitive demands, and extra emotional regulation.

Add in another schedule shift with kids home for winter break, plus any last-minute holiday tasks, and it's no wonder our brains are ready for a long winter's nap.

But instead of powering through, this is the time to decompress. Because the key to recovering from overstimulation is taking everything down a notch (or twelve) so our nervous system can reset instead of burning out. Some easy ways to reset include:

- Getting a good night's sleep
- Sitting in a quiet, dimly lit room
- Wearing comfortable clothes
- Spending some time alone
- Getting gentle movement like yoga or a nature walk

Feeling overstimulated doesn't mean we have to slam the brakes on all festivities and projects. But it does mean we should listen when our body is saying, "Hey, can we take a little break?"

Put It Into Practice:

Schedule decompression time in the next day or so…your nervous system needs it as much as your to-do list does.

Overstimulation, Self-Care, Mental Health

December 24

You Made Magic.

Many ADHD moms suffer from success amnesia, the tendency to focus on what's next or what went wrong instead of what we've actually achieved. This is likely due to our working memory, which makes it harder to hold onto our success and file it away for later, or our impulse control, which causes us to rush right past our wins and onto the next thing.

So today I'm reminding all of us (myself included) to take a moment to acknowledge and celebrate everything we've done to make the holiday season amazing for our families and beyond.

Spending just a few minutes intentionally acknowledging the specific efforts we've made over the past few weeks helps build self-esteem and encourages future effort. And when I say "effort," I mean effort…not outcome.

Because our perfectionism may try to sneak in and convince us to only celebrate what turned out exactly how we envisioned. But I'd bet there were plenty of moments where the work was immense, even if the outcome wasn't perfect.

Acknowledging and celebrating our effort helps build a growth mindset that reframes challenges and counteracts negative self-talk all year long.

Put It Into Practice:

Take some time today to reflect on the efforts you've made to make this holiday season memorable for your family.

Mindset, Mom Life

Presents and Presence.

Joy is what happens to us when we allow ourselves to recognize how good things really are. ~ Marianne Williamson

Sometimes it's hard to "be here now" when our ADHD brain wants to be here, there, and everywhere. But dwelling on the past or focusing on the future means what's happening now, in the moment, may fly right past.

Actively embracing the present helps us solidify memories because our working memory isn't being interrupted mid-processing. Grounding ourselves through mindful breathing or quick sensory check-ins can also make emotional regulation a little easier. And pausing to notice what we're grateful for in real time gives us a boost of dopamine and serotonin for whatever the day holds.

Presence doesn't have to be perfect to count. Even a ten-second pause to notice the sound of laughter, the warmth of a hug, or the look on your child's face can become a memory your brain actually keeps.

Staying present takes practice, especially for ADHD brains that are prone to wandering. But when we can recognize our mind wandering, we can gently bring it back.

Put It Into Practice:

Pick one "anchor moment" today. Take a breath, notice what you can see, hear, and feel, and let yourself actually be there for it.

Mindset, Mom Life

December 26
The Thank-You Boost.

Let us be grateful to people who make us happy, they are the charming gardeners who make our souls blossom. ~ Marcel Proust

As the holiday season winds down, it's the perfect time to revisit our old friend, gratitude. For ADHD moms, gratitude activates reward pathways (hello, dopamine), strengthens positive neural pathways, and supports emotional regulation through serotonin.

One especially powerful way to lock in that grateful feeling is to handwrite a thank-you note. Handwriting helps us process thoughts more deeply by activating more parts of the brain and gives our working memory a little support.

If the thought of writing a thank-you note feels overwhelming, here is a basic template to use to make the process easier:

- Greeting: Dear ____
- Thank you with a personal detail: Thank you for ____. It meant a lot because ____.
- Warm closing: With love/Gratefully/Sincerely, ____

Sending a text or telling someone how much you appreciate their gift or gesture absolutely works. But if you have a little downtime this week, write a quick thank-you note to someone who made the season special.

Put It Into Practice:

Write a thank-you note for a gift you received or something someone did for you during the recent holiday season.

Gratitude, Memory Support

The Great Reset.

You will burn and you will burn out; you will be healed
and come back again. ~ Fyodor Dostoevsky

A 2023 American Psychological Association poll[29] found that 89% of people feel overwhelmed and stressed during the holiday season. And since the holiday season is wrapping up, now is a great time for a little decompression.

The final week of the year is sometimes called "dead week" because, as one of my favorite memes says, we're "confused, full of cheese, and unsure of the day of the week."

And honestly? That's exactly where many ADHD moms need to be after a busy, overstimulating season. Slowing down gives our brains a chance to rest and reset, especially if we've been running on fumes.

We have permission to make things easy this week. Stay in our pajamas. Skip the full "get ready" routine. Simplify meals. Do whatever helps our nervous system take a breath.

Prioritize rest, but add a little gentle movement (walking or stretching) to reduce stress and start rebuilding your energy reserves.

Put It Into Practice:

Recover from holiday stress by focusing on resting and recharging this week.

Burnout, Self-Care

December 28

Brrrrrr.

---

*If you tiptoe into cold water, you'e missing out on the rush
of plunging in headfirst. ~ Simone Elkeles*

I absolutely hate winter. The shorter days and cold weather wreak havoc on my motivation and energy levels. But cold can have real benefits for us ADHDers.

Cold plunging has become increasingly popular for its potential to reduce inflammation, lower cortisol, and ease stress. And it's especially popular in neurodivergent communities because cold exposure can increase dopamine and norepinephrine, which may support focus, attention span, and mood regulation.

One study in 2000 found that cold water exposure significantly increased norepinephrine and dopamine levels in participants after prolonged exposure to cold water[30].

Now, I'm not recommending we jump in a cold lake or sit in a tub of ice outside for an hour. But if we're feeling sluggish from post-holiday winter blahs, we could try ending our shower with a 20-second cold burst.

Or we could work up to the suggested protocol from neuroscientist Andrew Huberman…about 11 minutes total per week, split into 2–4 sessions lasting 1–5 minutes.

Put It Into Practice:

Try a cold burst at the end of your shower to help boost your energy, focus, and mood levels.

Dopamine

Your ADHD Toolkit.

Our toolbox is simply a way for us to record the strategies and ideas we have for working with our ADHD—a place we can go and look at our intentions when we are off track. ~ William Curb

If we plan to build something, we need a plan *and* the right tools. And if we have goals and projects for the upcoming year, we also need both: a plan and the proper supports to follow through.

That's why an important first step in yearly planning is evaluating what tools our ADHD brain might need. Maybe we need better time management so we can realistically allocate the time required. Or stronger task initiation support so we can actually start the steps we intend to take. Perhaps we need external memory tools so we remember what we wanted to do in the first place.

Once we're aware of the supports our unique version of ADHD needs, we can seek out strategies through books, blogs, videos, podcasts, and groups. And remember…what works for one ADHDer may not work for you right away. We may need to adapt it to our brain, our lifestyle, and our season of life.

And don't forget to include tools that are already working (or have worked in the past). Keeping a running journal or digital note of coping strategies makes it easier to refresh our memory and reuse them when we need them again.

Put It Into Practice:

Make a list of areas where you may need more ADHD support to follow through on your goals in the upcoming year. Then research new strategies or revisit the ones that have worked for you before.

ADHD Symptoms

December 30

Know Your Why.

When you know your why, you'll know your way.
~ Michael Hyatt

'Tis the season for setting goals. And I'm all too familiar with an ambitious ADHD goal that starts strong...then slowly fizzles out as time goes by.

That's why getting clear on why you want to reach a goal matters, especially when your motivation starts to dwindle. Because let's be honest...there will come a time when your goal is no longer new, fun, or exciting to your ADHD brain.

Let's ask ourselves, "What's the best thing that could happen if I reach this goal?" We can dig deep and get specific about how this goal benefits our life.

For example, instead of "I want to make more money" try, "I want to take my family on a beach vacation where someone else cooks dinner." (Amen!)

When the excitement fades or something shinier comes along, our why becomes the thing that keeps us moving.

And once we've clarified it, we need to remind ourselves about it regularly. Type it up, print it out, and place it somewhere we'll see every day. Add it to our morning routine. Record it and listen to it while getting ready or before bed.

Put It Into Practice:

Write down the why behind one of your goals. Then choose one way to remind yourself of it regularly.

Goal Setting, Productivity, Taking Action

Look Back Before You Leap.

Tomorrow, is the first blank page of a 365 page book.
Write a good one. ~ Brad Paisley

We made it! Another year down and another on the horizon.

And when our ADHD brains are flying at lightning speed, it's easy to focus only on what's ahead without taking time to look back, acknowledge, and celebrate how far we've come.

So before we look forward, here are a few questions to help us reflect on the past year:

- What is something you're proud of from the past year?
- What is something new you tried?
- What is a challenge you overcame?
- What advice would you give future-you based on your experiences this year?
- What is something you'd like to do less of in the coming year?
- What is something you enjoy that you'd like to make more time or space for in the coming year?
- What is one small step you can take tomorrow to help make that happen?

Put It Into Practice:

Reflect on what you've learned and accomplished this year. Then choose one small step you can take tomorrow to move toward what you want more of in the next year…and take a moment to celebrate how far you've come.

Goal Setting, Taking Action

And now, return to January 1 to start your journey again…

You probably forgot some stuff or missed a few days anyway.

Attention Deficit Hyperactivity Disorder (ADHD) is a neurodevelopmental disorder characterized by symptoms of inattention, hyperactivity, impulsivity, and emotional dysregulation arising from executive dysfunction.

Body Doubling is productivity technique where a person works alongside someone else (in person or virtually) to stay focused on their own tasks.

Dopamine is a neurotransmitter and hormone in the brain and body, central to the brain's reward system, motivating behaviors like seeking pleasure, and also vital for functions such as mood, movement, memory, focus, and sleep.

Executive Function is a set of cognitive skills, managed by the brain's prefrontal cortex, that act as the brain's management system, enabling you to plan, focus attention, remember instructions, and juggle multiple tasks to achieve goals and manage daily life effectively.

Neurodivergent is a term used to describe those differing in mental or neurological function from what is considered typical or normal

Neuroplasticity is the ability of the brain to form and reorganize synaptic connections, allowing it to adapt, learn new skills, and recover from injury or disease by changing its structure and function in response to experiences, learning, or environmental changes.

Neurotransmitter is a chemical messenger that carries signals from one nerve cell to another, enabling communication throughout the brain and body for functions like thinking, moving, and feeling.

Neurotypical is a term used to describe those with brain functions, behaviors, and processing considered standard or normal.

Parasympathetic Nervous System (PNS) is a division of the autonomic nervous system that controls the body's "rest and digest" functions, promoting relaxation, conserving energy, and managing involuntary processes like digestion, heart rate, and breathing.

Prefrontal Cortex (or Lobe) is the forward most portion of the brain responsible for processing and adapting one's thinking in order to meet certain goals in different situations and allowing one to focus, control how they behave, and make different decisions.

Rejection Sensitive Dysphoria (RSD) is an intense emotional pain from actual or perceived criticism, rejection, or failure, often disproportionate to the situation, commonly linked with ADHD but not a formal diagnosis.

Sympathetic Nervous System (SNS) is the division of the autonomic nervous system responsible for the body's "fight-or-flight" response, preparing it for intense physical activity or stress by increasing heart rate, blood pressure, and breathing.

Time Blindness is a difficulty in perceiving, estimating, and managing the passage of time.

Time Horizon (ADHD) is the limited window of time into the future that feels real and actionable, which is often much shorter than for neurotypical people and may lead to time blindness.

Time Investments is the strategic allocation of time to activities that yield future benefits, growth, or returns.

Time Perception is the sense of time passing, which is measured by one's own assessment of the duration of the unfolding events

1. January 25 – Stop Paying for Nothing.
https://www.cnet.com/personal-finance/subscription-survey-2025/

2. February 25 – Think and Chew Gum.
Can, K. C., Tugba Ozel-Kizil, E., Colak, B., & Duman, B. (2022). Effects of gum chewing and repetitive motor activity on sustained attention in adults with attention deficit-hyperactivity disorder. Journal of Cognitive Psychology, 34(8), 1011–1021.
https://doi.org/10.1080/20445911.2022.2096623

3. March 14 – Address Your Stress.
Leiter, M. P., & Maslach, C. (1999). Six areas of worklife: a model of the organizational context of burnout. Journal of health and human services administration, 21(4), 472–489.

4. April 16 – Set It. Save It.
https://www.bankrate.com/banking/savings/emergency-savings-report/

5. April 19 – Move More. Sleep Better.
Min L, Wang D, You Y, Fu Y, Ma X. Effects of High-Intensity Interval Training on Sleep: A Systematic Review and Meta-Analysis. International Journal of Environmental Research and Public Health. 2021; 18(20):10973.
https://doi.org/10.3390/ijerph182010973

6. May 18 – Lean, Mean, Dopamine Machine.
Marques, A., Marconcin, P., Werneck, A. O., Ferrari, G., Gouveia, É. R., Kliegel, M., Peralta, M., & Ihle, A. (2021). Bidirectional Association between Physical Activity and Dopamine Across Adulthood-A Systematic Review. Brain sciences, 11(7), 829. https://doi.org/10.3390/brainsci11070829

7. May 20 – Warning: Burnout Ahead.
Ohio State University Wexner Medical Center. (2024, May 8). Pressure to be 'perfect' causing burnout for parents, mental health concerns for their children. ScienceDaily.
www.sciencedaily.com/releases/2024/05/240508093726.htm

8. June 10 – When Sips Set You Back
Wang, F. L., Pedersen, S. L., Joseph, H., Gnagy, E. M., Curran, P., Pelham, W. E., Jr, & Molina, B. S. G. (2019). Role of ADHD in the Co-Occurrence Between Heavy Alcohol Use and Depression Trajectories in Adulthood. Alcoholism, clinical and experimental research, 43(2), 342–352.
https://doi.org/10.1111/acer.13934

9. June 14 – Feed Your Focus.
   Thomas, J. R., Lockwood, P. A., Singh, A., & Deuster, P. A. (1999). Tyrosine improves working memory in a multitasking environment. Pharmacology, biochemistry, and behavior, 64(3), 495–500. https://doi.org/10.1016/s0091-3057(99)00094-5

10. June 19 – The Doorway Effect.
    Radvansky, G. A., Krawietz, S. A., & Tamplin, A. K. (2011). Walking through Doorways Causes Forgetting: Further Explorations. Quarterly Journal of Experimental Psychology, 64(8), 1632-1645. https://doi.org/10.1080/17470218.2011.571267

11. June 25 – Fidget to Focus.
    Zhao, X., Condron, P., Kumar, H., Kwon, E., Waters, G., Erb, C., Dudley, M., Taylor, D., Newburn, G., Maller, J., Shim, V., Wang, A., Holdsworth, S., Waldie, K., & Fernandez, J. (2023). Functional magnetic resonance imaging reveals fidgeting in ADHD improves prefrontal cortex activation during executive functioning [Abstract]. In Proceedings of the International Society for Magnetic Resonance in Medicine (ISMRM). ISMRM E-Library. Retrieved from https://archive.ismrm.org/2023/3343.html (accessed October 9, 2025).

12. July 12 – Work to the Music.
    Madjar, N., Gazoli, R., Manor, I., & Shoval, G. (2020). Contrasting effects of music on reading comprehension in preadolescents with and without ADHD. Psychiatry research, 291, 113207. https://doi.org/10.1016/j.psychres.2020.113207

13. July 16 – The Original Hard Drive.
    Van der Weel, F. R. R., & Van der Meer, A. L. H. (2024). Handwriting but not typewriting leads to widespread brain connectivity: A high-density EEG study with implications for the classroom. Frontiers in Psychology, 14, 1219945. https://doi.org/10.3389/fpsyg.2023.1219945

14. July 17 – Quiet Your Brain for a Boost.
    Kjaer, T., Bertelsen, C., Piccini, P., Brooks, D., Alving, J., Lou, H. (2002). Increased dopamine tone during meditation-induced change of consciousness. Cognitive Brain Research, 13(2), 255-259. https://doi.org/10.1016/S0926-6410(01)00106-9.

15. July 19 – Vent Before You Burst.
    Claponea, R. M., & Iorga, M. (2023). The Relationship between Burnout and Wellbeing Using Social Support, Organizational Justice, and Lifelong Learning in Healthcare Specialists from Romania. Medicina (Kaunas, Lithuania), 59(7), 1352. https://doi.org/10.3390/medicina59071352

16. September 1 – The Multitasking Myth
    Takeuchi, H., Taki, Y., Nouchi, R., Hashizume, H., Sekiguchi, A., Kotozaki, Y., Nakagawa, S., Miyauchi, C. M., Sassa, Y., & Kawashima, R. (2014). Effects of multitasking-training on gray matter structure and resting state neural mechanisms. Human brain mapping, 35(8), 3646–3660. https://doi.org/10.1002/hbm.22427

17. September 1 – The Multitasking Myth
    Francx, W., Llera, A., Mennes, M., Zwiers, M. P., Faraone, S. V., Oosterlaan, J., Heslenfeld, D., Hoekstra, P. J., Hartman, C. A., Franke, B., Buitelaar, J. K., & Beckmann, C. F. (2016). Integrated analysis of gray and white matter alterations in attention-deficit/hyperactivity disorder. NeuroImage. Clinical, 11, 357–367. https://doi.org/10.1016/j.nicl.2016.03.005

18. September 9 – 205 Times a Day.
    https://www.reviews.org/mobile/cell-phone-addiction/

19. September 15 – Tune In to Tune In.
    Melnichuk, A., Cooper, R.K. & Hawk, L.W. A parametric investigation of binaural beats for brain entrainment and enhancing sustained attention. Sci Rep 15, 4308 (2025). https://doi.org/10.1038/s41598-025-88517-z

20. September 16 – Mindfulness Builds Memory.
    Hölzel, B. K., Carmody, J., Vangel, M., Congleton, C., Yerramsetti, S. M., Gard, T., & Lazar, S. W. (2011). Mindfulness practice leads to increases in regional brain gray matter density. Psychiatry research, 191(1), 36–43. https://doi.org/10.1016/j.pscychresns.2010.08.006

21. September 19 – The Confidence Conundrum.
    Pedersen, A. B., Edvardsen, B. V., Messina, S. M., Volden, M. R., Weyandt, L. L., & Lundervold, A. J. (2024). Self-Esteem in Adults With ADHD Using the Rosenberg Self-Esteem Scale: A Systematic Review. Journal of attention disorders, 28(7), 1124–1138. https://doi.org/10.1177/10870547241237245

22. September 23 – Restless Legs Syndrome Day.
    Samuele Cortese, Eric Konofal, Michel Lecendreux, Isabelle Arnulf, Marie-Christine Mouren, Francesca Darra, Bernardo Dalla Bernardina, Restless Legs Syndrome and Attention-Deficit/Hyperactivity Disorder: a Review of the Literature, Sleep, Volume 28, Issue 8, August 2005, Pages 1007–1013, https://doi.org/10.1093/sleep/28.8.1007

23. October 22 – You Down with DPT.
    Lönn, M., Aili, K., Svedberg, P., Nygren, J., Jarbin, H., & Larsson, I. (2023). Experiences of Using Weighted Blankets among Children with ADHD and Sleeping Difficulties. Occupational therapy international, 2023, 1945290. https://doi.org/10.1155/2023/1945290

24. October 27 - G&hux$^Bnq.
    https://cybernews.com/security/password-leak-study-unveils-2025-trends-reused-and-lazy/

25. November 2 – Spark Your Serotonin.
    Rash, J. A., Matsuba, M. K., & Prkachin, K. M. (2011). Gratitude and well-being: Who benefits the most from a gratitude intervention? Applied Psychology: Health and Well-Being, 3(3), 350–369. https://doi.org/10.1111/j.1758-0854.2011.01058.x

26. November 4 – Lower Stress with Thankfulness.
    McCraty, R., Barrios-Choplin, B., Rozman, D., Atkinson, M., & Watkins, A. D. (1998). The impact of a new emotional self-management program on stress, emotions, heart rate variability, DHEA and cortisol. Integrative physiological and behavioral science : the official journal of the Pavlovian Society, 33(2), 151–170. https://doi.org/10.1007/BF02688660

27. November 5 – Sleep Better with Gratitude.
    Wood, A. M., Joseph, S., Lloyd, J., & Atkins, S. (2009). Gratitude influences sleep through the mechanism of pre-sleep cognitions. Journal of psychosomatic research, 66(1), 43–48. https://doi.org/10.1016/j.jpsychores.2008.09.002

28. November 24 – Thankful for ADHD?
    Nordby, E. S., Guribye, F., Nordgreen, T., & Lundervold, A. J. (2023). Silver linings of ADHD: a thematic analysis of adults' positive experiences with living with ADHD. BMJ open, 13(10), e072052. https://doi.org/10.1136/bmjopen-2023-072052

29. December 27 – The Great Reset.
    https://www.apa.org/news/press/releases/2023/11/holiday-season-stress

30. December 28 – Brrrr.
    Srámek, P., Simecková, M., Janský, L., Savlíková, J., & Vybíral, S. (2000). Human physiological responses to immersion into water of different temperatures. European journal of applied physiology, 81(5), 436–442. https://doi.org/10.1007/s004210050065

Recommended Reading:

1. **Driven to Distraction: Recognizing and Coping with Attention Deficit Disorder**, Edward M. Hallowell, M.D. and John J. Ratey, M.D.
2. **ADHD is Awesome: A Guide to (Mostly) Thriving with ADHD**; Penn and Kim Holderness
3. **Growth Mindset: The New Psychology of Success;** Carol S. Dweck, Ph.D
4. **365 Days of Good Morning, Good Life: Daily Reflections to Help You Go After the Life You Want**; Amy Schmittauer Landino and Sarah Mitchell McCain

Websites/Podcasts/YouTube:

1. **The ADHD Mompreneur** – theadhdmompreneur.com, youtube.com/theadhdmompreneur
2. **How to ADHD** - youtube.com/HowtoADHD
3. **ADDitude Magazine** - youtube.com/additudemag

Online Body Doubling Services:

1. **Flow Club** – flow.club
2. **Focusmate** – focusmate.com
3. **Deepwrk** – deepwrk.io

Password Managers:

1. **NordPass** – nordpass.com
2. **LastPass** – lastpass.com
3. **1Password** – 1password.com

I've created a resource page with downloads related to this book that I have produced for clients and my podcast. These free resources include (as of publishing):

- Home and Family Checklists
- Business Owner Checklists
- My TRIM Your To-Do List Flowchart
- Travel Checklist
- ChatGPT Prompts for Moms
- 10 Questions to Ask Before You Say "Yes"
- Back-To-School Planning Worksheets

I plan to continue to add to these resources as I create them so the list will continue to grow.

To see what's available and download your free printables, visit bit.ly/365bookdownloads or scan this QR code.

To my husband, Adam…thank you for picking up the slack around the house so I had the extra time and brainpower to make this book happen. I don't know how we would have eaten the last few months without you.

To my kiddos…thank you for always inspiring me to do more and be more. You motivate me to create a better world, not only for your generation, but for mine too.

To my WoWe ladies…I am sure this book would not have happened without your check-ins and cheering. When I told you I was doing it, not a single person questioned my crazy ambition. Instead, you asked how you could help. I wish every mom could have friends like you.

To every ADHD mom reading this book…thank you for sharing a bit of your time and bandwidth with me. I hope I've helped you see that you aren't alone in this beautifully chaotic ADHD mom journey.

And to keep in line with one of the major themes in this book, I also want to acknowledge myself. There were many times I was ready to throw in the towel, especially once the holidays hit. But luckily, I had the accountability and support to keep going and cross the finish line. Never forget…you can do big, hard things!

Christy Lingo is the founder and host of The ADHD Mompreneur and an executive function and accountability coach for ADHD mom business owners. She helps clients build the successful business they know is possible while juggling everything that comes with being a mom with ADHD.

She is diagnosed with combined-type ADHD and she is the parent of an ADHD child.

Christy's approach is practical, encouraging, and grounded in real life...because ADHD doesn't disappear just because you have goals. She believes success doesn't come from trying harder, but from building systems that actually work for your unique brain.

Whether she's helping clients with planning, consistency, follow-through, or home-life overwhelm, her goal is always the same...less shame, more support, and progress that feels sustainable.

When she's not coaching or creating content, she's a swim and soccer mom who loves British panel shows, baking, traveling, and hip-hop dance workouts.

You can connect with Christy at theadhdmompreneur.com or email her at christy@theadhdmompreneur.com.

www.ingramcontent.com/pod-product-compliance
Lightning Source LLC
Chambersburg PA
CBHW060402130626
46555CB00005B/1972